Illuminate Publishing

D0179132

WJEC AS Religious Studies

An Introduction to Philosophy of Religion & An Introduction to Religion and Ethics

Study and Revision Guide

Karl Lawson
Andrew Pearce

Published in 2012 by Illuminate Publishing Ltd, P.O. Box 1160, Cheltenham, Gloucestershire GL50 9RW

Orders: Please visit www.illuminatepublishing.com
or email sales@illuminatepublishing.com

© Karl Lawson, Andrew Pearce

The moral rights of the authors have been asserted.

All rights reserved. No part of this book may be reprinted, reproduced or utilised in any form or by any electronic, mechanical, or other means, now known or hereafter invented, including photocopying and recording, or in any information storage and retrieval system, without permission in writing from the publishers.

British Library Cataloguing in Publication Data

A catalogue record for this book is available from the British Library

ISBN 978-1-908682-07-9

Printed by 4edge Ltd, Hockley, Essex

08.13

The publisher's policy is to use papers that are natural, renewable and recyclable products made from wood grown in sustainable forests. The logging and manufacturing processes are expected to conform to the environmental regulations of the country of origin.

Every effort has been made to contact copyright holders of material reproduced in this book. If notified, the publishers will be pleased to rectify any errors or omissions at the earliest opportunity.

This material has been endorsed by WJEC and offers high quality support for the delivery of WJEC qualifications. While this material has been through a WJEC quality assurance process, all responsibility for the content remains with the publisher.

WJEC examination questions are reproduced by permission from WJEC

Editor: Geoff Tuttle

Design and layout: Nigel Harriss

Photograph and illustration credits

Shutterstock.com: p11 Olaf Speier, Federico Rostagno, Francesco83; p13 Efired, PeJo; p15 unkreativ, Alexander Trinitatov; p19 Georgios Kollidas, Nicku; p25 DAVIPIX, glasscuter; p29 Matusciac Alexandru; p39 SFerdon; p40 Joe Belanger, Roypix, Ken Tannenbaum, Fer Gregory, Mayovskyy Andrew, fpolat69; p44 Andy Dean Photography; p57 Matthew Cole; p58 Zvonimir Atletic; p77 Sue Smith, Panos Karapanagiotis; p83 iconspro, iralu; p84 akiradesigns; p97 wavebreakmedia; p108 Georgios Kollidas; p110 Olena Zaskochenko; p132 Monkey Business Images.

Wikimedia Commons: p15 (Blake); p20 (Kenny, Russell); p62 (Rumi); p111 (Mill).

Text credits

St. Thomas Aquinas , 'Treatise of the One God', *Summa Theologica*, translated by The Fathers of the English Dominican Province, Benziger Bros (1947)

p112, 113; *Catechism of the Catholic Church 2nd edition*, Doubleday (1995); English Translation for United States Catholic Conference, Inc. Libreria Editrice Vaticana © 1994

Acknowledgements

We are very grateful to the team at Illuminate Publishing for their professionalism, support and guidance throughout this project. Without their help, we would not have undertaken or completed this book. It has been a pleasure to work so closely with them.

The publisher would like to thank John Summerwill for his guidance and encouragement throughout.

Dedications

To Louise, Ben and Amy for their love, support and patience. In memory of Tom Heffer and a friendship that will never be forgotten. To my AS students Aaron, Emily, Eve, Georgia, Jonathan, Lauren B, Lauren R and Shauna for inspiring me and reminding why I became a teacher.

Andrew

For Helen, Rebecca and Jasmine – the love and light of my life

Karl

Contents

How to use this book

The contents of this study and revision guide are designed to guide you through to success in the WJEC 'An Introduction to Philosophy of Religion' (RS 1/2 PHIL) and 'An Introduction to Religion and Ethics' (RS 1/2 ETH) AS level examinations. This book has been written by experienced examiners so that you will be aware of what is required.

There are notes on each section of each of the examinations:

RS 1/2 PHIL

- The existence of God (i) – Cosmological Arguments
- The existence of God (ii) – Teleological Arguments
- Evil and Suffering
- An introduction to Religious Experience: Mysticism

RS 1/2 ETH

- Aquinas' Natural Law
- Situation Ethics
- Utilitarianism
- Applied Ethics

Knowledge and Understanding

The first section of the book covers the key knowledge required for the examination. Here you will find summary notes on all the topics in the specification. The evaluation skills required for the examination are also covered, with key elements relating to the issues raised in the specification being addressed for each topic.

In addition, we have tried to give you additional pointers so that you can develop your work:

- Glossary 'Key terms' found in the WJEC specification can often be used to form part of a question, so we have highlighted those terms and offered definitions. You could use these notes as the basis of revision cards.

- Grade Boost areas have also been identified. These are 'top tips' which try to give you clear guidance on best practice demonstrated by good candidates and common 'pitfalls' made by weaker candidates.

- We have also highlighted Key figures and Key quotes so you are reminded of the importance of referring to writers and evidence when writing your answers.

- There are Quickfire questions designed to test your knowledge and understanding of the material.

- We have offered examination advice based on experience of what candidates need to do to attain the highest grades.

Exam Practice and Technique

The second section of the book covers the key skills for examination success and offers you examples based on real-life responses to examination commands. First you will be guided to an understanding of how the examination system works, and then offered tips for success.

After that, there are a variety of sample answers to possible questions in the options. These are not model answers and you should not attempt to learn them. They offer a guide as to the standard that is required, and the commentary will explain why the responses gained the marks that they did. You will be offered advice on how to tailor your writing to produce an effective piece of extended writing.

Most importantly, we advise that you should take responsibility for your own learning and not rely on your teachers to give you notes or tell you how to gain the grades that you require. You should look for additional notes to support your study of WJEC RS: Philosophy and/or RS: Religion and Ethics.

We advise that you look at the WJEC website: www.wjec.co.uk. In particular, you need to be aware of the specification, trigger words and the AS glossary. Look for specimen examination papers and mark schemes. You may find past papers useful as well.

We would both like to take this opportunity to wish you all the best of luck with your revision.

Karl Lawson

Andrew Pearce

Knowledge and Understanding
Unit 1
What is Philosophy of Religion?

Introduction

Why are we here? What is the purpose of our lives? How do we know anything? Why do bad things happen to good people? Does God exist and, if so, what sort of God is s/he? Have you ever wondered about any of these questions? Well, if you have then you are in very good company as, for at least the last two and half thousand years, philosophers have been doing the same thing!

Philosophy has helped civilisation understand itself better and even led to the birth of modern science. If it had not been for the likes of Plato and Aristotle writing down their thoughts about how they believed the universe operated and what humankind's place within it was, then these questions might never have been considered by the likes of Aquinas, Descartes, Hume, Wittgenstein and others, and our world and our understanding of it would have been much the poorer.

Religious philosophy holds a special place within philosophy as a whole and has been contributed to by thinkers of many different religious backgrounds. Despite their differences the search for philosophical religious truths has remained the same and this course will give you a brief insight into some of their thoughts and why they said what they said.

Who said what when?

When you first start studying religious philosophy all of the names and dates can be very confusing – and that's before you've even had a chance to get to grips with their ideas. It's therefore a very good idea to have a diagram, somewhere in your notes, of the basic timeline of the main thinkers that you will be studying. It may look something like this:

Key Term

Philosophy = translated directly from the Greek for 'The Love of Wisdom', in its broadest sense it is the study of ideas about the world and humanity's place in it.

Grade boost

Remember always to say why a particular viewpoint is held – better explanations show your understanding of the subject!

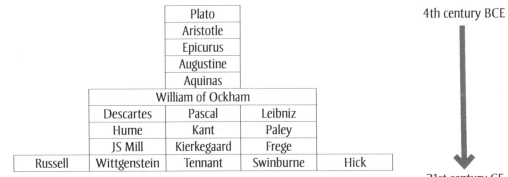

		Plato			4th century BCE
		Aristotle			
		Epicurus			
		Augustine			
		Aquinas			
	William of Ockham				
	Descartes	Pascal	Leibniz		
	Hume	Kant	Paley		
	JS Mill	Kierkegaard	Frege		
Russell	Wittgenstein	Tennant	Swinburne	Hick	21st century CE

1: Cosmological Argument

When revising the cosmological argument for the existence of God, you should focus on the main debates and issues. For example, you are expected to know the philosophical concepts of 'first cause', motion and contingency that the cosmological argument is based on. Furthermore, you will need to understand precisely how philosophers such as Aquinas, Leibniz and Craig have defined these philosophical concepts. In addition, you will need to understand the main philosophical objections to the cosmological argument and be able to articulate each of these fluently. Finally, you should be able to evaluate the issues that arise from the cosmological argument and be able to support any conclusion that you might draw with reference to the contributions of philosophers both ancient and modern.

Revision checklist

Tick column 1 when you have completed brief revision notes.
Tick column 2 when you think you have a good grasp of the topic.
Tick column 3 during final revision when you feel you have mastery of the topic.

			1	2	3
What contribution was made by the ancient Greek philosophers to this debate?	p8	Plato and the evidence for the existence of the gods			
	p9	Aristotle's concepts of motion and first mover			
What were Aquinas' Three Ways?	p11	First Way: motion or change including Aquinas' example of fire and wood			
	p12	Second Way: cause and effect, including the concepts of efficient, intermediate and ultimate cause			
	p14	Third Way: contingency, including the concept of a necessary being			
What was Leibniz's contribution to the cosmological argument?	p15	Principle of sufficient reason			
	p15	Example of the books of geometry			
What are the Kalam cosmological arguments?	p16	William Lane Craig – personal creator and infinity concepts			
	p18	Ed Miller – including example of categorical syllogism			
What are the arguments against the cosmological argument for the existence of God?	p19	Hume			
	p19	Kant			
	p19	Russell			
	p20	Kenny			
	p20	Big Bang			
	p20	Quantum theory			
What are the main issues that arise from the cosmological argument for the existence of God?	p21	Strengths vs. weaknesses			
	p21	How strong/convincing are the arguments?			
	p21	Do the arguments fail to establish God's existence?			
	p22	Is the cosmological argument sufficient to prove that God's existence is probable or not?			

Key Figures

Plato (c. 424–348 BCE)

Ancient Greek Philosopher, considered as the father of modern philosophy. He wrote mostly in the dialogue form and often speaks with the voice of Socrates, his teacher (who never recorded anything in writing himself). His works on the Forms, Logic and Epistemology were to form the bedrock of the development of Western thought for the next two millennia.

Aristotle (c. 384–322 BCE)

Ancient Greek Philosopher and student of Plato. However, his own philosophy diverged from Plato's in several significant areas. His contributions to science and ethics have known no parallel in Western civilisation and his ideas were heavily influential on medieval Christian theologians – particularly Aquinas.

Grade boost

Note that Plato's ideas put forward something that becomes a common strand of all future cosmological arguments (and is also the basis for Bertrand Russell's rejection of the argument in the 20th century!), i.e. the universe exists and therefore needs an explanation, which, invariably, is given the name 'God'. The theological standpoints of Plato and Aquinas may differ but their applications of logic to the argument are the same.

Historical background: Plato and Aristotle

Plato

One of the earliest forms of a cosmological argument can be found in Plato's writings: *Timaeus and The Laws* (Book X).

In *The Laws* we see the argument for the existence of the gods being posited as the very fact that the universe exists:

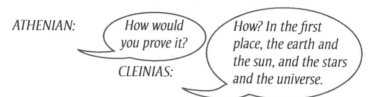

ATHENIAN: *How would you prove it?*

CLEINIAS: *How? In the first place, the earth and the sun, and the stars and the universe.*

The Laws also goes on to discuss the principles of change and motion. The point is made about where these principles need to arise from:

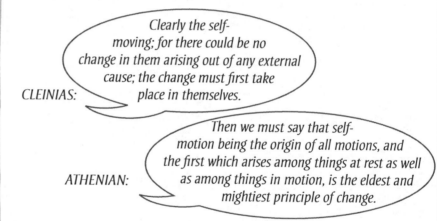

CLEINIAS: *Clearly the self-moving; for there could be no change in them arising out of any external cause; the change must first take place in themselves.*

ATHENIAN: *Then we must say that self-motion being the origin of all motions, and the first which arises among things at rest as well as among things in motion, is the eldest and mightiest principle of change.*

Plato is not claiming the existence of God by virtue of this argument instead he is positing the necessity of a 'self-moved' mover – an essential first step for the formulation of cosmological arguments that were to follow.

In *Timaeus* it is claimed that:

> *'Now everything that becomes or is created must of necessity be created by some cause, for without a cause nothing can be created.'*

Summary

This establishes not only the philosophical notion that cause and effect are necessary mechanisms for the universe to exist in the way that it does but also implies the necessity of a first cause which starts everything else off. In *Timaeus* this 'first cause' is named as the 'creator' or 'demi-urge', and everything created originates from him. More properly speaking, Plato's demi-urge 'fashioned' the universe out of already created matter by observing the perfect forms, rather than creating all things '*ex nihilo*' (out of nothing).

Aristotle

'Everything that is in motion must be moved by something. For if it has not the source of its motion in itself it is evident that it is moved by something other than itself, for there must be something else that moves it.'

Aristotle, *Physics*

In both his *Physics* and his *Metaphysics*, Aristotle takes great care in outlining the changes that can occur within the universe and everything in it in terms of motion, changes of state and movements in distance. Aristotle's specific contribution to Aquinas' work will be dealt with in subsequent chapters but the words written in the Physics are fundamental to the developments that Aquinas will make, in his quest to bring the works of 'the Philosopher' (as Aquinas refers to Aristotle in his writings), a case which is evident in the following:

'(Motion, we say, is the fulfilment of the movable in so far as it is movable) Since everything that is in motion must be moved by something, let us take the case in which a thing is in locomotion and is moved by something that is itself in motion, and that again is moved by something else that is in motion, and that by something else, and so on continually: then the series cannot go on to infinity, but there must be some first mover.'

Aquinas: background and *Summa Theologica*

For much of your work in philosophy and ethics at AS in Religious Studies you will need to study the work, ideas, thoughts and theories of St Thomas Aquinas. The chances are that before AS level study you will not have come across this thinker specifically. However, his works and his ideas have been so massively influential in the development of Western civilisation that it is impossible that Aquinas' contributions have not, in some way, touched your life, even before you started thinking of what it was you wanted to study at A level! (Consider your ideas of what is right and wrong; how the modern world fights its wars, the way that a law is defined as 'just', etc.)

His early life

Born into a wealthy family in Italy in the first part of the 13th century in a place called Aquino (this is where his 'surname' comes from), he was a disappointment to his parents, who sought for their son to gain high office in the Catholic Church, for young Thomas had settled on the life of a monk in the Dominican order – a relatively new monastic movement in the Church and one that was renowned for insisting on the vow of poverty from its members (unlike the Benedictine order that Thomas had originally been schooled in).

quickfire

(1) According to Plato's *The Laws*, what reason is given as evidence for the existence of the gods?

(2) Which medieval philosopher was influenced by Aristotle?

Grade boost

It should be remembered, however, that, for Aristotle, whilst there was a first mover to start all motion off within the universe (or, rather 'cosmos' to Aristotle), he believed the universe itself to have been eternal, it did not come into being at any one point. The rather complex notion of a series of spheres (of which the Earth was at the centre) comprised his view of the universe, a geo-centric model that was influential for hundreds of years afterwards.

Grade boost

You will not be given any academic credit in an essay at AS for writing anything about his biography as it is his ideas and works that you need to be familiar with – not his life story. Candidates often waste valuable essay writing time giving mini biographies of Aquinas' life but this is ultimately to be avoided as the specification does not allow a question that asks about his life.

Grade boost

In your own AS studies you will notice that Aristotle's ideas are often referred to as the groundwork for Aquinas' ideas. This is especially true in reference to the concepts of First Mover, Efficient Cause and Natural Law – amongst several other key ideas.

So, unimpressed with their son's new career choice, his parents had him kidnapped and locked up in a room with a renowned prostitute of the time who was charged with seducing Thomas into breaking his monastic vows and therefore (in his parents' minds at least) 'rescuing' him from the Dominicans. Thomas, however, refused to be tempted and allegedly used an iron poker that had been heated in the fireplace to fend off her advances!

Eventually his parents relented and he was free to join the Dominicans without further intrusion from his family. The rest of his life was spent studying, writing and (again, somewhat infamously) eating. Aquinas nickname in the order was that of 'The Dumb Ox' – a reference to the fact that he was studiously quiet and with a physique that was on the larger side than the other monks.

Aquinas and Aristotle

Perhaps Aquinas' most noteworthy achievement, in his own lifetime, is that he 'Christianised' the works of Aristotle (who the Christian Church had long held as a heretic and worthy only of rejection and condemnation). However, Aquinas saw no contradiction in his own belief that reason, as a gift from God, could not be used to support the faith that was the foundation stone for belief at this point of time. Aristotle's works were therefore brought into a Christian framework and much of the *Summa Theologica* contains these re-workings.

Aristotle was not the only great thinker outside of the usual Christians to be referred to by Aquinas; he also made use of Maimonides the great Jewish philosopher and Avicenna the Muslim thinker, amongst others. In fact, the *Summa Theologica* contains references to so many other thinkers from across different cultures and time periods that it is almost a miracle in itself that Aquinas managed to read, reflect, evaluate and respond to these.

In our own age of libraries, internet search engines and endless easily accessible information it is worth taking a moment to reflect on how Aquinas, a single individual working mostly alone, managed to access all of this material (much of which was frowned upon by the Church) with none of our advantages.

Aquinas died 1274CE. His *Summa Theologica* was unfinished. The Church, initially, did not understand Aquinas' work and therefore it was some years before they fully realised its brilliance as a rational defence of the Christian faith. With the massive upheaval that was sweeping through Europe at the time – politically and religiously, Aquinas' work could not have come at a more opportune time, so as to preserve the Church's dogmatic identity. It was to this end that the process to make Thomas of Aquino into Saint Thomas Aquinas, was begun in 1323. The rest, as they say, is history!

Aquinas: First Way

Aquinas' First Way is often referred to as 'motion' or 'change'. Basically, Aquinas said that when we observe the universe we notice that things tend to be in a state of change or motion. From this observation Aquinas noted that things do not do this of their own accord but are instead 'moved' (or 'changed') by something else. In this, Aquinas is restating what Aristotle said.

Aquinas said that if we looked back down this sequence of movements/changes we would eventually have to come to something which started the whole sequence off. Now, as all things in the universe (that are observable) are either moving or movers, we need to find a point that started these things – and that means, necessarily, looking outside of the universe – i.e. to something which has not been moved by anything else and is in fact incapable of being moved/changed by anything else but is responsible for initiating the whole sequence of movement/change.

Aristotle named this the Prime Mover, and Aquinas developed this into the 'Unmoved Mover' – *'that which all men call God'*.

To illustrate this point further, Aquinas builds on Aristotle's examples and explanations. Aristotle speaks of things moving from a state of **'potentiality'** (i.e. something that it has a possibility of moving/changing into) towards a state of **'actuality'** (where it actually achieves or reaches its potential).

Key quote

It is certain, and evident to our senses, that in the world some things are in motion. Now whatever is in motion is put in motion by another, for nothing can be in motion except it is in potentiality to that towards which it is in motion; whereas a thing moves inasmuch as it is in act. For motion is nothing else than the reduction of something from potentiality to actuality. But nothing can be reduced from potentiality to actuality, except by something in a state of actuality.

St Thomas Aquinas, *Summa Theologica*

However, both Aristotle and Aquinas both noted that this change could only happen if something that already possessed a state of actuality acted on that which was in its state of potentiality. This third party is known as the **'efficient cause'**.

Aristotle used the example of a block of marble (potential) becoming a statue (actual) but only when acted upon by the sculptor (efficient cause).

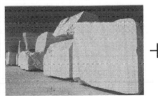 +  =

Block of Marble
(potential)

Sculptor
(efficient cause)

Statue
(actual)

Key Terms

Potentiality = the ability to be able to become something else.

Actuality = when something is in its fully realised state.

Efficient cause = the 'third party' that moves potentiality to actuality.

Key Figure

St Thomas Aquinas
A 13th-century Dominican priest from Italy who is regarded by many as the greatest medieval religious philosopher to have ever lived. He is particularly well known for using the philosophical works of Aristotle (considered heretical by many in the Church at the time) and putting them into a Christian framework. His philosophical style is most commonly referred to as Natural Theology.

Grade boost

Always use <u>examples</u> to <u>explain</u> your answers – it shows you <u>understand</u> the work and helps satisfy the trigger word 'Explain' in a question.

quickfire

③ What new name did Aquinas give Aristotle's prime mover?

④ What is an efficient cause?

Key terms

Efficient cause = this simply refers to the cause of an effect.

Intermediate cause = this refers to a cause that relies on something else to have triggered it (remember the 2nd domino in the line!).

Ultimate cause = in the sense of Aquinas' writings, this is the end cause in a sequence that could not have occurred had there not been preceding efficient and intermediate causes. (Think about this as the penultimate domino in the line to fall.)

Grade boost

The idea of motion does not necessarily mean movement in terms of velocity or direction; it can also mean the motion that an object has as it changes its state (e.g. H_2O molecules are in motion when heated and change from water to steam).

Aquinas uses the example of wood becoming hot in order to illustrate this point:

Key quote

Thus that which is actually hot, as fire, makes wood, which is potentially hot, to be actually hot, and thereby moves and changes it. Now it is not possible that the same thing should be at once in actuality and potentiality in the same respect, but only in different respects. For what is actually hot cannot simultaneously be potentially hot; but it is simultaneously potentially cold. It is therefore impossible that in the same respect and in the same way a thing should be both mover and moved, i.e. that it should move itself.

(St Thomas Aquinas, *Summa Theologica*)

In this, Aquinas is stating that the fire that makes wood hot must already have the property of hotness within itself in order, in turn, to make the wood hot. Were it to have any other state (e.g. coldness) within itself then it would be impossible to make the wood hot.

Aquinas: Second Way

Aquinas' Second Way deals with the concept of cause and effect. Everything observable in nature is subject to this law, according to Aquinas, although the idea that this chain of cause and effect could be traced back infinitely is seen as impossible by him. This then leads to the question: 'What was the first cause?' and, for Aquinas, the answer is 'God'.

Key Quote 1

*The second way is from the nature of the **efficient cause**. In the world of sense we find there is an order of efficient causes. There is no case known (neither is it, indeed, possible) in which a thing is found to be the efficient cause of itself; for so it would be prior to itself, which is impossible.*

St Thomas Aquinas, *Summa Theologica*

Aquinas states here, not only the idea that cause and effect is a simple, undeniable, law of the universe but also that it is impossible for anything within the universe to cause itself. (It would be like you being your own parent – you cannot exist before you exist – you need something else to bring you into existence.)

Key Quote 2

*Now in efficient causes it is not possible to go on to infinity, because in all efficient causes following in order, the first is the cause of the **intermediate cause**, and the intermediate is the cause of the **ultimate cause**, whether the intermediate cause be several, or only one. Now to take away the cause is to take away the effect. Therefore, if there be no first cause among efficient causes, there will be no ultimate, nor any intermediate cause.*

St Thomas Aquinas, *Summa Theologica*

Imagine a line of dominoes. The first (efficient cause) is the one that causes the second (intermediate cause) one to fall, which in turn causes the third (ultimate cause) one to fall. However, the third one would not have fallen, had the first one not have hit the second one. Aquinas' idea of efficient cause followed by intermediate cause and ending at ultimate cause can seem confusing at first, but by using the domino analogy (see diagram) it gives a suitable visual expression of the philosophical idea.

Ultimate cause

Intermediate cause

Efficient cause

quickfire

⑤ According to Aquinas, what law is everything observable in nature subject to?

⑥ Why, according to to Aquinas, was it impossible not to have a first cause?

Key Quote 3

But if in efficient causes it is possible to go on to infinity, there will be no first efficient cause, neither will there be an ultimate effect, nor any intermediate efficient causes; all of which is plainly false. Therefore it is necessary to admit a first efficient cause, to which everyone gives the name of God.

St Thomas Aquinas, *Summa Theologica*

Aquinas states clearly here that he rejects the idea of an infinite series of causes and effects existing within the universe (imagine an infinite row of dominoes – if it was infinite, where would the first domino be to push all of the others over?) and concludes that it is therefore essential for there to be a first cause to start everything else off. Aquinas characteristically names the first cause as 'God'.

Grade boost

Ed Miller in his *Questions that Matter* makes the point that when Aquinas is arguing against an infinite series of causes and effects he is not thinking of a temporal series, or one that stretches infinitely backwards in time, but rather a hierarchical series, or one that extends infinitely upwards in being. This would therefore be based on an assumption that all things have their source in an ultimate cause (or, in Aquinas' words: 'God'). This idea also closely relates to the ideas of both Plato and Aristotle.

Key Terms

Contingent = anything that depends on something else (in the case of a contingent being – it is contingent upon another being for its existence, e.g. a child is contingent upon its parent).

Necessary being = the philosophical concept of an existent being that cannot not exist. It is the source of existence for all other contingent beings.

quickfire

⑦ What is the difference between a contingent being and a necessary being?

Aquinas: Third Way

Aquinas' Third Way deals with the concept of contingency and necessity. Again, Aquinas notes that everything that exists has the possibility of not existing (i.e. it is contingent) and draws the conclusion that if this were true of everything in existence then nothing would ever have come into existence. This is because in order for **contingent** beings to exist there has to be a non-contingent (i.e. necessary) being that brought everything else into existence. For Aquinas, this **necessary being** is 'God'.

Key Quote 1

The third way is taken from possibility and necessity, and runs thus. We find in nature things that are possible to be and not to be, since they are found to be generated, and corrupted, and consequently, they are possible to be and not to be. But it is impossible for these always to exist, for that which is possible not to be at some time is not. Therefore, if everything is possible not to be, then at one time there could have been nothing in existence ... it would have been impossible for anything to have begun to exist; and thus even now nothing would be in existence ... which is absurd.

St Thomas Aquinas, *Summa Theologica*

Aquinas states that all things in nature are limited in their existence. They all have beginnings and endings. Following this idea to its logical conclusion Aquinas notes that this means at one point in history nothing existed and that, even now, nothing would exist – which is plainly not the case.

A way of thinking of this idea is to consider the relationship of the parent and the child. Without the existence of the parent, the child cannot come into existence. Or, to put it another way, the child is contingent on the parent for its existence.

Key Quote 2

Therefore, not all beings are merely possible, but there must exist something the existence of which is necessary. But every necessary thing either has its necessity caused by another, or not. Now it is impossible to go on to infinity in necessary things which have their necessity caused by another, as has been already proved in regard to efficient causes. Therefore we cannot but postulate the existence of some being having of itself its own necessity, and not receiving it from another, but rather causing in others their necessity. This all men speak of as God.

St Thomas Aquinas, *Summa Theologica*

Aquinas states that the only possible solution to this dilemma is that something must exist that is unlike everything else in existence – in that it has no beginning and no end, in other words, it has necessary existence. This necessary existence is needed to bring about the existence of everything else. For Aquinas this being was 'God'.

Leibniz: Principle of sufficient reason

Leibniz's argument comes in two parts. Firstly he takes Parmenides' original observation '*ex nihilo, nihil fit*' (out of nothing, nothing comes) and then asks: 'Why is there something rather than nothing?' (the assumption upon which all cosmological arguments ultimately rest). Leibniz then states that there must be some reason for the existence of everything. He uses the example of a succession of editions of the same book (see illustration) and suggests that it is impossible to give a full explanation as to where the book came from by merely looking at the previous edition. In effect Leibniz claims that unless you posit an author then you will never have a full explanation ('**sufficient reason**') for why the book existed in the first place. He then compares this to the world and states that, like the book, the world is nothing more than a succession of itself from earlier 'editions'. Unless a 'creator' (whom Leibniz calls 'God') is posited then, just like the books, a 'sufficient reason' can never be given for its existence.

Key Terms

Partial reason = an explanation which gives part of the reason why something is the way it is. However, this is not a full (sufficient) explanation for an idea or event and further information is required to substantiate it.

Sufficient reason = where a full explanation for any given idea or event is provided. No other explanation is required to substantiate what the sufficient reason provides.

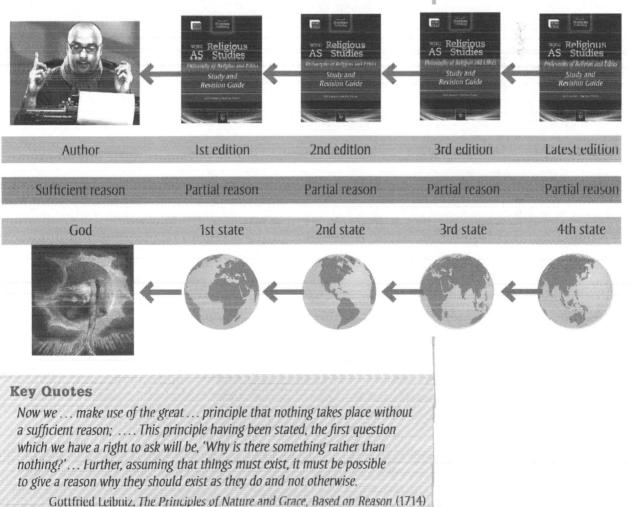

Author	1st edition	2nd edition	3rd edition	Latest edition
Sufficient reason	Partial reason	Partial reason	Partial reason	Partial reason
God	1st state	2nd state	3rd state	4th state

Key Quotes

Now we … make use of the great … principle that nothing takes place without a sufficient reason; …. This principle having been stated, the first question which we have a right to ask will be, 'Why is there something rather than nothing?' … Further, assuming that things must exist, it must be possible to give a reason why they should exist as they do and not otherwise.

Gottfried Leibniz, *The Principles of Nature and Grace, Based on Reason* (1714)

Grade boost

Don't forget to link Leibniz's example of the books to the existence of the universe. It is essential to do this to show that you have understood Leibniz's point and therefore his contribution to the cosmological argument.

quickfire

⑧ What is Latin for 'Out of nothing, nothing comes'?

> *Let us suppose a book … to have existed eternally, one edition having always been copied from the preceding: it is evident then that, although you can account for the present copy by reference to a past copy which it reproduces, yet, however far back you go … you can never arrive at a complete [explanation].*
>
> Gottfried Leibniz, *On the Ultimate Origination of the Universe* (1697)

> *Now this sufficient reason for the existence of the universe cannot be found in the series of contingent things …. Although the present motion … arises from preceding motion, and that in turn from motion which preceded it, we do not get further however far we may go, for the same question always remains. The sufficient reason, therefore, which needs not further reason, must be outside of this series of contingent things and is found in a substance which … is a necessary being bearing the reason for its existence within itself; otherwise we should not yet have a sufficient reason with which to stop. This final reason for things is called God.*
>
> Gottfried Leibniz, *The Principles of Nature and Grace, Based on Reason* (1714)

Key Figure

William Lane Craig (b. 1949) is an American philosopher and Christian **apologist**. He is particularly well known for his contribution to the cosmological argument with his version of the 'Kalam' argument. He has regularly debated publicly with proponents of views that are in opposition to his own – notably atheist apologists Christopher Hitchens and Richard Dawkins.

Key Terms

Apologist = an individual who writes or speaks in defence of a particular cause or belief.

Temporal = things relating to time.

Kalam arguments (1): William Lane Craig

In 1993 Craig stipulated his argument thus:

1 Everything that begins to exist has a cause of its existence.

2 The universe began to exist.

3 Therefore, the universe has a cause of its existence.

4 Since no scientific explanation (in terms of physical laws) can provide a causal account of the origin of the universe, the cause must be personal (explanation is given in terms of a personal agent).

This is a (relatively) straightforward and easy to follow argument. However, in order to answer challenges to the idea that the universe might be considered infinite, Craig developed the following defence to his second point:

i) An actual infinite cannot exist.

ii) A beginningless **temporal** series of events is an actual infinite.

iii) Therefore, a beginningless temporal series of events cannot exist.

In order to explain this, an example of a library is often referred to: Imagine a library with an actually infinite number of books. Suppose that the library also contains an infinite number of red and an infinite number of black books, so that for every red book there is a black book, and vice versa. It follows that the library contains as many red books as the total books in its collection, and as many red books as red and black books combined. But this is absurd; in reality the subset (i.e. red or black) cannot be equivalent to the entire set (i.e. red and black). Hence, actual infinites cannot exist in reality.

However, critics point out that this is ignoring the fact that there are two types of infinity recognised in standard mathematics – 'actual' and 'potential'. Craig only refers to the impossibility of the first, not the second in his initial argument. Craig responded by recognising that if an **actual infinite** was impossible, a **potential infinite** confirmed the fact that the universe had a beginning. This forms the second part of his argument.

Craig's Kalam argument is often seen as very confusing, not least because it depends on an understanding of the concepts of infinity that are, in themselves, difficult to grasp. However, in its simplest form it is straightforward and appealing – to such a degree that it has had massive influence in the rational theistic defence against atheistic arguments – especially in the evangelical Christian churches of America.

Key Quote

I think that it can be plausibly argued that the cause of the universe must be a personal Creator. For how else could a temporal effect arise from an eternal cause? If the cause were simply a mechanically operating set of necessary and sufficient conditions existing from eternity, then why would not the effect also exist from eternity? For example, if the cause of water being frozen is the temperature being below zero degrees, then if the temperature were below zero degrees from eternity, then any water present would be frozen from eternity. The only way to have an eternal cause but a temporal effect would seem to be if the cause is a personal agent who freely chooses to create an effect in time. For example, a man sitting from eternity may will to stand up; hence, a temporal effect may arise from an eternally existing agent. Indeed, the agent may will from eternity to create a temporal effect, so that no change in the agent need be conceived. Thus, we are brought not merely to the first cause of the universe, but to its personal Creator.

William Lane Craig, 'The Existence of God and the Beginning of the Universe', Leadership University, Copyright © 2012 William Lane Craig

Key Terms

Actual infinite = something that is actually infinite in extent or in extent of the operations performed.

Potential infinite = the potential infinite is something that could continue on, were effort to be applied. E.g. it would be possible to always continue a number line if we wanted to, or we could always come up with a bigger number.

quickfire

(9) What did Craig state was true for everything that begins to exist?

(10) What is the main difference between an actual infinite and a potential infinite?

(11) Which movement within Christianity has been particularly supportive of Craig's argument?

Grade boost

Successful candidates are not expected to be able to go into great detail regarding Craig's concepts of infinity. As long as they can show that they understand how his Kalam argument is formulated, along with the basic differences (as explained in Key terms) of potential and actual infinites, then that is sufficient to meet the criteria for a top-level answer.

Key Term

Syllogism = a form of logical, deductive, reasoning. It usually contains two premises (one major, one minor) and a conclusion that follows from these premises.

Key Figure

Professor Edward L. Miller

A 21st-century American theologian and religious philosopher. He is best known internationally for his book *Questions that Matter*, which examines the history and development of a wide number of issues related to religious philosophy. He is most commonly associated with the University of Colorado, Boulder, where he has taught for over thirty years. His contribution to the Kalam cosmological argument is associated, like Craig, with the philosophical necessity to believe in the beginning of the world, rejecting the possibility of an infinite universe.

quickfire

⑫ What is the philosophical basis for Miller's Kalam argument?

Kalam arguments (2): Ed Miller

Ed Miller summarises the cosmological argument into five basic steps:

First stage

1. There exists the world (or, literally, all of space and time).
2. It could not be the cause of itself (as it would have to exist before itself, which is impossible).
3. It could not come from nothing (because of '*ex nihilo, nihil fi*t').
4. It could not be an effect in an infinite series of causes and effects.
5. Therefore, it must be caused by something outside space and time, something uncaused and ultimate.

Second stage

He goes on to point out that the argument can even be formulated as a type of categorical **syllogism**:

1. All contingent (or caused) beings depends for their existence on some uncaused being.
2. The cosmos is a contingent being.

Therefore:

3. The cosmos depends for its existence on some uncaused being.

He does, however, recognise that the strength of any deductive reasoning is only as good as its premises and recognises that the uncaused cause does not necessarily have to be God!

Conclusion

Miller, like Craig, considers that it is philosophically necessary to arrive at the conclusion that the cosmos has a beginning. He states:

> 'If the world *has* always existed, then an infinite number of years (or months, minutes or whatever) has *already gone by*. But surely this is a self-contradictory claim. For an *infinite* series of years (or whatever) can never (by its very nature as being *infinite*) go by or be completed. How can one claim that prior to this moment (what lies in the future is irrelevant) the world has *passed through* an infinite numbers of years? Of course, you can *think* of an infinite number of years, but you can't count them; you can entertain the *idea* of an infinite series, but you can't actually *pass through* one and come out the other end. Or try this: If the universe has always existed, then it has taken *forever* to reach this point. But then it could never reach this point. But here we are! So it *didn't* take forever.'
>
> Ed L Miller, Jon Jensen, *Questions that Matter: An Invitation to Philosophy*, McGraw-Hill Higher Education (1985)

Miller's point is that it is impossible that the world has existed for an infinite amount of time because that would mean an infinite number of years had already gone by and, as that is self-contradictory, there must have been a point, in the past, where the world had a starting point, a beginning.

Arguments against the cosmological argument

Having existed for over 2,500 years, the cosmological argument has attracted not only supporters but also those who wish to show its shortcomings. Scientific developments, particularly in the last 100 years, have taken our conventional understanding of a cause and effect universe and turned it upon its head. Quantum physics, chaos theory and similar radical progressions in our understanding of the workings of the universe have all had a role to play in diminishing the claims made by supporters of the cosmological argument, even though they are not always wholly successful. Indeed, some scientific theories, including most notably the Big Bang theory, have even been used to support parts of the cosmological argument – not least in demonstrating the concept that the universe had a starting point.

Summary of criticisms

Hume

1. Just because we observe cause and effect IN the universe does not mean that this rule applies to the universe itself! (Russell used the example 'Just because every human has a mother does not mean the whole of humanity has a mother') This is often called the '**fallacy of composition**'.
2. Whilst we can talk about things that we have experience of with some certainty, we have no experience of creating a universe and therefore cannot talk meaningfully about that.
3. There is not enough evidence to say whether the universe had a cause and definitely not enough to make any conclusion as to what the cause might have been.
4. Even if 'God' could be accepted as the cause of the universe, there is no way to determine what sort of God this would be and certainly no way of determining if it was the **God of classical theism**.

Kant

5. The idea of cause and effect only applies in the realm of sense experiences – if we have not experienced something with our senses we can make no claim on it.
6. To suggest God as the cause of the universe is equally nonsensical as he also lies outside of the realm of sense experience.

20th century

7. (Russell) Suggested that the existence of the universe was a 'brute fact' and that, as the cosmological argument depended entirely on asking the question 'how did the universe begin?' then by removing the question the argument is pointless.

Key Terms

God of classical theism
= the God that is generally associated with the Western monotheistic religions of Christianity, Islam and Judaism.

Fallacy of composition
= philosophical notion that what is true of the parts is not necessarily true of the whole (i.e. atoms are colourless but this does not mean that a cat, which is made of atoms, is colourless).

Key Figures

David Hume (1711–1776) Scottish enlightenment philosopher who, as an empiricist, demonstrated a number of the flaws in the main theistic arguments for God's existence. Most significant work in relation to this is his *Dialogues Concerning Natural Religion*.

Immanuel Kant (1724–1804) German enlightenment philosopher who attempted to reconcile the empirical and rational realms in his philosophy. He saw God as a natural postulate of reason but refused to accept that it was empirically possible to 'prove' God's existence.

A posteriori = that which is based on empirical evidence or experience.

A priori = that which is not based on empirical evidence or experience.

quickfire

⑬ What problem did Hume raise for those who stated that a god was the cause of the universe?

⑭ Whose law did Anthony Kenny invoke to show Aquinas' First Way to be inaccurate?

⑮ What basic contradiction lies at the heart of most theistic cosmological arguments?

⑯ As a strength, what question does the cosmological argument satisfy?

⑰ Why is the cumulative case argument suspect?

8. (Kenny) The physical principle highlighted in Newton's First Law of Motion '… wrecks the argument of the First Way.' This is because the principle of inertia can be used to show how animals have the capacity to move themselves without being moved by another.

General

9. Aquinas' suggestion (after Aristotle) that only like causes bring about like effects is widely dismissed in the modern scientific world. E.g. the friction that results from rubbing two sticks (cold) together produces heat, whereas using Aquinas' model it should be that only more cold could be produced.

10. Both traditional and modern cosmological arguments assert that the universe is finite but God is infinite. This assumption underlies the arguments. This is, however, a contradiction – to deny the possibility of infinite for one (i.e. the universe) but not the other (i.e. God) is a philosophical fallacy.

11. (Scientific) The Big Bang theory is often used as a 'proof' that it was the random action of quantum particles that caused the beginning of the universe, not God. However, many theists suggest that this interaction was not random but caused by God.

Key Figures

Bertrand Russell (1872–1970) Welsh-born analytical philosopher who saw religion as an outdated superstitious practice that impeded mankind's intellectual development. Most famously associated with the cosmological argument due to his 'famous' radio debate with Father Frederick Copleston on the existence of God.

Anthony Kenny (b.1931) English philosopher who has written extensively on Aquinas. His 1969 work *The Five Ways: St Thomas Aquinas' Proofs of God's Existence* is an essential text for understanding how the modern world has recognised the flaws in Aquinas' work due to progress in scientific understanding.

Strengths and weaknesses of the cosmological argument

Evaluations often consider the strong and weak points of arguments and ideas. As such it is important to know what those ideas are before a proper evaluation can take place. Consider the points presented in the 'Strength /Weaknesses' diagram: Are they all equally valid? Do some make sense to everyone or only to religious believers? Do these arguments cancel each other out? etc. Your ability to ask and answer each of these questions will strengthen your evaluation in your essay.

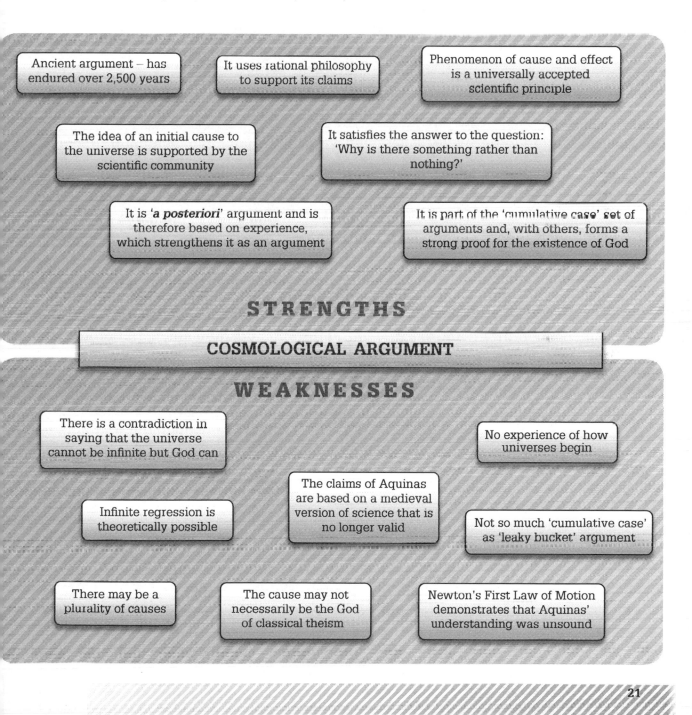

STRENGTHS

Ancient argument – has endured over 2,500 years

It uses rational philosophy to support its claims

Phenomenon of cause and effect is a universally accepted scientific principle

The idea of an initial cause to the universe is supported by the scientific community

It satisfies the answer to the question: 'Why is there something rather than nothing?'

It is 'a posteriori' argument and is therefore based on experience, which strengthens it as an argument

It is part of the 'cumulative case' set of arguments and, with others, forms a strong proof for the existence of God

COSMOLOGICAL ARGUMENT

WEAKNESSES

There is a contradiction in saying that the universe cannot be infinite but God can

No experience of how universes begin

Infinite regression is theoretically possible

The claims of Aquinas are based on a medieval version of science that is no longer valid

Not so much 'cumulative case' as 'leaky bucket' argument

There may be a plurality of causes

The cause may not necessarily be the God of classical theism

Newton's First Law of Motion demonstrates that Aquinas' understanding was unsound

Summary: Cosmological argument

We have identified the key points on the WJEC AS specification and, combined with the information in this topic, represented them as a diagram which shows the main things that you need to know. You may want to fill in further details to elaborate and personalise this content.

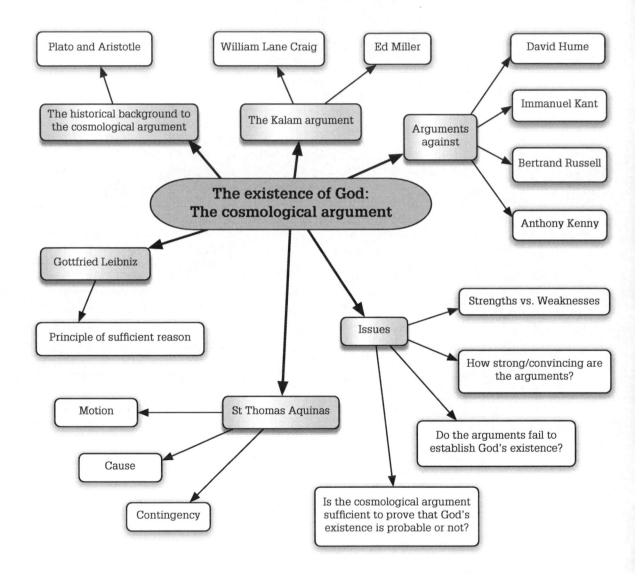

2: Teleological Argument

When revising the teleological argument for the existence of God, you should focus on the main debates and issues. For example, you are expected to know the philosophical concepts of order, design and purpose as originated by Plato, Aristotle and Aquinas. You will also need to understand precisely how philosophers such as Paley and Tennant have developed these concepts. In addition, you will need to understand the main philosophical objections to the teleological argument and be able to articulate each of these fluently. Finally, you should be able to evaluate the issues that arise from the teleological argument and be able to support any conclusion that you might draw with reference to the contributions of philosophers both ancient and modern.

Revision checklist

Tick column 1 when you have completed brief revision notes.
Tick column 2 when you think you have a good grasp of the topic.
Tick column 3 during final revision when you feel you have mastery of the topic.

			1	2	3
What is the historical background to the teleological argument?	p24	Plato – concept of the demi-urge			
	p24	Aristotle – concept of complexity and possibilities of divine handiwork.			
What was the contribution from Aquinas?	p25	The Fifth Way – from the governance of things			
	p25	Explanation of archer and arrow analogy			
How did William Paley further the argument from design?	p26	Analogy of watch and watchmaker			
	p26	Design qua purpose			
	p26	Design qua regularity			
What is the Anthropic principle?	p28	Weak anthropic principle			
	p28	Strong anthropic principle			
	p28	Tennant			
	p28	Polkinghorne			
	p29	Swinburne			
What is the aesthetic argument?	p29	Appeal to the presence of beauty as evidence for a benevolent designer			
What are the arguments against the teleological argument for the existence of God?	p30	Hume – Seven critiques			
	p32	Kant – Limits of human reason			
	p32	Mill – Problem of evil			
	p33	Darwin – Evolution and natural selection			
	p33	Dawkins – Regular processes of natural world and the blind watchmaker			
What are the main issues that arise from the teleological argument for the existence of God?	p34	Strengths vs. weaknesses			
	p34	How persuasive is the teleological argument?			
	p34	Do the arguments against make the teleological argument ineffective?			
	p34	Does the evidence from science discredit the teleological argument?			

Historical background: Plato and Aristotle

quickfire

① What name did Plato give to the designing creator?

② What evidence does Aristotle suggest points towards the existence of the gods?

Plato

Plato believed in a universe that was pre-existent. Within this universe there existed a being who had the power to shape worlds – Plato names this being the demi-urge. For Plato, this demi-urge is responsible for all things on earth – having fashioned them out of the pre-existent matter of the early universe. This for Plato was the rational explanation as to why there existed order, rather than chaos, in the world around him. However, whilst this superficially appears to be a similar universe view to those that believe in the God of classical theism there are (at least) two important differences. Firstly, Plato's demi-urge does not create (or design) *ex nihilo* – he is working within an established universe, of which he is a part. Secondly, for Plato perfection was only to be found within the world of the Forms which was beyond this world. All things within creation may move towards trying to emulate the Forms but, as they had been made from the material universe, this venture was in vain.

Aristotle

In turn, Aristotle considered that, based on all his observations of the world around him and the stars above him, the only possible explanation for all the complexity and beauty that the world contains was a divine intelligence. Aristotle put forward an argument in his *Metaphysics* that there had to be a First Unmoved Mover responsible for, and the source of, all order that exists in the universe. Such a god was also viewed as possessing intelligence, goodness, eternity yet remained incorporeal.

Key Quote

This ordered world is of mixed birth; it is the offspring of a union of Necessity and Intellect. Intellect prevailed over Necessity by persuading it to direct most of the things that come to be toward what is best, and the result of this subjugation of Necessity to wise persuasion was the initial formation of this universe.

Plato, *Timeaus* trans. Donald Zeyl, Hackett (2000)

Key Quote

Can any sane person believe that all this array of stars and this vast celestial adornment could have been created out of atoms rushing to and fro fortuitously and at random? or could any other being devoid of intelligence and reason have created them? Not merely did their creation postulate intelligence, but it is impossible to understand their nature without intelligence of a high order ....

Cicero, *On the Nature of the Gods*

Key Quote

When thus they would suddenly gain sight of the earth, seas, and the sky; when they should come to know the grandeur of the clouds and the might of the winds; when they should behold the sun and should learn its grandeur and beauty as well as its power to cause the day by shedding light over the sky; and again, when the night had darkened the lands and they should behold the whole of the sky spangled and adorned with stars; and when they should see the changing lights of the moon as it waxes and wanes, and the risings and settings of all these celestial bodies, their courses fixed and changeless throughout all eternity – when they should behold all these things, most certainly they would have judged both that there exist gods and that all these marvellous works are the handiwork of the gods.

Aristotle, *On Philosophy*

Aquinas: Fifth Way

Key Term
Telos = the term can have a number of meanings but generally refers to the 'end' (as in final destination); 'goal' or 'purpose' of something. The term is frequently found in Aristotle's philosophy.

Aquinas' teleological argument can be found in the fifth of his 'Five Ways' in the *Summa Theologica*. Here Aquinas states that something that lacks intelligence cannot move towards fulfilling a useful end, unless something with intelligence has moved them.

Imagine, for example, that you need to write your essay with a pen. The pen itself is non-intelligent and cannot (however much you may wish it!) write your essay for you. The only way that it will do this is if you (as an intelligent being) pick up the pen, hold it in a way that is appropriate for writing and then apply it to the paper, moving it to make the required shapes (i.e. writing) that are required to communicate your ideas.

Aquinas' own example was that of the arrow and the archer – archery was a frequent pastime in his day, either as a sport or as a way of killing other people in war and therefore his analogy would have been easily understood.

Key Quote

The fifth way is taken from the governance of the world. We see that things which lack knowledge, such as natural bodies, act for an end, and this is evident from their acting always, or nearly always, in the same way, so as to obtain the best result. Hence it is plain that they achieve their end, not fortuitously, but designedly. Now whatever lacks knowledge cannot move towards an end, unless it be directed by some being endowed with knowledge and intelligence; as the arrow is directed by the archer. Therefore, some intelligent being exists by whom all natural things are directed to their end; and this being we call God.

St Thomas Aquinas, *Summa Theologica*

③ Why did Aquinas believe it was necessary to suggest a guiding intelligence behind the natural workings of the universe?

Aquinas stated that the arrow, by itself, cannot reach the target. It needs to be fired by the archer in order for this to happen. He relates this to the workings of the universe and states that everything in the universe follows natural laws, even if they possess no intelligence (i.e. the regular movement of the stars in the sky – which in Aquinas' time people had no rational 'scientific' explanation for). The fact that these things also tend to follow these laws and, in doing so, fulfil some purpose or end goal (their '*telos*') yet don't have the ability to 'think' for themselves, suggests that (as with the arrow) they have been 'directed' by something else. For Aquinas, the only possible explanation was that this guiding intelligence was God.

Key Terms

Natural world = the world of nature, comprising all objects, organic and inorganic.

Qua = Latin word meaning by virtue of, e.g. design *qua* purpose = design *by virtue of* purpose.

quickfire

④ How did Paley compare the stone and watch?

⑤ Outline how the watchmaker and universe-maker are linked by Paley.

⑥ Give two examples of design qua purpose.

Grade boost

Candidates frequently retell Paley's analogy without providing the final conclusion that the universe's designer (God) is analogous to the watchmaker. As this is the whole point of Paley's argument, ensure that you do not make the same mistake!

William Paley: Analogy of the watchmaker and other arguments

William Paley, Archdeacon of Carlisle, is widely credited with proposing the design argument in its popular modern form. He proposed his version in *Natural Theology*, published in the early 1800s. His basic argument was that, were we to discover a stone whilst walking, we might enquire how it came to be and, through considering natural events, would come to a conclusion of how it was formed. However, were we to discover a watch, we would not come to the same conclusions. Paley was interested in pointing out why this was the case.

A watch of around this time would have been made up of a watch-face with numerals and hands that pointed towards the time. The inner workings of the watch were a complex system of cogs, springs and gears. Simply because they were complex, these mechanisms would point towards the conclusion that this watch had been designed by a being of intelligence and was not the result of random chance.

Paley states that we could draw this conclusion even if we were unaware of the purpose of the watch; if the watch went wrong or even if we didn't understand what some of the parts of the watch actually did. In summary, the complex watch needs an intelligent watchmaker to explain how it came into being.

Paley then widens his argument and states that the universe in which we live (and using the **natural world** as evidence) is likewise complex and therefore also suggests it had a designer. Paley spends a large amount of time detailing the workings of the eye and suggests that the incredible complexity of this unit within the human body alone is evidence for a designing intelligence.

Paley also details how other examples in nature seem to point towards the same conclusion. For example, he points out how the instincts of birds ensures that they sit on their eggs whilst the young are growing inside them, thereby providing the perfect incubating environment, or how moths and butterflies lay their eggs on precisely the sort of plant that their larvae need to feed on to survive and grow to maturity.

All of these arguments talk about how God, as the designer, designed the natural world so that everything in it not only had a purpose but was also capable of fulfilling that purpose. For this reason, some commentators refer to this part of Paley's argument as 'design **qua** purpose'.

Paley also referred to other types of phenomena observable within the natural world to support his argument and these form his 'design qua regularity' argument.

In his *Natural Theology* Paley refers to the motion of the planets observable in the night sky and states that even though their motion may be due, in some part, to their relative proximity to each other, the conclusion was inescapable that some guiding intelligence had pre-determined their place so as to allow that regularity of motion.

Paley asserts that this guiding intelligence was as responsible for creating the purpose of all living things on the earth as it was for the regular movement of things above the earth, and this for him, was God the author, in nature, of infinitely various expedients for infinitely various ends.

Key Quote

In crossing a heath, suppose I pitched my foot against a stone, and were asked how the stone came to be there, I might possibly answer, that, for any thing I knew to the contrary, it had lain there for ever: nor would it perhaps be very easy to shew the absurdity of this answer. But suppose I had found a watch upon the ground, and it should be enquired how the watch happened to be in that place, I should hardly think of the answer which I had before given, that, for any thing I knew, the watch might have always been there. Yet why should not this answer serve for the watch as well as for the stone?

Key Quote

... when we come to inspect the watch, we perceive (what we could not discover in the stone) that its several parts are framed and put together for a purpose, e.g. that they are so formed and adjusted as to produce motion, and that motion so regulated as to point out the hour of the day; that, if the several parts had been differently shaped from what they are, of a different size from what they are, or placed after any other manner, or in any other order, than that in which they are placed, either no motion at all would have been carried on in the machine, or none which would have answered the use that is now served by it ... the inference, we think, is inevitable, that the watch must have had a maker: that there must have existed, at some time and at some place or other, an artificer or artificers who formed it for the purpose which we find it actually to answer; who comprehended its construction, and designed its use ... every manifestation of design, which existed in the watch, exists in the works of nature; with the difference, on the side of nature, of being greater and more, and that in a degree which exceeds all computation.

Key Quote

This is the scale by which we ascend to all the knowledge of our Creator which we possess, so far as it depends upon the phenomena or the works of nature. Take away this, and you take away from us every subject of observation and ground of reasoning; I mean, as our rational faculties are formed at present. Whatever is done, God could have done without the intervention of instruments or means; but it is in the construction of instruments, in the choice and adaptation of means, that a creative intelligence is seen. It is this which constitutes the order and beauty of the universe.

William Paley, *Natural Theology*, printed for R Faulder (1802)

Key Term

Anthropic = as relating to humans (from the Greek *anthropos*, a human being).

Anthropic principle

Key Term

Anthropic = as relating to humans (from the Greek *anthropos*, a human being).

Key Quote

Scientists are slowly waking up to an inconvenient truth – the universe looks suspiciously like a fix. The issue concerns the very laws of nature themselves. For 40 years, physicists and cosmologists have been quietly collecting examples of all too convenient 'coincidences' and special features in the underlying laws of the universe that seem to be necessary in order for life, and hence conscious beings, to exist. Change any one of them and the consequences would be lethal ... Like Baby Bear's porridge in the story of Goldilocks, the universe seems to be just right for life.'

Paul Davies, 'Yes, the universe looks like a fix. But that doesn't mean that a god fixed it', *The Guardian*, 26/6/2007. © Guardian News & Media Ltd 2007

Key Quote

The central insight of the Anthropic Principle (AP) is that the specific character of lawful necessity had to have a very particular form – often expressed in the metaphor of a 'fine-tuning' of the laws of nature .... In other words, simple evolutionary exploration of what might happen (chance) would not have been sufficient if the lawful regularity of the universe (necessity) had not taken the very specific form required for biological potentiality. The universe was billions of years old before life appeared in it, but it was pregnant with that possibility from the beginning.

John Polkinghorne, 'The Anthropic Principle and the Science and Religion Debate', *The Faraday Papers No.4* © 2007 The Faraday Institute for Science and Religion, St Edmund's College

quickfire

⑦ Who coined the term 'Anthropic principle'?

⑧ What were Tennant's three pieces of evidence to support his Anthropic principle?

Grade boost

It is a common mistake to say that Tennant invented the Anthropic principle. Make certain when referencing Tennant that you always use the term 'developed' rather than invented!

One of the more persistent forms of the design argument in the contemporary world is that of the Anthropic principle. (In actual fact there are many anthropic principles but, for sake of simplicity, we shall subsume them under one umbrella term.) The term was first coined by astrophysicist Brendon Carter, who proposed a weak and strong form of the Anthropic principle.

The weak form runs thus:

We must be prepared to take into account the fact that our location in the universe is necessarily privileged to the extent of being compatible with our existence as observers.

Whereas the strong form states:

The Universe (and hence the fundamental parameters on which it depends) must be such as to admit the creation of observers within it at some stage.

Whilst not using the specific term 'Anthropic principle', in his 1928 work *Philosophical Theology* Frederick Tennant developed a set of evidences which are widely recognised as anthropic principles today. The evidence included beliefs such as:

1. The very fact that the world in which we live provides precisely the things that are necessary for life to be sustained.

2. The fact that the world in which we live can not only be observed but holds itself up for rational analysis from which we can deduce its workings.

3. The fact that the process of evolution, through natural selection, has led to the development of intelligent human life – to the degree that that intelligent life can observe and analyse the universe that it exists in.

John Polkinghorne supports the Anthropic principle and suggests that it is the only reasonable explanation for the existence of carbon-based life forms that also have intelligence and the ability to rationally observe the universe that they are living in.

Richard Swinburne's Anthropic principle is related to the idea that the existence of humankind in an ordered, rational universe is too improbable for it to be the result of random chance. He thus concluded that the simplest conclusion was to say it was the result of the deliberate decision of a divine designer.

Aesthetic argument

Tennant's **aesthetic** argument relates to the natural appreciation that human beings have for things that are considered to be 'beautiful' and asks why we have such an appreciation as part of our nature. When looking at the rest of the natural world there appears to be no other species which reacts to its surroundings in this way. In fact, this can also be extended to the appreciation that humans have for music, art, poetry and other forms of literature as well as an appreciation for things like fashion, cosmetics and other such things that are said to enhance human beauty.

If a purely rational approach is taken towards human beings as a species then only those things which are necessary for our survival are necessary for us to have in the world around us. Our understanding of the natural world informs us that living organisms operate on a 'survival of the fittest' mechanism and anything that does not aid evolution is quickly rejected by a species as it develops through time. Why then do we, as human beings, have an appreciation of beauty? Why are aesthetics so important to us?

Tennant's response was to claim that this appreciation was a direct result of a benevolent God. Having designed the world so that it led to the development of intelligent human life (*see Anthropic principle*), God not only wanted this creation to live in the world, but also to enjoy living in it. Beauty and its appreciation were not necessary for humans to survive. For Tennant the existence of beauty in the world was its own evidence for God's existence and led, by way of revelation, to the enquiring mind discovering the fact of God's existence for themselves.

Key Term
Aesthetic = related to the concept and appreciation of beauty.

Key Quote

The aesthetic argument for theism becomes more persuasive when it renounces all claims to proof and appeals to a logical probability. And it becomes stronger when it takes as the most significant fact ... the saturation of Nature with beauty .... God reveals himself in many ways; and some men enter His Temple by the Gate Beautiful.

F R Tennant, *Philosophical Theology Volume 2*, Cambridge University Press (1930)

quickfire

(9) Why did Tennant consider that an appreciation of beauty led to the conclusion that the designer of the world was benevolent?

An aesthetic dimension for human beings was proof of the existence of a benevolent designer according to Tennant.

Key Figures

Charles Darwin

English naturalist who revolutionised the Western world's understanding of how life developed. His most famous work, *On the Origin of Species*, published in 1859, set forward the idea that life on earth had developed through processes of natural selection and evolution. The theory made no mention of life developing as part of the work of a divine creator and was met with varying degrees of opposition from the religious establishment upon its publication.

Richard Dawkins

Evolutionary biologist sometimes referred to as Darwin's 'Bulldog'. As an atheist, Dawkins has written a number of books which reject the need for a religious worldview and campaign for the adoption of a wholly scientific view of the universe and its workings by modern society. Most notable works are *The Selfish Gene* (1976); *The Blind Watchmaker* (1986) and *The God Delusion* (2006).

See also Hume and Kant on page 19.

Arguments against the teleological argument

Tracing its origins to the earliest of Western civilisation's greatest thinkers, the design or teleological argument represents one of religious theists' most stalwart defences. The idea that the universe is far too complex, contains purpose for all things within it and has produced a life-form capable of observing, analysing and even philosophising about it and that none of these things seem likely to have happened by chance, all seems to point towards the existence of God; or so religious believers would like to claim. However, like the cosmological argument, this too has its detractors. It is argued that we lack sufficient experience to make such claims about a grand design; that the analogies used do not hold up to scrutiny; that if the universe were designed it would not have so many flaws. As well as the alternative solutions proposed by scientific enquiry, all these arguments need serious consideration.

Summary of criticisms

1   Hume – Analogies

Hume criticises the use of human analogies to demonstrate the fact that the universe is designed. He uses the example of a house and an architect/builder and says that just because we know how a house is designed/built it does not mean that we can infer from this how the universe is designed/built. The house and the universe are just too different to draw that point of comparison, no matter the general resemblances that they may have in other ways. Analogies normally work on the following basis:

a. X and Y are similar

b. X has the characteristic Z

c. Therefore Y has the characteristic Z

However, to claim what is true of Y based purely on a similarity to X is only as strong as the point at which X and Y are similar. If the similarity between them is weak, then the conclusion drawn by the analogy is likewise weak. Hume concludes that, as the universe is unique, no analogy is sufficient to explain its origins.

2   Hume – Experience

Any analogy made by human beings is necessarily based on the experience that human beings have. If we lack experience of the thing that the analogy is being used to 'prove' then how can we be certain that the analogy is sound? As human beings have no experience of how the universe was designed then any analogy put forward to try to prove this matter is ultimately futile.

3 Hume – Organic universe

The suggestion that the universe is comparable to some artificial construct such as a house or a machine is also rejected. The universe demonstrates greater similarities to the living organisms within the natural world than it does to a static artificial construct.

> 'And does not a plant or animal, which springs from vegetation or generation, bear a stronger resemblance to the world, than does any artificial machine, which arises from reason and design?'
>
> Hume, *Dialogues*

4 Hume – Apparent design

In his *Dialogues Concerning Natural Religion* Hume suggests there is fallacy in assuming that the universe is designed just because it seems so. He makes the distinction between authentic design and apparent design. In the first case, this would be the claim made by the classical theist – that God is responsible for the design of the universe. However, in the latter case what we have is an appearance of design where none actually exists. Indeed, this is the point that Hume makes through Philo, the character in the *Dialogues* that most commentators associate with Hume's own view. Philo makes reference to the Epicurean Hypothesis. This is a belief, stated by Epicurus, that the current so-called order in the universe that exists, is nothing more than the random association of atoms that had previously been in a chaotic state, but, through the principal nature of the universe (which is change), these atoms re-organise themselves infinitely, and occasionally do so in a way that resembles order (and, thereby, design).

5 Hume – Poor design

Even if we assume that the universe has a designer, as we have no universes to compare this one to, how do we know that it has been designed well? It may be that were we able to make such a comparison, we would find the designer of this one to be lacking in skill. Hume makes the comparison with a ship builder. If one saw a ship for the first time, one might assume that the ship builder was a genius to have made such a thing. However, if one were to investigate further they will find that the ship they are observing is nothing more than an imitation of other ships and, in comparison, it's not even that good. Neither does it take into account the various other ships that this ship builder may have tried to make along the way in perfecting his art. Relating this to the work of a god in designing the universe, Hume observes that there may be better universes out there; that this designing god is a poor designer in comparison to others and that, in practising his art, he has produced a series of worlds and universes that have been '*botched and bungled, throughout an eternity, ere this system was struck out*'. (Hume, *Dialogues*)

Key Quote

Nearly all the things which men are hanged or imprisoned for doing to one another, are nature's every day performances. Killing, the most criminal act recognized by human laws, Nature does once to every being that lives; and in a large proportion of cases, after protracted tortures such as only the greatest monsters whom we read of ever purposely inflicted on their living fellow-creatures.

John Stuart Mill, *Nature, the Utility of Religion and Theism*, Longmans, Green, Reader, and Dyer (1874)

Key Quote

But nothing obliges us to suppose that either the knowledge or the skill is infinite. We are not even compelled to suppose that the contrivances were always the best possible. If we venture to judge them as we judge the works of human artificers, we find abundant defects. The human body, for example, is one of the most striking instances of artful and ingenious contrivance which nature offers, but we may well ask whether so complicated a machine could not have been made to last longer, and not to get so easily and frequently out of order.... The divine power may not have been equal to doing more.

John Stuart Mill, *Nature, the Utility of Religion and Theism*, Longmans, Green, Reader, and Dyer (1874)

Grade boost

Remember that Hume lived before Paley. Some candidates mistakenly state that Hume was criticising Paley but this was not the case. Make certain you are aware of the chronological order in which the main philosophers lived so that you do not make the same mistake!

 **quickfire**

⑩ How many criticisms does Hume make?

⑪ Outline why Hume rejects the use of analogy to prove the existence of a divine designer.

⑫ How does the existence of suffering in nature pose a problem for JS Mill?

6 Hume – Many builders

After referring to the ship/shipbuilder analogy, Philo suggests that, as a house or ship has many builders, surely it makes sense to say that there were many builders likewise involved in constructing the universe. In making this assertion, Hume is demonstrating that the use of human analogies is a double-edged sword for those theists who rely on them to show the likelihood of the existence of a designing creator God.

7 Hume – Absent designer

Furthermore, after a ship or house builder has completed their task they move on. Perhaps this is also true of the supposed designer of the universe? He may well have left the universe to its own devices (this is very similar to the Deist position), or perhaps may even have died. There is no necessity for such a designer to have to exist for eternity, just because that which he has designed does.

8 Kant – Restricted experience

Human reason is only capable of making certain conclusions about the phenomenal or empirical world (i.e. the world around us that is directly available to us through our senses and experiences). To make any statement about those things which are beyond those two worlds is to make statements that we cannot be certain about. Such statements therefore have no validity. Thus any statements made about the universe's origins, or about whether it has been designed, are equally futile.

9 Mill – Suffering and cruelty

In his essay *Nature and the Utility of Religion*, Mill remarked that the way in which nature allowed so much suffering and cruelty as part of everyday life seemed to suggest that either there was no designer or the designer was limited in his ability to prevent evil and suffering (see Key quotes, page 31). The problem of evil and innocent suffering is a major attack on the idea that the world has been designed by a kind and loving God. Many philosophers, both before and after Mill, have recognised this. For a fuller treatment of this issue, which can then be added to the criticisms against the teleological argument, see Section 3 'Evil and Suffering' (pages 37–43).

10 Darwin – Random chance

In his *Origin of Species*, Darwin notes that it was random chance that organises life in the universe, according to the principles of evolution and natural selection. This was a challenge to the majority of people in the 19th century, who believed that God was the prime mover of the universe – not chance. However, in referring to the principle of natural selection, Darwin is stating that his notion of chance was not a reference to things 'just happening' but rather that they were happening according to a specific principle – however unpredictable it may be.

11 Darwin – Adaptation

The reason for species being so well suited to their environment was not, as had been previously thought, due to a benevolent designer but was because of their ability to adapt to their surroundings and to pass on the favourable characteristics that allowed this adaptation to be successful. Darwin admitted that he did not know what mechanism caused these useful traits to be passed from one generation to another but, with the discovery of DNA in the 20th century, this problem has been largely overcome.

12 Dawkins – Nature not God

Supporting Darwin's theory, Dawkins observed that everything that Paley had said about God, in terms of his designing abilities, could be attributed to the realm and laws of Nature. There was no need to posit belief in a divine being for what, he believed, were nothing more than the regular everyday occurrences of the natural world.

Grade boost

Referring to criticisms of the design argument is NOT the same as evaluating it. It is important to recognise that evaluations arise from the strengths and the weaknesses. Criticisms **on their own** are AO1 material – and belong only in part 'a' of your essay.

quickfire

⑬ What was the main idea behind Darwin's theory of natural selection?

Key Quote

All appearances to the contrary, the only watchmaker in nature is the blind forces of physics albeit deployed in a very special way. A true watchmaker has foresight: he designs his cogs and springs, and plans their interconnections, with a future purpose in his mind's eye. Natural selection, the blind, unconscious, automatic process which Darwin discovered, and which we now know is the explanation for the existence and apparently purposeful form of all life, has no purpose in mind. It has no mind, and no mind's eye. It does not plan for the future. It has no vision, no foresight, no sight at all. If it can be said to play the role of watchmaker in nature, it is the blind watchmaker.

Richard Dawkins, *The Blind Watchmaker*, Longman (1986)

Strengths and weaknesses of the teleological argument

Remember that good evaluations depend on you analysing the strengths and weaknesses of the argument. Take each argument in turn and consider whether it can be supported by other parts of the strengths/weaknesses section. If so, it is likely to be a stronger argument. If not, it is likely to be a weaker argument. This method does not work in all cases – especially where an argument is unique, but it can be very useful in helping link arguments together to present a more persuasive or convincing case.

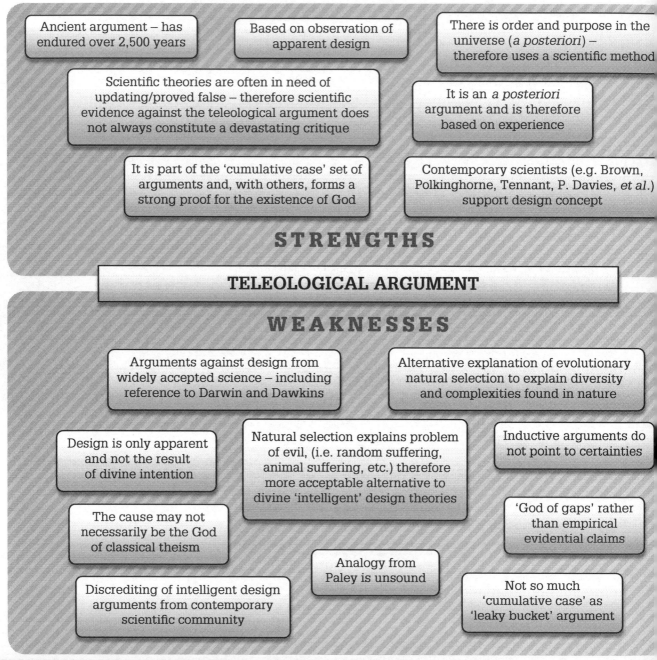

Ancient argument – has endured over 2,500 years

Based on observation of apparent design

There is order and purpose in the universe (*a posteriori*) – therefore uses a scientific method

Scientific theories are often in need of updating/proved false – therefore scientific evidence against the teleological argument does not always constitute a devastating critique

It is an *a posteriori* argument and is therefore based on experience

It is part of the 'cumulative case' set of arguments and, with others, forms a strong proof for the existence of God

Contemporary scientists (e.g. Brown, Polkinghorne, Tennant, P. Davies, *et al.*) support design concept

STRENGTHS

TELEOLOGICAL ARGUMENT

WEAKNESSES

Arguments against design from widely accepted science – including reference to Darwin and Dawkins

Alternative explanation of evolutionary natural selection to explain diversity and complexities found in nature

Design is only apparent and not the result of divine intention

Natural selection explains problem of evil, (i.e. random suffering, animal suffering, etc.) therefore more acceptable alternative to divine 'intelligent' design theories

Inductive arguments do not point to certainties

The cause may not necessarily be the God of classical theism

'God of gaps' rather than empirical evidential claims

Analogy from Paley is unsound

Discrediting of intelligent design arguments from contemporary scientific community

Not so much 'cumulative case' as 'leaky bucket' argument

Summary: Teleological argument

We have identified the key points on the WJEC AS specification and, combined with the information in this topic, represented them as a diagram which shows the main things that you need to know. You may want to fill in further details to elaborate and personalise this content.

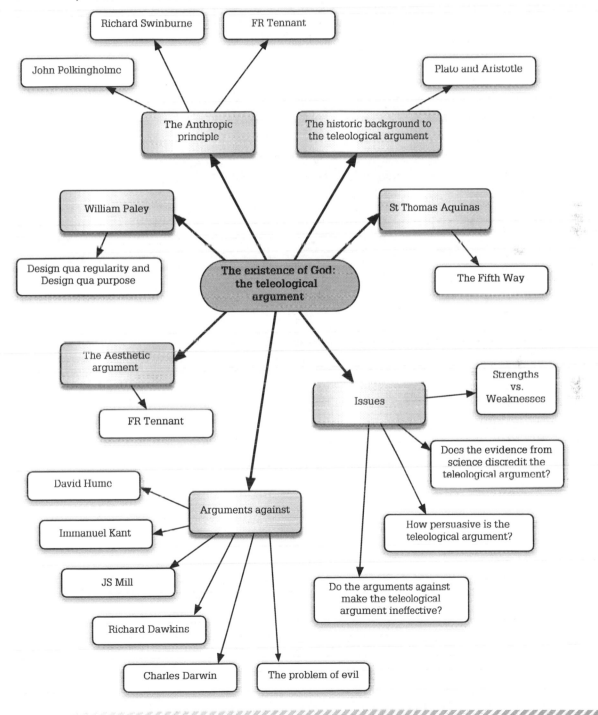

3: Evil and Suffering

The unit on 'Evil and Suffering' requires you to focus your revision on the main challenges presented to believers in the God of classical theism by the existence of evil and suffering in the world. For example, you will need to articulate the problem of evil as defined in the inconsistent triad and refer to those philosophers who have offered comment on this particular problem. You are also expected to be able to explain the nature of evil with relevant examples relating to both moral and natural forms of evil. Furthermore, you will need to understand the main philosophical debates surrounding the challenges presented by animal, innocent and immense suffering. Your ability to explain the responses to the problem of evil from Augustine and Irenaeus is essential and you should be aware of both classical and modern presentations of these theodicies. Finally, you should be able to evaluate the issues that arise out of these areas and be aware of the main ideas that both support and detract from these issues.

Revision checklist

Tick column 1 when you have completed brief revision notes.
Tick column 2 when you think you have a good grasp of the topic.
Tick column 3 during final revision when you feel you have mastery of the topic.

			1	2	3
What is meant by the problem of evil?	p37	Epicurus – a classical definition			
	p37	Characteristics of the God of classical theism			
	p37	Mackie's inconsistent triad			
How can the nature of evil be classified?	p39	Moral and Natural evil			
What are the particular challenges caused by the existence of evil?	p41	Animal suffering			
	p42	Innocent suffering			
	p43	Immense suffering			
What is a theodicy?	p44	The justification of God in the face of evil			
	p44	Free-will defence			
What is the Augustinian theodicy?	p45	Perfect creation and Story of the Fall			
	p45	Evil as a privation			
	p46	Seminal presence			
	p46	Happy mistake			
What are the main criticisms of the Augustinian theodicy?	p47	Logical problems			
	p48	Historical/scientific problems			
What is the Irenaean theodicy?	p49	Genesis 1:26 – image and likeness			
	p49	Evil as a means of developing moral goodness and spiritual perfection			
	p49	God as craftsman			
	p50	Hick's epistemic distance			
	p50	Hick's universal salvation			
What are the main criticisms of the Irenaean theodicy?	p51	Causing suffering inappropriate expression of love			
	p51	Unequal distribution of suffering			
	p51	Concept of universal salvation unfair			
What are the main issues related to the problem of evil and suffering?	p52	Is there an adequate religious answer to the problem of evil?			
	p52	Are problems raised by animal, innocent and immense suffering strong proofs against the existence of the God of classical theism?			
	p53	Do the theodicies of Augustine and Irenaeus fail to explain the existence of evil and suffering in a world supposedly created and controlled by God?			

The problem of evil: The problem stated

The problem of evil is an ancient philosophical and theological one. If a belief system suggests that the universe was created deliberately, out of nothing, by a God that is all-powerful, all-knowing and all-loving, then how is it possible that things within that universe can go wrong? Not only that, why is it that within that universe, the created beings, which are again deliberately made by this God, suffer – often to appalling extremes?

Key Quote

Either God wants to abolish evil, and cannot; or he can, but does not want to.
If he wants to, but cannot, he is impotent.
If he can, but does not want to, he is wicked.
If God can abolish evil, and God really wants to do it, why is there evil in the world?

Epicurus, *The Wrath of God*

Any response would seem to throw up some kind of philosophical contradiction to the characteristics of this God and this is why, despite numerous attempts by religious believers, theologians and philosophers, it remains a constant challenge to those that would believe in such a God (commonly referred to as the God of classical theism).

The Australian philosopher J L Mackie formulated the problem of evil into an 'inconsistent triad' which runs thus.

1. God is omnipotent
2. God is omnibenevolent
3. Evil exists

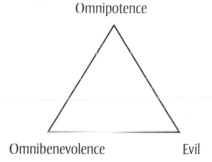

Key Terms

Omnipotent = all powerful.

Omnibenevolent = all-loving.

Evil = that which causes suffering or harm.

Key Figure

JL Mackie
Born in Sydney, Australia in 1917, his 1955 work *Evil and Omnipotence* dealt with the inconsistencies of evil's existence alongside the traditional characteristics of the God of classical theism and that this resulted in a devastating blow to the integrity of the main monotheistic religions. Teaching for much of his academic life in Australia, he was eventually elected as a fellow of University College, Oxford in 1967. He died in 1981.

Mackie points out that it is logically inconsistent for these three statements to exist simultaneously. This is because if God were omnipotent God would have the power to remove evil, as God's omnipotence means that God is capable of any feat. The characteristic of omnipotence also includes the notion that God could have created a universe where there was no evil.

If God were omnibenevolent then God, in loving kindness towards God's creation, would want to remove evil so that creation did not suffer. The idea that any omnibenevolent being would deliberately tolerate evil, and the horrendous suffering that it causes, is anathema to the very idea of omnibenevolence.

However, the existence of evil is so tangible in its effects and its scope that any denial of its existence would be nonsensical. Thus it is not possible for the three statements to co-exist.

An alternative solution to the problem is to try to resolve the inconsistent triad by removing one of the three points. Any such solution would read like so:

quickfire

① What is meant by the term the God of classical theism?

② What is the problem of evil?

③ Explain what philosophers mean by the term 'inconsistent triad'.

Grade boost

Always make certain that you fully explain the inconsistent triad and how it could be solved by removing any one corner of the triangle. Candidates often lose marks because they do not explain this properly.

1 Not all-powerful

If we removed the characteristic of omnipotence from God, then we can understand why evil exists because, whilst God loves creation and wants to prevent evil, God does not have the power to do so. This solution echoes the philosophical stance taken by process theologians such as Whitehead, who claimed that God was part of the universe and was responsible for starting off the evolutionary process that led to humanity, and as such was responsible for what happened to God's creation. However, such a God, as part of the universe, did not have sufficient power to remove evil. Process theologians regard this God as 'the fellow sufferer who understands' – being as much part of the universe as humanity. However attractive this solution appears, ultimately it does not satisfy those religious believers who believe that their God was responsible for creating the universe *ex nihilo* – and is therefore greater than all that exists within the universe.

2 Not all-loving

So some suggest that we should remove the characteristic of omnibenevolence. In this case evil exists and God is omnipotent. Having the power to remove evil does not mean that God wants to. If God is not 'all-loving' then why should God care if God's creation suffers? Such a God may even be considered as malicious, and may even enjoy seeing God's creation suffer. However, such a God is so far from the imagination of all classical theistic religions as to be unrecognisable; the problem therefore remains.

3 No evil

Finally then we can remove the fact that 'evil exists'. In doing so, God retains the characteristics of omnipotence and omnibenevolence and there is no contradiction for believers, in terms of God's characteristics. The assertion is that evil does not exist. After all, it may be our perception that is at fault. If we were able to see the universe from a God's-eye view, then we might see that the suffering that creation faces is not the evil that we think it is, but rather has a purpose that we do not understand because we do not have God's perspective.

4 Example

Imagine the situation of a toddler playing in the kitchen whilst the parent is using the oven. The toddler's curiosity is piqued by the oven and he wanders over to it. Standing against the oven he reaches up to try and pull the pan off the top of the oven in order to see what is inside it. At this point the parent, alarmed and seeing what is about to happen, may smack the toddler's hand away from the oven. In doing so, the toddler suffers from having a smacked hand. He cannot understand why the parent has just smacked the hand and is upset by the incident. He may even consider the parent to be cruel and unfair. However, what the toddler was unaware of was that the pan on top of the oven was full of boiling water and, had he succeeded in pulling it off the oven top, he would have been severely injured and suffered a far greater degree of pain than was caused by the smacking of the hand. The toddler did not have the parent's perspective, and, like the toddler, creation does not share God's (as the parent) perspective.

5 Problems

Attractive as this idea may at first appear, it has been largely rejected for the simple reason, as Hume points out, that the effects of evil are felt too widely, and its presence attested too vividly for it to be dismissible.

For many philosophers the problem of evil is simply insurmountable. The inconsistent triad presents a simple but devastating critique of the question of why an all-loving, all-powerful God would allow God's creation to suffer. However, this view has been challenged by a number of theists who maintain that the inconsistent triad and the problem of evil rest on assumptions which, if challenged, can open the debate.

6 Solutions?

For instance, one such assumption is the notion that just because God is all-powerful and all-loving, it does not follow that God would necessarily want to remove evil immediately from the universe. Perhaps it does indeed serve some greater purpose of which we are currently unaware.

Aquinas, referencing his work on our understanding of God's nature, points out that what we understand as all 'goodness' (or even evil for that matter) may not be the same as what God understands as goodness. After all, our understanding of goodness is often relative to the time and culture within which we live. We are limited by time as finite beings and the world and society that we live in is always changing. God, as a perfect being, is not subject to such change and therefore God's understanding of concepts such as good and evil are likewise immutable, and may be very different from our own; in such case there is no logical contradiction within the 'inconsistent triad'.

The Nature of Evil

Key Quote

Good and Evil are the overarching opposites of all experience. They form a syzygy, paired opposites. Each exists only in relationship to the other. Without their relationship, both would cease to exist.

James A Hall and Jeffrey Raff, 'Thoughts on the Nature of Evil', *Journal of Jungian Theory and Practice*, Vol 8 No 1 2006, C G Jung Institute of New York

Overview

Evil is often considered to be anything that causes suffering. This suffering can occur in many different forms and can be the result of a moral action or an event that occurs in nature. As such, the nature of evil presents philosophical issues. Consider the images in the diagram – what sort of evil do they represent? What is the suffering that is caused by these types of evil? How do they differ?

Broadly speaking evil can be categorised in two main ways: moral evil and natural evil.

Grade boost

In order to demonstrate the higher level skills, candidates should always explain fully any example of evil that they might use in an answer to illustrate moral or natural evil. This explanation must demonstrate how the example chosen causes suffering and is therefore considered as evil.

Moral evil

Any suffering that is brought about through the actions of a free-will agent. Free-will agents have the ability to choose 'good' or 'evil'. As such, their actions can result in the suffering of others. It is important to realise that one of the main philosophical issues that is raised by this type of evil is that if evil is caused by an individual *that could have chosen to do good instead,* does that mean that God cannot be held accountable for evil's existence in the world?

Examples of moral evil include murder, theft, violence, rape, slavery, child abuse, animal cruelty, terrorism, adultery, dishonesty, any form of negative discrimination, genocide, etc.

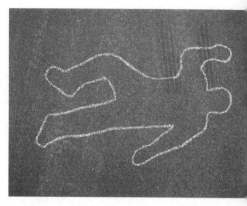

quickfire

④ Name the two main types of evil.

⑤ Give an example of moral evil and of natural evil.

Natural evil

Any suffering that is brought about as a consequence of the events outside of the control of free-will agents – most commonly those which occur as part of the natural order. (Occasionally free-will agents can set in motion a series of events that result in suffering that were not intended. It is therefore highly debatable as to whether this suffering constitutes moral evil or not.)

Examples of natural evil include the suffering that results from earthquakes, tsunamis, drought, tornados, hurricanes, extremes of temperature – hot and cold, disease, ageing, crop failure, forest fires, etc.

Particular problems (1): Animal suffering

Key Quote

Who trusted God was love indeed
And love Creation's final law
Tho' Nature, red in tooth and claw
With ravine, shriek'd against his creed

Alfred Lord Tennyson, *In Memoriam A. H. H.* (1850)

In a system where the God of classical theism is regarded as allowing evil to exist in the world to serve a purpose for humanity, the question is often raised as to why animals suffer.

The Western religions of Christianity, Judaism and Islam all assert that humankind has a higher status in the created order than animals and also believe that animals do not possess the spiritual quality of a 'soul'.

Eastern religions such as Buddhism and Hinduism have a different outlook and consider that animals, whilst spiritually in many ways different from humankind, do in fact possess a spiritual nature and are subject to the laws of reincarnation/rebirth in the similar way to humans. In such a case, animal suffering may indeed have a 'higher purpose'. For the Western religions there is no such explanation though and so alternative solutions need to be presented.

- The existence of natural selection within the natural order proves that nature, as Tennyson stated, was 'red in tooth and claw'.
- Dawkins re-used the phrase in *The Selfish Gene* (1976) to sum-up the behaviour of all living beings.

Specific issues relating to animal suffering include:

- Humans have free-will and can choose good or evil: suffering is a consequence of this. Animals do not have this moral capacity, so why should they suffer?
- Surely God could have created a world where animals do not need to suffer as part of the natural order?
- If suffering is meant to improve the quality of one's soul, and if animals have no souls, then why should they suffer?

Some religious thinkers have tried to provide justifications for why animals suffer, such as:

- Pain is a necessary event for any living thing to learn how best to survive within the natural order.
- The suffering caused as part of natural selection benefits the species as a whole in terms of evolution.
- The suffering of animals is an additional punishment to humankind (in empathetic terms) because of humanity's evil actions.
- Animal suffering allows human beings to practise compassion and develop positive spiritual qualities.

 quickfire

⑥ Give two reasons as to why animals suffer.

Key Quote

Then Job answered the Lord: I know that you can do all things and that no purpose of yours can be thwarted. Who is this that hides counsel without knowledge? Therefore I have uttered what I did not understand, things too wonderful for me, which I did not know.

(Job 42 v1–3)

Grade boost

Making reference to key religious texts to support your reasoning is an important skill in all aspects of religious studies. It is important that any explanation of the text is accurate and is supported by reference to appropriate scholarship.

⑦ What is meant by the term 'innocent suffering'?

Particular problems (2): Innocent suffering

When individuals do something wrong, they can expect to be punished, and suffer as a result, if their wrongdoing is discovered. Society works on this principle of justice, that every person should be treated in the way that they deserve. The issue of innocent suffering, however, is one that raises problems as the very nature of the 'innocent' is one that is blameless and guiltless and therefore totally undeserving of any form of 'punishment' or suffering. When young children are shown as the victims of famine or war, there tends to be a strong reaction to the blatant unfairness of their suffering. This issue of 'injustice' is at the root of the problem of innocent suffering: Why does an omnipotent and omnibenevolent God allow the innocent to suffer?

Job

The book of Job deals with the story of how Job, a 'righteous' man, has huge suffering put upon him as the result of a heavenly 'bet' between God and Satan. Despite the fact that Job suffers, at no point does he sin – he remains innocent. His friends try to tell him that his suffering is a result of some past misdemeanour that he hasn't faced up to, despite Job's protestations that this is not true. This is an important point because, in Jewish philosophy, a person could suffer at a future date for some sin which had been committed far in the past. The concept of God's justice meant that all individuals would have to pay for any sin that they had committed, at some point in their life. Job, however, was not guilty. When, at the end of the story, Job is faced with God and asks why he suffers, God's reply is that he suffers because God has a reason for him to suffer – and just because Job does not understand that reason, it does not mean that he is suffering unjustly. Job's response is to accept that he does not understand the ways of God and the story finishes with God blessing Job and rewarding him for his faithfulness by restoring his fortunes two-fold.

The story therefore illustrates that innocent suffering may seem unjust now but we need to understand that humanity's view of the universe is narrow and limited and that even the suffering of innocents has its place in God's ultimate plan for his creation.

Particular problems (3): Immense suffering

The final particular problem caused by the problem of evil is that of immense suffering. Sometimes the suffering is not restricted to one individual but can affect many – in some cases millions. The last hundred years have seen humanity produce weapons of huge destructive power; the victims of such weapons are more often civilians than they are military targets. Medical conditions such as HIV and AIDS, as well as cancer, cholera and malaria, cause untold suffering to millions of people in the 21st century.

Genocide

Genocides in Rwanda, Bosnia, Tibet, Somalia, Ethiopia and Cambodia account for the deaths of millions between them; the often quoted, but nonetheless appalling systematic persecution and destruction of European Jewry in the Second World War; all of these are examples of immense suffering.

Questions

The philosophical questions that are raised by these events are numerous but amongst them is the question: 'Why so many?' If lessons need to be learnt by suffering, surely it could be learnt by fewer people suffering and dying? Did six million Jews really need to die? Why not just two million – this would still have been an appalling human tragedy at this number, so why increase it further?

How can the existence of such widespread suffering ever be an expression of love from an omnibenevolent God? Surely there must be alternatives to the immensity of this suffering?

Leibniz

It is appropriate, at this point, to consider Leibniz's suggestion that God had a choice of the sort of world to create. Leibniz maintained that God is omnipotent, omnibenevolent and just, and chose to create this world as the one that had the optimum conditions for humanity to grow towards God. The existence of evil and suffering allows humanity to respond in positive ways to the suffering of others, to develop qualities such as charity, courage and dignity. Were this world not the way that it is, then these things would not be possible. This is one philosophical solution to why there is immense suffering in the world – in order to provoke immense positive responses from humanity.

Key Term

Genocide = the deliberate extermination of a racial group or society.

Key Quote

This is the best of all possible worlds.

Gottfried Leibniz

quickfire

(8) What is the point that Leibniz makes in order to justify why there is immense suffering present in the world?

Introduction to theodicies (including free-will defence)

Key Terms

Theodicy = a defence which justifies God in allowing evil and suffering to exist in the world.

Free-will = the belief that human beings, as moral agents, have the ability to freely choose their actions.

quickfire

(9) What does Swinburne mean when he refers to the concept of 'a toy world'?

Religious believers who hold a belief in the God of classical theism have developed a number of responses to the problem of evil over the centuries. These defences of God are known as a **theodicy** and there are two classical Christian theodicies that need to be understood for the purposes of this specification.

There is a defence which underpins both theodicies and extends beyond the Christian world view. It relates to the concept held in the Judeo-Christian tradition that God created humankind and gave the gift of **free-will** – that is, the ability to freely choose to do good or to do evil. This ability makes human beings moral creatures and, as such, we can be held accountable for our moral actions.

As you will recall from the previous discussion on the nature of evil, moral evil is that evil or suffering which occurs as a result of the actions of free-will agents. In this sense the question is then posed: 'Is all the evil actually worth it? Would it not be better for God to have created us to always choose to do good, rather than evil, and therefore have a world which contains no suffering?'

Swinburne's view

Richard Swinburne suggests that had God chosen to create such a world then, in effect, any action which a human being chose to do would be very limited in scope of its consequences. Swinburne calls this 'a toy world'. How would human beings ever develop qualities such as compassion and courage if there was never any opportunity to face real adversity and suffering? Swinburne also cites the fact that death brings an end to all suffering and is in fact the mark of a compassionate creator who limits the suffering of his creation by allowing them to die. It also places a limitation on the number of opportunities that each individual has to choose to do the right thing, exercising their free-will in a way that benefits others. The teachings of the major world religions strongly echo this idea that the ability to make the right moral choice in this life is essential if the afterlife is to be one of reward – whether that be paradise or a favourable rebirth/reincarnation.

Conclusion

The value of the free-will defence hinges upon the perspective of the individual yet it remains one of the most significant defences for the God of classical theism in the face of the terrible suffering faced by his creation.

← Good Choice
Bad Choice →

The Augustinian theodicy

Despite several modern presentations to the contrary, Augustine's theodicy is not a compact singular work but rather a strand that runs throughout much of his literary output. It has been observed by some of his commentators that Augustine was obsessed with the problem of evil and wrestled with it throughout his life – even before his conversion to Christianity. Therefore it must be remembered that any presentation of his theodicy, which is demonstrated in a book such as this, is a necessary simplification of Augustine's thoughts. The actual specifics can only be gained by reading through his vast writings – and taking on board the influences that he had from Manichaeism, Neo Platonism and other competing thought systems that he found himself exposed to during his eventful life.

Overview

- According to Augustine, God's creation was originally free from evil. It did not exist before the sin of angels and humans. It first came into existence when angels, followed by humans, misused their wills and turned from God, their creator.
- It is a fact of the created universe that God has called all things into existence *ex nihilo* and, through corruption and decay, they will all eventually lapse back into nothingness.
- Humans and angels are both part of the created order and therefore they are susceptible to change and so have the capability of turning away from God.
- It is precisely this turning – which involves an act of free-will (namely, of choosing a lower rather than a higher good) – that brings about evil.
- However, the cause of human and angel willingness to do this remains a mystery beyond human understanding, according to Augustine.
- As the gift of free-will necessarily entails the concept of moral responsibility, it is humans that are ultimately responsible for sin and, consequently, evil – not God. This is because humans voluntarily choose sin.
- It is important to realise, however, that evil is not in any way a 'substance' or part of the created order. Instead, evil indicates an absence or **privation** of part of God's created order. E.g. when humans or angels 'turn away' from God it is this turning away that is a privation of God's original created order and purpose. The 'turning away' is then 'evil'.
- From the viewpoint of God, the whole of creation is beautiful, harmonised and good.
- Human perception of evil is due to our limited existence and inability to see 'the whole picture' as God does. Augustine compares the presence of evil in the universe with the presence of the 'colour' black in a picture. On its own, black is not considered by most to be a pleasant colour; however, it is in the

Key Term

Privation – the absence or loss of something that is normally present (e.g. a privation of health means that a person is ill and not healthy).

Key Quote

Nature therefore which has been corrupted, is called evil, for assuredly when incorrupt it is good; but even when corrupt, so far as it is nature it is good, so far as it is corrupted it is evil.

Augustine, *Concerning the Nature of Good, Against the Manichaeans*

Grade boost

Show awareness in your answers on this theodicy that Augustine's ideas were founded on a complex set of intellectual ideas that were combined with biblical teachings to produce his theodicy. Do not instantly dismiss his theodicy as 'simplistic' or 'naïve' because in doing so you are revealing your own understanding of Augustine to be flawed. He is regarded as being one of the greatest Christian thinkers that ever lived – so be cautious in your criticism and show respect to his views. (You don't have to agree with them but neither should you dismiss them as worthless either!)

Key Term

Redemption = the act of saving something or someone. In the Christian context it refers to Jesus saving humanity from evil and sin.

Key Quote

the Almighty God, who … has supreme power over all things, being Himself supremely good, would never permit the existence of anything evil among His works, if He were not so omnipotent and good that He can bring good even out of evil. For what is that which we call evil but the absence of good? … Just in the same way, what are called vices in the soul are nothing but privations of natural good.

Augustine, *Enchiridion*

quickfire

⑩ On what did St Augustine base his theodicy?

⑪ What is meant by a privation?

⑫ Why is the Fall of Humanity a 'happy mistake'?

picture because the artist has a specific purpose for its being there and, if it were absent, the beauty of the whole picture would be spoilt.

- The reason that humans tend to be offended at the order of existing things is their finiteness, which does not allow seeing the whole picture.

- As all human beings are ultimately descended from Adam (in Augustine's words 'seminally present') then all humans share Adam's guilt and sin. As we all share his guilt and sin, we all deserve to face the same punishment. We suffer through 'moral evil' as that is humankind's fault through actions performed on the basis of free-will.

- The suffering that humans face as part of the natural world (i.e. natural evil) is a direct result of the 'absence of good' created in creation by the 'turning away' from God and therefore bringing corruption into the created order.

- As an ultimate response to the question: 'Why did God choose to create this particular universe, even though he knew that human beings would abuse their freedom and sin?' Augustine replies: 'God judged it to be better to bring good out of evil, than to not permit any evil to exist'.

- It is this point 'to bring good out of evil' that many Christians refer to as the 'Happy mistake' (*Felix culpa*). In this is the Christian belief that, were it not for the events of The Fall of Adam and Eve (and therefore, all humans), then God would never had needed to send Jesus into the world to save it from its sin.

- Those who freely chose to accept Jesus as their saviour would be redeemed and, after this life, be reunited with God in heaven.

- Augustine believes that this chance for humanity to seek **redemption**, through Christ, not only demonstrates that God is merciful but also that it underlines God's Justice.

Key Figure

Augustine of Hippo Born in North Africa in 354CE, Augustine had a pagan father and Christian mother. He had a Christian education but rebelled in his teenage years and rejected Christianity. He spent many years trying to find a thought system that made sense to him and followed several (at the time) influential teachings. He spent much of his time also indulging himself in the 'pleasures of the flesh' (much to the despair of his Christian mother) until he came under the influence of Ambrose of Milan, a Christian bishop. He renounced his other beliefs and in 387CE was baptised. Eventually in 396 he became Bishop of Hippo, in North Africa. He produced a vast amount of writing, chiefly in defence of Christianity against a number of heresies popular at the time, although he also wrote very influentially on Christian belief and doctrine. His best known works are *City of God*, *Confessions* and his *Enchiridion*. He died in 430CE.

Criticisms of the Augustinian theodicy

Overview

Augustine's theodicy relies heavily on his interpretation of the accounts of the Creation and the Fall as depicted in the biblical book of Genesis, chapters 1–3. For the literalist Christian believer this means that the accounts are plausible and rooted in the revelation of divine scripture. Humankind's place in the created order, and the suffering that it faces, are clearly accounted for in the Genesis accounts. However, as soon as any other view of scripture is taken, Augustine's theodicy becomes problematic.

If this part of scripture is viewed as non-literal and mythological, then any claim of historicity relating to the accounts of creation and fall become suspect. It is from this viewpoint that the most devastating attacks upon the theodicy arise. John Hick in his *Evil and the God of Love* (1966) considers many of these problems and invokes the work of German theologian Friedrich Schleiermacher in considering these issues. Other scholars have contributed to these criticisms and what follows is a summary of some of the main critiques:

Grade boost

Make certain that you can confidently explain the difference between literal and non-literal interpretations of the bible; this will help improve any evaluation of Augustine's arguments that are based on his views of the biblical text of Genesis.

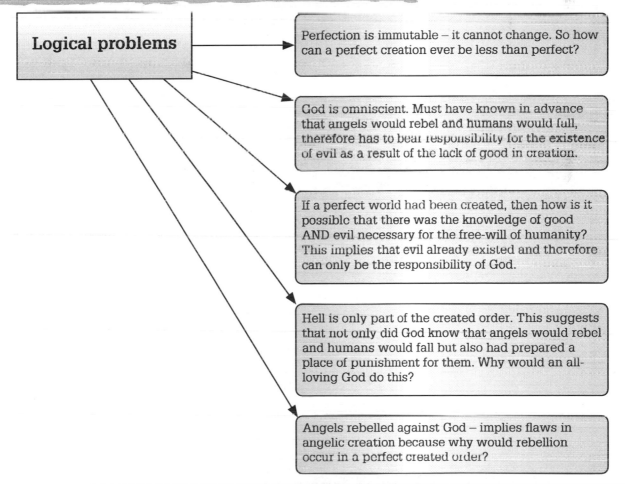

Logical problems

Perfection is immutable – it cannot change. So how can a perfect creation ever be less than perfect?

God is omniscient. Must have known in advance that angels would rebel and humans would fall, therefore has to bear responsibility for the existence of evil as a result of the lack of good in creation.

If a perfect world had been created, then how is it possible that there was the knowledge of good AND evil necessary for the free-will of humanity? This implies that evil already existed and therefore can only be the responsibility of God.

Hell is only part of the created order. This suggests that not only did God know that angels would rebel and humans would fall but also had prepared a place of punishment for them. Why would an all-loving God do this?

Angels rebelled against God – implies flaws in angelic creation because why would rebellion occur in a perfect created order?

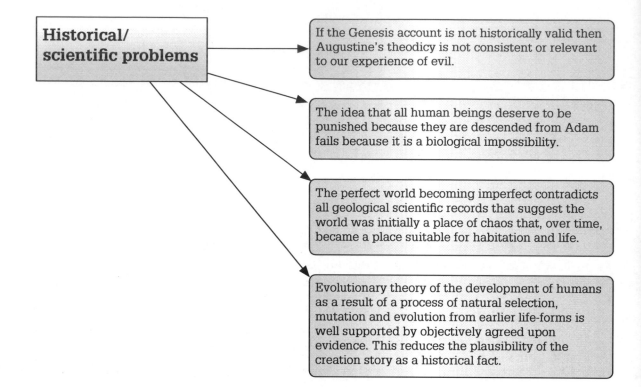

Historical/ scientific problems

If the Genesis account is not historically valid then Augustine's theodicy is not consistent or relevant to our experience of evil.

The idea that all human beings deserve to be punished because they are descended from Adam fails because it is a biological impossibility.

The perfect world becoming imperfect contradicts all geological scientific records that suggest the world was initially a place of chaos that, over time, became a place suitable for habitation and life.

Evolutionary theory of the development of humans as a result of a process of natural selection, mutation and evolution from earlier life-forms is well supported by objectively agreed upon evidence. This reduces the plausibility of the creation story as a historical fact.

Conclusion

Debate about the validity of Augustine's theodicy still continues in modern religious philosophy, however. Modern supporters such as Plantinga and Miller suggest that much depends on how we interpret what Augustine meant by terms such as privation and free-will. Others, such as Hick, consider that it is simply a product of its time and has no real relevance to the way in which we understand the world today.

quicKᖴire

⑬ Describe one logical problem with Augustine's theodicy.

⑭ Why does evolutionary theory undermine Augustine's theodicy?

The Irenaean theodicy

Overview

Unlike Augustine, who held that the responsibility for the existence of evil was due to the actions of free-will agents deliberately turning away from God, Irenaeus maintained that the presence of evil in the created order was a deliberate action of an omnibenevolent God who wanted God's creation to develop the qualities that would make them spiritually perfect. His ideas are a result of his interpretation of Genesis 1v26. However, like Augustine, his theodicy was never presented as a complete work but rather arose from his ideas about the place of humankind in the universe and the relationship that they have with God.

Image and likeness

Irenaeus regards this life as a place where human beings develop their potential and grow from the 'image' (possessing the potential qualities of God's spiritual perfection) to the 'likeness' (actualising those qualities) of God, through the trials and tribulations that they face and the decisions that they make. For every moral decision faced where a good choice is freely made, then the individual develops more fully towards spiritual maturity.

Human development

Evil is a necessary facet of life that enables humans to develop. Without it, decisions in life would have no real value. For instance, a person would never really appreciate being in good health unless they had experienced being ill. Virtues such as courage, patience and perseverance could never be developed if there were not the challenges in life that tested such virtues. Suffering not only enables humans to become stronger: it also allows them to appreciate goodness more. For Irenaeus, the ability for human beings to be able to freely choose to do good was therefore instrumental in achieving God's purpose for his creation.

Analogy

Irenaeus makes use of an analogy of God as a craftsman working with human beings as his material and suggests that humans should allow God to mould them into perfection by acting in faith towards God and allowing the experiences of life, both good and bad, to make us into a perfectly crafted item. He also makes the point that those who resist God will be punished in the next life. Unlike Augustine, Irenaeus allows for God's mercy to continue into the next life where individuals who have rejected God in this life will have the opportunity to earn his forgiveness and develop into spiritual perfection in the next.

Key Figure

Irenaeus of Lyons
Second third century Early Christian Bishop who is chiefly remembered for his writings against the heresy of Gnosticism – a major threat to Christian orthodoxy in the first few centuries of the Church's history. He also influentially stated that human beings had been made imperfect and needed to grow towards perfection, which he believed could only be done by making the proper response to God through Christ.

quickfire

(15) Which biblical verse is the foundation of the Irenaean theodicy?

(16) What is the role of evil in the Irenaean theodicy?

Key Quote

Then God said, 'Let us make humankind in our image, according to our likeness.'

Genesis 1v26

Key Terms

Epistemic distance = a distance measured in terms of knowledge rather than space or time.

Soul making = a process where the soul is developing towards spiritual perfection by gaining the wisdom to always make the correct moral choices when faced with the ambiguities of life as a human being.

Key Figure

John Hick
Born 1922, Hick was one of the most influential religious philosophers of the 20th and early 21st centuries. His most famous works include *Faith and Knowledge* (1957); *Evil and the God of Love* (1966); *Death and the Eternal Life* (1976); *Philosophy of Religion* (various editions – most recently 4th edition, published 1990) and *The New Frontier of Religion and Science Religious Experience, Neuroscience and the Transcendent* (2006). He died in February 2012.

Hick's development

John Hick developed Irenaeus' theodicy in his book *Evil and the God of Love* (1966). Hick describes Irenaeus' theodicy as a '**soul-making**' theodicy (a reference to John Keats' idea that the world was a proving ground for human beings who earned their salvation, not simply by belief in a saviour figure, but rather by working through the trials and tribulations of everyday existence). Hick also makes the point that in order to be truly free, human beings had to be created at an '**epistemic distance**' from God, in this, humans were placed in a situation where the existence and non-existence of God were equally likely. This therefore allowed true human freedom to exist in terms of how they then responded to God. God could not create humans who were spiritually perfect or who were immediately aware of his existence for the simple reason that, in the first instance, goodness developed through free choice is more valuable than goodness that is 'ready-made' and, secondly, this would restrict choices made as humanity would be constantly aware of being 'watched' and would therefore make all decisions in the light of this knowledge. Hick also accepted the idea that God's mercy would allow for all human beings to complete the process of developing spiritual perfection – if not in this life, then in the next.

Key Quotes

God made man a free [agent] from the beginning, possessing his own power, even as he does his own soul, to obey the behests of God voluntarily, and not by compulsion of God. For there is no coercion with God, but a good will [towards us] is present with Him continually.

Irenaeus, Chapter 37,
Against Heresies, Book IV

He shall overcome the substance of created nature. For it was necessary, at first, that nature should be exhibited; then, after that, that what was mortal should be conquered and swallowed up by immortality, and the corruptible by incorruptibility, and that man should be made after the image and likeness of God, having received the knowledge of good and evil.

Irenaeus, Chapter 38,
Against Heresies, Book IV

And the harder we strive, so much is it the more valuable; while so much the more valuable it is, so much the more should we esteem it.

Irenaeus, Chapter 37,
Against Heresies, Book IV

The common cognomen of this world among the misguided and superstitious is 'a vale of tears' from which we are to be redeemed by a certain arbitrary interposition of God and taken to Heaven – What a little circumscribed straightened notion! Call the world if you please 'The vale of Soul-making'

John Keats, letter to George and
Georgiana Keats, 3 May 1819

Criticisms of the Irenaean theodicy

quickfire

⑰ Give one criticism of the Irenaean theodicy.

Overview

The modern re-workings of this theodicy, with its sympathies towards scientific appreciation of the development of life on earth, have given it a lease of life and plausibility that the Augustinian theodicy has not been able to enjoy to the same extent. Developing into spiritual maturity has a resonance with faiths outside of the Christian framework – and possibly echoes Hick's own views on religious pluralism. However, despite many of its attractions, the Irenaean theodicy has also attracted fierce criticism.

Grade boost

Remember that criticisms of any argument can weaken or strengthen depending on the viewpoint that a person holds. For example, one of the criticisms of soul-making is only a strong criticism if a person holds to a Christian view of the atonement. If they don't then it holds no value as a criticism.

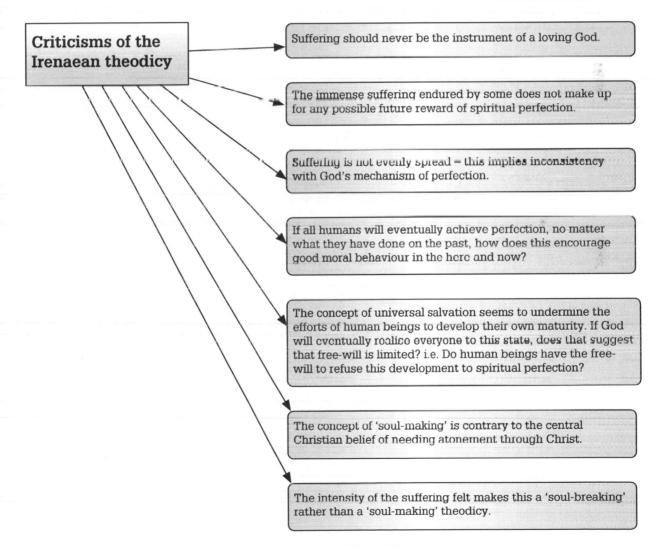

Criticisms of the Irenaean theodicy

- Suffering should never be the instrument of a loving God.

- The immense suffering endured by some does not make up for any possible future reward of spiritual perfection.

- Suffering is not evenly spread – this implies inconsistency with God's mechanism of perfection.

- If all humans will eventually achieve perfection, no matter what they have done on the past, how does this encourage good moral behaviour in the here and now?

- The concept of universal salvation seems to undermine the efforts of human beings to develop their own maturity. If God will eventually realise everyone to this state, does that suggest that free-will is limited? i.e. Do human beings have the free-will to refuse this development to spiritual perfection?

- The concept of 'soul-making' is contrary to the central Christian belief of needing atonement through Christ.

- The intensity of the suffering felt makes this a 'soul-breaking' rather than a 'soul-making' theodicy.

K | Evaluative issues

The following tables demonstrate typical responses to the debates surrounding the evaluative issues relating to the problem of evil. There is, inevitably, a certain degree of crossover in material that can be used to support or deny the propositions that can be made relating to the debate.

1: 'There is no adequate religious answer to the problem of evil.' Assess this view.

Adequate

- The Augustinian theodicy is consistent with the biblical tradition of a wholly good creator God
- Consistent with human experience of cause/effect – i.e. sin leads to suffering
- Responsibility for suffering becomes humanity's rather than God's
- The Irenaean theodicy provides purpose for suffering
- Compatible with scientific view of evolution and natural selection
- Involves genuine human responsibility respecting human free-will
- Maintains belief in life after death as suffering will be overcome in next life

Not adequate

- Concept of hell as part of universe's design implies foreseen flaw, therefore world not made perfect
- Scientific evidence disagrees with the concept of a 'fallen' nature – development of species over time/ evolutionary developments, etc.
- Biological impossibilities of all humans being 'seminally present' in Adam
- Evil not merely absence of good but real entity/ experience
- Questions omnibenevolence of God when purpose of life is to grow through suffering
- Fails to explain uneven distribution of suffering
- If all go to heaven, there is no incentive to do good rather than evil

2: 'Animal, immense and innocent suffering prove that the God of classical theism does not exist.' Assess this view.

For

- The omnibenevolent/omnipotent characteristics of God would prohibit animal, immense and innocent suffering
- Animal suffering has no theological or philosophical basis in classical theism
- Innocent suffering denies the concept of a 'just' God
- Immense suffering counters the theological proofs of a designing/creating God of classical theism

Against

- Animal, immense and innocent suffering questions God's characteristics not his existence
- Augustinian theodicy explains animal and innocent suffering in terms of disruption of natural order due to Fall and deserved punishment through Adam
- The Irenaean theodicy regards all suffering as necessary for moral and spiritual development
- Animal, innocent and immense suffering explained by free-will conflicts
- Proof of God's existence rooted in faith as well as natural theology – evil and suffering often interpreted as tests of faith

3: 'The Augustinian theodicy successfully resolves the problem of evil.' Assess this view.

Successful
- Augustinian theodicy is consistent with the biblical tradition of wholly good creator God
- Consistent with accounts in Bible of Fall and Atonement
- Consistent with human experience of cause/effect
- Responsibility for suffering becomes humanity's rather than God's

Unsuccessful
- Criticisms of theodicy based on concepts relating to logical, scientific and moral error
- Concept of hell as part of universe's design implies foreseen flaw, therefore not made perfect
- If humans were created perfect then evil choice would not have been made
- Scientific evidence disagrees with 'fallen' nature – development of species over time/evolutionary developments
- Biological impossibilities of all humans being 'seminally present' in Adam
- Failure to justify innocent and animal suffering
- Evil not merely absence of good but real

4: 'The Irenaean theodicy successfully resolves the problem of evil.' Assess this view.

Successful
- The Irenaean theodicy provides a purpose for suffering
- It is compatible with the scientific view of evolution
- Involves genuine human responsibility and is respecting of human free-will
- Promotes human growth/development in achieving moral virtue
- Maintains belief in life after death – and that all suffering will ultimately be rewarded so that justice is achieved

Unsuccessful
- God is partly responsible for evil
- Questions omnibenevolence of God when the purpose of life is to grow through suffering
- It is incompatible with biblical accounts of Creation, Fall and Atonement
- Idea of suffering leading to moral/spiritual development is not a universal experience but often leads to more evil/suffering (therefore can be described more accurately as soul-breaking rather than soul-making)
- The excessive extent of evil/suffering is not accounted for and it fails to justify the suffering of the 'innocent'
- There is no explanation as to why animals suffer
- Fails to explain uneven distribution of suffering
- If all go to heaven, then there is no incentive to do good rather than evil – this is incompatible with most religious moral frameworks

▲ Grade boost

There is never any requirement to favour one side of the debate rather than another in this module. The essential quality of a good evaluation is that both sides are carefully represented and then a conclusion, **which is based on the evidence presented**, can be drawn. Conclusions are an essential feature of all successful AO2 responses.

5: 'Augustine's theodicy is less convincing than that of Irenaeus.' Assess this view.

Less convincing

- Scientific evidence disagrees with Augustine's concept of a 'fallen' nature – development of species over time/evolutionary developments, etc.
- Biological impossibilities of Augustine's view that all humans were 'seminally present' in Adam
- Evil not merely absence of good but real entity/ experience
- Whereas the Irenaean theodicy provides purpose for suffering
- Irenaean theodicy is compatible with scientific view of evolution and natural selection
- Irenaeus' theodicy involves genuine human responsibility respecting human free-will
- Irenaeus also maintains belief in life after death as suffering will be overcome in next life

Not less convincing

- The Augustinian theodicy is consistent with the biblical tradition of a wholly good creator God
- Religious believers can appreciate Augustine's view of a fallen (spiritually) creation therefore can be convincing to them
- If Irenaeus is accepted then this questions omnibenevolence of God when purpose of life is to grow through suffering
- Irenaeus fails to explain uneven distribution of suffering and if all go to heaven, there is no incentive to do good rather than evil
- Both theodicies are dependent on an interpretation of the bible. If sacred writings are not accepted (i.e. non-believers) then neither theodicy is convincing

6: 'Both Augustine and Irenaeus fail to provide a satisfactory theodicy.' Assess this view.

Fail

- Concept of hell as part of universe's design implies foreseen flaw, therefore world not made perfect
- Scientific evidence disagrees with the concept of a 'fallen' nature – development of species over time/evolutionary developments, etc.
- Biological impossibilities of all humans being 'seminally present' in Adam
- Evil not merely absence of good but real entity/ experience
- Questions omnibenevolence of God when purpose of life is to grow through suffering
- Fails to explain uneven distribution of suffering
- If all go to heaven, there is no incentive to do good rather than evil
- Both theodicies presume the benevolence of God – if this is rejected (i.e. by non-believers) then the theodicies fail

Do not fail

- The Augustinian theodicy is consistent with the biblical tradition of a wholly good creator God
- Consistent with human experience of cause/effect – i.e. sin leads to suffering
- Responsibility for suffering becomes humanity's rather than God's
- The Irenaean theodicy provides purpose for suffering
- Compatible with scientific view of evolution and natural selection
- Involves genuine human responsibility respecting human free-will
- Maintains belief in life after death as suffering will be overcome in next life
- Both satisfy believers from the Christian tradition as ideas are consistent with several Christian doctrines

Summary: Evil and Suffering

We have identified the key points on the WJEC AS specification and, combined with the information in this topic, represented them as a diagram which shows the main things that you need to know. You may want to fill in further details to elaborate and personalise this content.

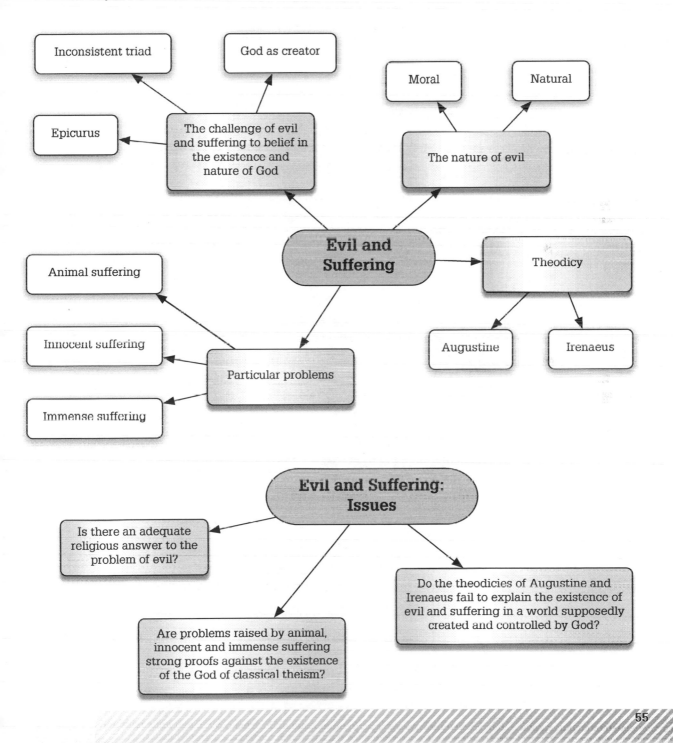

4: Religious Experience: Mysticism

When revising mysticism, you should focus on the main beliefs and practices associated with this form of religious experience. For example, you are expected to know the main types of mystical experience, including reference to the types described by William James. In addition, you will need to be familiar with how one religious mystic showed mysticism in practice, so for instance, you may choose to present what you have learned about Teresa of Avila's experiences of prayer. Furthermore, you will need to understand the main philosophical debates surrounding the challenges of objectivity and authenticity to mysticism and be able to show how these can present a challenge to a belief in mystical experiences. Finally, you should be able to evaluate the issues that arise out of these areas and be aware of the main ideas that both support and detract from these issues.

Revision checklist

Tick column 1 when you have completed brief revision notes.
Tick column 2 when you think you have a good grasp of the topic.
Tick column 3 during final revision when you feel you have mastery of the topic.

			1	2	3
What is meant by the nature of mystical experience?	p57	Brief history of mysticism			
	p57	Definitions and characteristics of mystical experience			
	p57	Mystical ascent and unity with the divine			
What can be learnt about mysticism in practice?	p58	St Teresa of Avila			
	p60	Meister Eckhart			
	p62	Rumi			
What are the main types of mystical experience?	p63	Kataphatic vs. apophatic			
	p64	Extrovertive and introvertive			
	p64	Monistic mysticism			
	p64	Theistic and non-theistic			
	p65	Theurgic vs. non-theurgic mysticism			
	p65	Union with God			
What contributions did William James make to the study of mysticism?	p66	Ineffability			
	p 66	Noetic quality			
	p67	Transciency			
	p67	Passivity			
What are the main challenges to mysticism in relation to objectivity and authenticity?	p68	Nature of the subjectivity of mystical experiences			
	p69	Challenges of verification and falsification to the use of language to describe a mystical experience			
	p70	Caroline Franks-Davis: three categories of challenge			
	p70	Naturalistic explanations			
What are the main issues related to a study of mystical experiences?	p72	Challenges for mysticism in an empirical world			
	p73	How can religious belief relate to mysticism?			
	p73	Should challenges of authenticity be allowed to devalue mystical experiences?			

Introduction to and nature of mystical experience

A religious experience can include a number of varied phenomena but, for the purposes of this unit, we shall be focussing on one aspect of religious experience, i.e. mystical experiences. The term mysticism has become somewhat loosely interpreted in recent times to refer to a range of experiences, often erroneously attributed to a vague kind of 'new-age' approach to religious practices and experiences. Whilst there may well be veins of mystical experiences to be found within such areas, the history of such things is older by far. Mystical experiences are described in the most ancient religious traditions that we know of. From ancient texts such as the Bhagavad Gita in Hinduism to accounts of medieval mystics such as Julian of Norwich and Meister Eckhart, mysticism has a rich and diverse history.

Miller's definition

What then is the *nature* of mystical experience? To this question there are numerous responses but certain themes run throughout all of them. Ed Miller regards it as *'the pursuit of a transcendent, unitive experience with the absolute reality'* (*Questions that Matter*, Miller, 1995) and offers the following helpful summary:

1. *Transcendent:* Not localisable in space or time
2. *Ineffable:* Not expressible in language
3. *Noetic:* Conveying illumination, truth
4. *Ecstatic:* Filling the soul with bliss, peace
5. *Unitive:* Uniting the soul with reality

Miller is not alone in making use of these particular terms to define mystical experiences. Commentators such as William James (who makes use of several of the above categories) and Walter Stace define mystical experiences in different ways but admit to a series of common features that all such experiences are said to have.

Climbing the ladder

Religious mystics also often speak of a mystical ascent, in some ways similar to the Platonic view of reality, where there is, effectively, a ladder or staircase. These steps begin in the earthly, mundane world but, with regular practice and divine assistance, the individual can transcend their own reality and make an ascent of this ladder, to gain unity with the ultimate reality. It is often described metaphorically as a journey from darkness to light.

The Divine

Earthly Self

Key Quotes

The most important, the central characteristic in which all fully developed mystical experiences agree, and which in the last analysis is definitive of them and serves to mark them off from other kinds of experiences, is that they involve the apprehension of an ultimate nonsensuous unity in all things, a oneness or a One to which neither the senses nor the reason can penetrate. In other words, it entirely transcends our sensory-intellectual consciousness.

W. T. Stace – *The Teachings of the Mystics*, New American Library, 1960

The mystical experience is a transient, extraordinary experience marked by feelings of being in unity, harmonious relationship to the divine and everything in existence, as well as euphoric feelings, noesis, loss of ego functioning, alterations in time and space perception, and the sense of lacking control over the event.

David Lukoff,
www.spiritualcompetency.com

quickfire

① What, according to Miller, are the five main characteristics of all mystical experiences?

An overview of selected religious mystics

St Teresa of Avila (1515–1582)

Beginnings

She was born on 15 March 1515 in Spain. Her family inspired the young Teresa to take her religious life seriously and in 1535 she joined an order of Carmelite nuns. After a severe illness, which left Teresa partially paralysed for three years, she became somewhat disillusioned with her religious practices, especially prayer. However, a vision of the 'sorely wounded Christ' was to re-energise Teresa's spiritual journey and inspire her to write her great works on prayer.

Approach

Teresa's approach to mystical experience was through her four stages of prayer. She believed that true union with God could only be achieved by intense concentration and disciplining oneself through a life of prayer that would, by a series of stages, allow a person to reach that union:

> *To say something, then, of the early experiences of those who are determined to pursue this blessing and to succeed in this enterprise... it is in these early stages that their labour is hardest, for it is they themselves who labour and the Lord Who gives the increase. In the other degrees of prayer the chief thing is fruition, although, whether at the beginning, in the middle or at the end of the road, all have their crosses, different as these may be. For those who follow Christ must take the way which He took, unless they want to be lost.*
>
> The Autobiography of St. Teresa of Avila

The Garden analogy 1

Teresa firmly believed that it was not possible for an individual to achieve that union by themselves but that, only through God's grace, could a person move through the various stages:

> *The beginner must think of himself as of one setting out to make a garden in which the Lord is to take His delight, yet in soil most unfruitful and full of weeds. His Majesty uproots the weeds and will set good plants in their stead. Let us suppose that this is already done – that a soul has resolved to practise prayer and has already begun to do so. We have now, by God's help, like good gardeners, to make these plants grow, and to water them carefully, so that they may not perish, but may produce flowers which shall send forth great fragrance to give refreshment to this Lord of ours, so that He may often come into the garden to take His pleasure and have His delight among these virtues.*
>
> The Autobiography of St. Teresa of Avila

quickfire

② What vision did Teresa see that inspired her to a life of prayer?

③ What metaphor does Teresa of Avila employ to describe the various stages of prayer?

The Garden analogy 2

Teresa is often associated with her teaching on the various stages of prayer. She compares these stages to the ways in which a garden can be watered (the metaphor that she has already established to represent the state of a person's spiritual self):

> *The garden can be watered in four ways: by taking the water from a well, which costs us great labour; or by a water-wheel and buckets, when the water is drawn by a windlass . . . ; or by a stream or a brook, which waters the ground much better, for it saturates it more thoroughly and there is less need to water it often, so that the gardener's labour is much less; or by heavy rain, when the Lord waters it with no labour of ours, a way incomparably better than any of those which have been described.*
>
> The Autobiography of St. Teresa of Avila

In an article for a Catholic journal, Father Larry Lapointe sums up what these water metaphors mean on a spiritual level:

> *Teresa says beginners should use determination to overcome distractions while praying and devoutly contemplate Christ. At the second stage, the soul has quieted and gains greater clarity. The will is lost in God but other human faculties, such as imagination, remain distracted. In the third stage, Christ becomes the gardener; the soul is given over to God blissfully but the union with God remains incomplete. The fourth stage is a trance. Union with God is complete; the senses stop and consciousness of the body fades.*
>
> Fr Larry LaPointe, *Teresa of Avila, Living Faith: Mind, Body & Soul*, Connecticut College (9/9/2006)

The Interior Castle

Overview

Whilst her definitions of prayer from her autobiography are highly significant, many observers believe that the real insight into mystical experience is found in Teresa's final work: *The Interior Castle*. Moving on from her analogy of a watered garden, Teresa now considers the soul to be like a castle which contains seven suites or mansions (the original Spanish term, which is often used in English considerations of Teresa's teachings is *las moradas*). The first three mansions refer to the type of prayer that Teresa speaks about in detail in earlier works such as her *Autobiography*. These prayers, whilst allowing the individual to come closer to God, do not give the same level of union that can eventually be gained. This union is to be found within the fourth to the seventh mansions, where Teresa represents the various degrees of mystical prayer.

The fourth mansion

The first of these, found in the fourth mansion, is the prayer of consolations from God, better known as the Prayer of Quiet. Teresa describes this as a state where the human will is completely captivated by God's Love. This now has the individual operating on the mystical level and, as such, they now experience,

Grade boost

When writing about these mystics in an essay, it is very important that you demonstrate to the examiner how they showed 'mysticism in practice'. This means talking about their contributions to mystical experiences and the various ways that they may have done this. You should make frequent references to their writings where appropriate to support your comments.

quickfire

④ How many mansions were in the Interior Castle and what did they represent?

Key Quote

We should desire and engage in prayer, not for our enjoyment, but for the sake of acquiring the strength which fits us for service .... Believe me, Martha and Mary must work together .... I will end by saying that we must not build towers without foundations, and that the Lord does not look so much at the magnitude of anything we do as at the love with which we do it. If we accomplish what we can, His Majesty will see to it that we become able to do more each day.

St. Teresa of Avila, Chapter 4 *The Interior Castle: Seventh Mansions*

quickfire

(5) Which is the more intense state of prayer – mystical marriage or spiritual marriage?

peace and spiritual delight. Sometimes the experience is so intense that the individual can faint or appear semi-comatose – this state is referred to by St Teresa as a 'sleep of the faculties'.

The fifth mansion

Within the fifth mansion Teresa describes the next stage as the prayer of simple union: 'God implants himself in the interior of the soul is such a way that, when it returns to itself, it cannot possibly doubt that God has been in it and it has been in God.'

The sixth mansion

The sixth mansion contains the longest of Teresa's mystical descriptions and is occasionally disputed as to precisely what was being described. It is commonly known as the stage of spiritual marriage. The main experiences associated with this stage can include rapture, feelings of painful longing, spiritual ecstasy and visions. The over-riding characteristic is the sense of wanting to be able to spend every possible moment alone with the divine 'spouse' and the complete rejection of all things that can get in the way of such moments.

The seventh mansion

The seventh and final mansion is regarded as the highest possible state of prayer that is achievable on earth. The soul is regarded as having reached a state of transforming union or, as it is more commonly known, the stage of 'mystical marriage'. It is the stage where complete unity with the divine is felt, to the extent where an intimate and perceptive awareness, knowledge and understanding of the person of the divine are intuitively felt.

Meister Eckhart (c.1260–1328)

Educated as a member of the Dominican order in the Catholic Church, Meister Eckhart was no stranger to controversy and was accused of heresy on a number of occasions. He died whilst under investigation from Pope John XXII, who condemned some of Eckhart's works as heretical, although these were not confirmed until after Eckhart's death. Largely ignored for many years, Eckhart has enjoyed a revival in terms of his teachings not least thanks to an English psychotherapist, Ursula Fleming, who in the 1990s wrote a series of books that, amongst other things, encouraged people to engage with the works of Eckhart. She recognised that his works were difficult to understand but, following advice given to her by her own spiritual advisor, she states in her book:

Don't try to understand Eckhart too much.
Don't try to work it all out. Just read it.
  Meister Eckhart, *The Man From Whom God Hid Nothing*, edited by Ursula Fleming, Fount (1988)

Uniting with God

According to Eckhart, each individual's quest in life was to find a way to unite their soul with God's. However, and this was one of the ideas that led to him attracting controversy in his own time, Eckhart did not believe that the teachings and traditions of the Church were sufficient to bring about this unification but that a personal independence was required where individuals could be free to find God in their own way, and understand God in the way that was appropriate to them – only in this way could a soul achieve that sought-after unity.

Overcoming obstruction

Eckhart stated that the main obstruction between God and humankind was the basic human nature that centred on greed, selfishness and an indifference to love and justice. For Eckhart, that obstruction could only be overcome by a complete and utter devotion to God – he himself believed that God could be found in everything in nature and that we only had to open ourselves to find this truth.

Preaching

Eckhart preached on four inter-related themes:

> When I preach, I am careful to speak about detachment and that a person should become free of self and of all things.
>
> Secondly, that one should be reformed in the simple good that is God.
>
> Thirdly, that one should think of the great nobility which God has placed in the soul, so that person may thereby come to God in a wonderful way.
>
> Fourthly, concerning the purity of divine nature   there is such brilliance in it that it is inexpressible.
>
> Meister Eckhart, *Sermons*

Detachment

The detachment that Eckhart speaks of (interestingly also one of the reasons that Eckhart's teachings have sometimes been compared with those of the historical Buddha) is essential in the individual's quest of becoming one with God. One of Eckhart's recurring themes is of the need for God being born into the individual in order for this unification to be realised fully. The basic truth stated in Eckhart's teaching is the unity granted by grace between the all-powerful God and the 'nothing' of human beings.

Via negativa

Eckhart also presented a form of language to describe God that some describe as a '**via negativa**'. For Eckhart, applying any kind of finite language to God was inappropriate for it did not encompass the quality of God being infinite. Therefore, Eckhart would often say that God was 'not-"X"' (X being the finite quality). In this Eckhart was not denying that God had the quality 'X' just that God did not possess that quality in a finite sense. Thus when Eckhart makes the claim that God is non-existent, he means that God has none of the qualities of finite existence, not that he doesn't exist.

Key Term

Via negativa = a form of negative language: a way of describing what something is not like, in order to try and reach an understanding, through negative language, of the reality of something.

Key Quote

Why do we pray, why do we fast, why do we do all our works, why are we baptised, why (most important of all) did God become man? – I would answer, in order that God may be born in the soul and the soul be born in God. For that reason all the scriptures were written, for that reason God created the world and all angelic natures …

Meister Eckhart, *Sermons*

quickfire

(6) Which order did Meister Eckhart belong to?

(7) How many themes did he normally preach on?

(8) Which other mystic is Eckhart sometimes compared with?

Rumi (c.1207–1273)

Sufism, a mystical group within Islam, that focuses on divine union with Allah through meditation, dance, and other mystic practices, was the tradition that Rumi, a 13th-century Persian poet, found himself associated with. Born Jalāl ad-Dān Muḥammad Balkhā, but known to the English speaking world simply as 'Rumi', his poems have been well received and preserved throughout the ages, making him, arguably, the most significant poet ever to have come from the Persian region.

Becoming a Sufi

He was not born into the Sufi tradition but became involved with it when he was introduced to Shams-eTabrizi, an Iranian Sufi mystic and teacher. They formed a strong friendship and teacher–student bond.

Rumi (inspired by his own experiences) believed that all individuals have a yearning within them that is due to the feeling of separation that all beings instinctively feel. He recognised that whilst Allah was both high in the heavens and closer to man than his own jugular vein, humankind was still separated from Allah and only by spiritual purification through love could union with God (tawhid) be truly achieved. Rumi believed that the human spirit was designed for the singular underlying purpose to draw into a deeper relationship with God.

Belief and practice

Taught by Shams, he developed the practice known as Sema, a sacred dance, where Sufis constantly turn on the left foot; (the turning, according to Rumi, is a metaphor for *a blessed state of every fibre of an individual's being turning on the axis of the merciful and compassionate creator and sustainer of all things')*, this turning is meant to generate a spiritual ascent to Allah. This message of yearning to be united with Allah forms the central message in his poem *The Song of the Reed Flute*. Here Rumi invites the listener to understand the secret of human existence by hearkening to the message hidden in the plaintive tones of the reed flute. (The first few lines are represented in the Key quotes section.)

If, reasoned Rumi, the most basic purpose of the human spirit was to put a person in relationship with the divine then all other relationships within the created order, especially those with other human beings, are mystical gateways into a closer relationship with the creator. This highly significant part of Rumi's mystical experience was played out in his own relationship with his mentor, Shams. He noted how through this close relationship he felt that he became closer in his relationship with Allah.

Rumi wrote many poems of devotion centred on the theme of Allah's love, and on the essential quest of seeking spiritual union with that love directly. Rumi's major work is *Masnavi-ye Manavi*, a six-volume poem about spiritual unity with the 'beloved', the illusion of separation from this source, and Rumi's longing to experience reunification. It is regarded as one of the most important pieces of mystical poetry ever produced. Rumi believed poetry, music, and dance were all direct doorways to the divine and, due to these convictions; he founded the Mevlevi order of Sufis, famous for their Whirling Dervishes.

Key Quotes

1. *Now listen to this reed-flute's deep lament*
   About the heartache being apart has meant:
2. *Since from the reed-bed they uprooted me*
   My song's expressed each human's agony,
3. *A breast which separation's split in two*
   Is what I seek, to share this pain with you:
4. *When kept from their true origin, all yearn*
   For union on the day they can return.

Jalal Al-Din Rumi, *The Masnavi, Book One*, translated by Jawid Mojaddedi, Oxford University Press (2004)

quickfire

⑨ In which medium did Rumi communicate his mystical experiences?

⑩ How did Rumi come to view human relationships?

⑪ What is a Sema?

Types of mystical experience

Overview

Notoriously difficult as an area for philosophers to agree on, mystical experiences have nonetheless been an area of fascination for religious commentators for many years now. What follows is an attempt to cover some of the main types of mystical experiences as recognised by a majority of academics. It is, however, entirely possible that your own research will find other categorisations, as well as those who disagree with some (or even all) of the classifications that follow.

A useful summary of some of these issues is presented by Philip Almond:

- *Radhakrishnan: There is one kind of religious experience, the mystical.*
- *Zaehner: There are three kinds of mystical experience: panhenic, monistic and theistic.*
- *Smart: There are two kinds of religious experience: mystical and numinous (theistic).*
- *Stace: There are two kinds of mystical experience, extrovertive and introvertive, the first of which is on the path to the second.*

Philip C Almond, *Mystical Experience and Religious Doctrine: An Investigation of the Study of Mysticism in World Religions*, Mouton (1982)

Kataphatic vs. apophatic

In kataphatic mysticism the mystic feels able to make claims about their experiences with the divine. It emphasises the importance of images, symbols, and sensation in mystical experience. The *Spiritual Exercises* of Ignatius of Loyola and Teresa of Avila's meditations on water to explain prayer are two examples.

In apophatic mysticism the mystic feels unable to communicate anything of their experience of the divine. The apophatic mystic believes that there are no words and no images that can adequately describe the indescribable divine. This form of mysticism is a form of via negativa. Meister Eckhart and St John of the Cross are two particularly notable exponents of apophatic mysticism.

Christianity has both a strong kataphatic and apophatic mystical tradition.

Some philosophers have stated that the two forms are mutually exclusive but Roman Catholic writer Thomas Keating states:

'... [there is] a misleading distinction suggesting opposition between the two, in fact, a proper preparation of the faculties (kataphatic practice) leads to apophatic contemplation, which in turn is sustained through appropriate kataphatic practices.'

Thomas Keating, *Open Mind, Open Heart*, Continuum International Publishing Group Ltd 20th Anniversary edition (2007)

Grade boost

Being able to write clearly and confidently about these types of mystical experiences is key to a successful answer – you can do this by using an example to define each type and giving an appropriate quotation from a religious mystic to further strengthen your material.

 quickfire

⑫ Define kataphatic and apophatic mysticism.

Key Terms

Extrovertive = outward looking.

Introvertive = inward looking.

Monism = the metaphysical idea that all things in the universe are connected or part of the same single unity.

Theistic = relating to belief in a god.

Extrovertive and introvertive

These are the types of mystical experience that W T Stace classified:

> One may be called **extrovertive** mystical experience, the other **introvertive** mystical experience. Both are apprehensions of the One, but they reach it in different ways. The extrovertive way looks outward and through the physical senses into the external world and finds the One there.
>
> The introvertive way turns inward, introspectively, and finds the One at the bottom of the self, at the bottom of human personality. The latter far outweighs the former in importance both in the history of mysticism and in the history of human thought generally.
>
> The introvertive way is the major strand in the history of mysticism, the extrovertive way a minor strand.

W. T. Stace, *The Teachings of the Mystics*, New American Library (1960)

⑬ Which philosopher defined mystical experiences as extrovertive and introvertive?

Monistic mysticism

This experience is where the individual describes the whole world as revolving around a central point. Everything about that individual, both external and internal, is somehow attracted towards or emanates from that central point.

The **monistic** mystical experience has been described in this way: 'It is like seeing everything fall away and being absorbed. I was able to see an infinite becoming and an infinite disappearing in the same eternal moment.'

The Hindu Upanishads express monastic mysticism in the declaration 'I am Brahman' and 'That Thou Art' – expressions of the all-pervading principle and the eternal nature of the soul respectively. Taoism is another expression with the quest of seeking unity with the indescribable way, Tao.

Theistic and non-theistic

A distinction in experience that has been popular with philosophers of Europe and North America, including notably Ninian Smart, a **theistic** mystical experience is one where the individual feels a mystical understanding of God, yet remains distinct from God. These are known as numinous theistic experiences, as opposed to mystical theistic experiences which tend towards the experience being where the individual claims a unitive 'at-one-ness' with God (cf Teresa of Avila). Non-theistic experiences tend to refer to an experience of some kind of ultimate reality or an awareness of a concept of nothingness (cf Siddhartha Gautama).

Theurgic vs. non-theurgic mysticism

The practice of **theurgy** is an ancient practice that involves ritualistic behaviour intended to somehow invoke the presence of the divine in order to bring about mystical union between the divine and the self. Some regard Jewish kabbalism as the most well-known form of alleged theurgy. In kabbalistic practice the individual seeks to bring about a mystical union through invoking the sephirot, the ten emanations of the divine.

Non-theurgic mysticism represents the mystical experiences of those who do not attempt to evoke or invoke the divine but instead practise mysticism in a way that attempts to make sense of reality as it is. An example of non-theurgic mysticism can be found in the Zen school of Buddhism.

Union with God

This type of mystical experience tends to cover a range of similar types of experiences, rather than describing a single identifiable experience. The concept of union involves a removal of the separation between the individual and God. Many Christian mystics have claimed such experiences, including St Bernard of Clairvaux, the French Cistercian Abbot, who described the experience as a 'mutuality of love'; the German mystic (and student of Meister Eckhart), Henry Suso, stated that the experience was like a man who:

> '...is entirely lost in God, has passed into him, and has become one spirit with him in all respects, like a drop of water which is poured into a large portion of wine. Just as this is lost to itself, and draws to itself and into itself the taste and colour of the wine, so it likewise happens to those who are in complete possession of blessedness.'
>
> Henry Suso, *Little Book of Eternal Wisdom*

Key Term

Theurgy = the belief that a supernatural intervention into the lives and experiences of humans is possible.

Grade boost

Many of these key terms can appear very confusing at first. Constantly revising the spelling and meanings of these key terms, and then making regular use of them in your practice essays, will not only help you become more comfortable with their use but it will also help you improve performance by correctly using technical language.

⑭ How does Suso define union with God?

Key Terms

Ineffable = that being of which a person cannot speak as no words can describe the experience.

Noesis = knowledge gained through mystical experience that would otherwise not be available to the recipient through ordinary means.

Key Figure

William James

Born to a wealthy family in North America in 1842, and brother to the notable American novelist Henry James, William explored several academic disciplines during the first part of his life before settling on the relatively new discipline of psychology. His work inspired many of the 20th century's greatest thinkers, including Ludwig Wittgenstein. (Allegedly the only book written by a modern philosopher that Wittgenstein would have on his own bookshelf was James' *Varieties of Religious Experience*!)

A philosophical pragmatist, James nonetheless stated his belief that religious experience was ultimately beyond the realm of empirical science to ever prove as 'true'. Of such experience he observes:
the further limits of our being plunge, it seems to me, into an altogether other dimension of existence from the sensible and merely 'understandable' world

(James, *Varieties of Religious Experience*, 1902)

William James' *Varieties of Religious Experience* (1902) is still regarded as one of the most significant and influential studies of religion of the 20th century. Amongst other subjects, James details a classification of mysticism within lectures 16 and 17 of the work. These are instrumental observations of mystical experience and no serious study of the subject can be undertaken without reflecting on James' contributions.

Here follows the explanations of the classifications in James' own words (quotes from James' *Varieties of Religious Experience*):

1. *'**Ineffability** – The handiest of the marks by which I classify a state of mind as mystical is negative. The subject of it immediately says that it defies expression, that no adequate report of its contents can be given in words. It follows from this that its quality must be directly experienced; it cannot be imparted or transferred to others. In this peculiarity mystical states are more like states of feeling than like states of intellect. No one can make clear to another who has never had a certain feeling, in what the quality or worth of it consists. One must have musical ears to know the value of a symphony; one must have been in love one's self to understand a lover's state of mind. Lacking the heart or ear, we cannot interpret the musician or the lover justly, and are even likely to consider him weak-minded or absurd. The mystic finds that most of us accord to his experiences an equally incompetent treatment.'*

James' first class of mystical experience is the one most commonly cited by mystics such as Teresa of Avila, Eckhart, Rumi and others. It is atypical of a mystical experience that it is so profound that mundane language cannot express it. It also represents, as James acknowledges, the greatest challenges to the authenticity of the experience. However, James continues, just because it cannot be 'proved' should not detract from its value; indeed, he implies, it is more to do with the deficiency of the empiricist than it is with any such deficiency of the mystic, that the experience cannot be described.

2. *'Noetic quality – Although so similar to states of feeling, mystical states seem to those who experience them to be also states of knowledge. They are states of insight into depths of truth unplumbed by the discursive intellect. They are illuminations, revelations, full of significance and importance, all inarticulate though they remain; and as a rule they carry with them a curious sense of authority for after-time.'*

The gaining of a special kind of knowledge, or insight, is another hallmark of the work of mystics down the ages and this is what James refers to when he considers the **noesis** (gaining of knowledge) of the mystics' experiences.

3. 'Transiency — *Mystical states cannot be sustained for long. Except in rare instances, half an hour, or at most an hour or two, seems to be the limit beyond which they fade into the light of common day. Often, when faded, their quality can but imperfectly be reproduced in memory; but when they recur it is recognized; and from one recurrence to another it is susceptible of continuous development in what is felt as inner richness and importance.'*

In the third classification, James relates the fleeting nature of the mystical experience and demonstrates, through the evidence that he collects, that such experiences may be very intense and have lasting consequences for the recipient, yet in terms of the time in which they take, they are relatively short-lived.

4. 'Passivity — *Although the oncoming of mystical states may be facilitated by preliminary voluntary operations, as by fixing the attention, or going through certain bodily performances, or in other ways which manuals of mysticism prescribe; yet when the characteristic sort of consciousness once has set in, the mystic feels as if his own will were in abeyance, and indeed sometimes as if he were grasped and held by a superior power. This latter peculiarity connects mystical states with certain definite phenomena of secondary or alternative personality, such as prophetic speech, automatic writing, or the mediumistic trance. When these latter conditions are well pronounced, however, there may be no recollection whatever of the phenomenon and it may have no significance for the subject's usual inner life, to which, as it were, it makes a mere interruption. Mystical states, strictly so called, are never merely interruptive. Some memory of their content always remains, and a profound sense of their importance. They modify the inner life of the subject between the times of their recurrence. Sharp divisions in this region are, however, difficult to make, and we find all sorts of gradations and mixtures.'*

The fourth and final classification notes the important feature that the experience tends to be 'done to' the recipient and that, even when the recipient goes searching for the experience, the actual moment itself is governed by a being or force external to the will of the mystic. The suggestion is also that these events have a transformative effect on the individual, whose life will very often be changed after the experience.

quickfire

⑮ What are the four identifying features of mystical experiences, according to William James?

Key Quotes

One may say truly, I think, that personal religious experience has its root and centre in mystical states of consciousness…

Mystical states indeed wield no authority due simply to their being mystical states. But the higher ones among them point in directions to which the religious sentiments even of non-mystical men incline. They tell of the supremacy of the ideal, of vastness, of union, of safety, and of rest. They offer us hypotheses, hypotheses which we may voluntarily ignore, but which as thinkers we cannot possibly upset. The supernaturalism and optimism to which they would persuade us may, interpreted in one way or another, be after all the truest of insights into the meaning of this life.

William James, *Varieties of Religious Experience: A Study in Human Nature* (1902)

Problems of objectivity and authenticity: challenges to religious mysticism

Key term

Authenticity = where something is undisputedly credible.

Overview

The very nature of mystical experiences (whatever their type and whoever undergoes them), seems to belong to a bygone era. Reading accounts of mystical experiences in ancient religious texts seems perfectly natural, as does considering the experiences of the famous mystics from the traditions of the various world religions. However, when faced with such claims in an age seemingly dominated by empiricism, science, rationality and evidential proofs, scepticism tends to come into play and doubt as to their occurrences, or at least, to the authenticity of such experiences, seems to be the automatic response.

What follows is a brief consideration of some of the main issues around the debate of objectivity and **authenticity**.

Nature of the subjectivity of mystical experiences

In trying to establish the reliability of any mystical experience, some criteria for establishing truth must first be agreed upon. However, due to the very nature of mystical experiences, most philosophers agree that such criteria are virtually impossible to have universal agreement on. This is due to the fact that, by their very nature, mystical experiences are subjective and not objective.

Objectivity

If something is objective, it is something that relates to external facts that can be agreed upon by the observers – it is possible to prove by one or more of the five senses, it is something that can be described and multiple observers will come to the same conclusion about the same thing, e.g. the colour of the car is red.

Subjectivity

If something is subjective then it tends to be based upon opinion, personal judgement, belief or assumption. It is likely to be interpreted in different ways by multiple observers and these views may change according to time and context, e.g. this is the best car in the world to drive.

Conclusion

Due to the very fact that communicating mystical experiences depends entirely on the perception of the experience by the recipient – or in some cases the witnesses of the recipient – it is considered as a subjective experience. As scientific empiricism tends to reject subjective accounts out of hand, then this presents a serious challenge to the 'truth' of any mystical experience.

Challenges of verification and falsification to the use of language to describe a mystical experience

Verification

The work of the **Vienna Circle** and the **logical positivists** did much to help clarify our understanding of how language is used to convey knowledge and ideas, as well as the conditions where that language could be considered either meaningful or meaningless. Any claim made by a religious believer about a mystical experience may seem to be an ordinary claim about their perception of the state of reality (whichever reality they may be referring to) but as their claim lacks any empirical evidence to support it, and as such experiences are neither analytic *a priori* nor synthetic *a posteriori*, they are considered by the logical positivists to be meaningless.

Falsification

A further difficulty is posed by Anthony Flew's falsification principle, which stated that propositions could be made meaningful if there was some evidence that could count against them. However, Flew stated that as religious believers allow nothing to count against their beliefs, then all religious statements, including those of the mystic, were ultimately meaningless. He used John Wisdom's *Parable of the Gardener* to support his point:

> *Once upon a time two explorers came upon a clearing in the jungle. In the clearing were growing many flowers and many weeds. One explorer says, 'Some gardener must tend this plot'. The other disagrees, 'There is no gardener'. So they pitch their tents and set a watch. No gardener is ever seen. 'But perhaps he is an invisible gardener.' So they set up a barbed-wire fence. They electrify it. They patrol with bloodhounds. (For they remember how H. G. Wells' The Invisible Man could be both smelt and touched though he could not be seen.) But no shrieks ever suggest that some intruder has received a shock. No movements of the wire ever betray an invisible climber. The bloodhounds never give cry. Yet still the Believer is not convinced. 'But there is a gardener, invisible, intangible, insensible, to electric shocks, a gardener who has no scent and makes no sound, a gardener who comes secretly to look after the garden which he loves.' At last the Sceptic despairs, 'But what remains of your original assertion? Just how does what you call an invisible, intangible, eternally elusive gardener differ from an imaginary gardener or even from no gardener at all?'*
>
> Antony Flew, 'Theology and Falsification', *University*, 1950–51

Flew's point was that for a religious believer, they would always offer a qualification as to why no evidence could be found to count against their own beliefs and, as mystical experiences, are essentially ones where there is no clear and agreed upon criteria which can be used to count against them, they too must, according to Flew's criteria, be considered meaningless.

Key terms

Logical positivism – a form of empiricism that bases all knowledge on sense experience.

Vienna Circle = a hugely influential group of philosophers who initially met and worked from the University of Vienna in the early 1920s.

A posteriori = that which is based on empirical evidence or experience.

A priori = that which is not based on empirical evidence or experience.

quickfire

(16) Why are mystical experiences considered to be 'meaningless' when applying the criteria established by the logical positivists?

Key terms

Anthropology = the study of humans, their society and cultures.

Naturalistic = that which arises from real life or the world of nature.

Sociology = the study of the way in which human society works.

quickfire

⑰ What are Caroline Franks-Davis's three categories of challenge?

Caroline Franks-Davis: three categories of challenge

Caroline Franks-Davis in her 1989 work *The Evidential Force of Religious Experience*, listed three distinct forms of challenge to the validity of claims of religious (mystical) experiences. These were:

1 Description-related

When any event is described that claims itself to be an experience of 'God' or 'The Divine' then a claim is being made for which there is no proof. This description is therefore not valid. Furthermore the claim is inconsistent or contradictory with normal everyday experience and, for this reason, should be rejected. It is not a claim that is in any sense valid, merely a misunderstanding of the experience on the part of the recipient.

2 Subject-related

In this challenge, the recipient (subject) of the religious experience is put under suspicion. It may be claimed that they are unreliable as a source, they may be considered to be suffering from a mental illness or to have been suffering delusions brought about by some sort of substance misuse. In such cases they are not in a position to properly understand what they have experienced and, as such, must have their claims dismissed.

3 Object-related

The final type of challenge focuses on the alleged object of the experience. The challenge is that the likelihood of having experienced something such as the recipient claims is so unlikely as to be entirely untrue. The suggestion of God (the object) having been experienced is no more likely than a claim of having seen an 8 ft green alien or a flying antelope. As we are unlikely to believe anyone that claimed experience of the latter two examples, why then should we believe the claim of someone who was said to have experienced God?

Naturalistic explanations

Using alternative explanations, based on the objective worlds of science and nature, is nothing new in terms of critiquing events that fall into the religious and mystical sphere. When considering the possibility of miracles occurring, David Hume in *An Enquiry Concerning Human Understanding* (1748) stated that it was not impossible that miracles could occur: it was merely impossible to ever prove that one had in fact occurred. Transferring this **naturalistic** view to mystical experiences, a similar problem is faced. Due to their highly individualistic nature (for the most part) mystical experiences are not open to rational enquiry, and, thus, are treated with suspicion at best and derision at worst.

The scientific fields of **sociology**, psychology and **anthropology** have all made huge advances in understanding the human condition within the past century and, in doing so, have all examined the religious dimension of humankind's existence and sought to offer alternative theories as to what is actually being experienced.

Anthropology

For instance, studies by the anthropologist Ioan Lewis have shown a close and intelligible connection in pre-industrial societies between the incidence of religious ecstasy and the need of individuals and groups to legitimatise claims made upon the larger society. In the spirit of such observations, it has been suggested that it was no coincidence that St Teresa of Avila claimed the experiences that she did, precisely at a time in history when the Catholic Church was undergoing an upheaval due to the effects of the Protestant Reformation.

Psychology

Sigmund Freud held the view that all mystical experiences were nothing more than the result of the repression of sexual urges. Re-interpreting Teresa's vision of the angel piercing her soul in the light of Freudian imagery is very easy to do but has come under criticism itself for being too reductionist.

Wendy Dossett puts Freud's position forward thus:

> *In a book called* Civilisation and its Discontents *Freud engages with a writer friend, Romain Rolland, who had told him about the mystical experience, to be found in many religious traditions, in which the mystic has the overwhelmingly powerful experience of him or herself becoming 'one' with God or the Universe. Rolland had described this as the Oceanic Feeling, a term also used by the Hindu mystic Ramakrishna. Instead of finding this persuasive, Freud argues that in fact it is evidence of the true nature of religion which is mere 'wish-fulfilment'. This idea had also been a strong theme of his earlier book* The Future of an Illusion. *Humans cannot cope with life as independent beings. They find it isolating and threatening. As infants they did not need to be individuals with egos. They relied completely on their mother. The most comforting and connected state of course is inside the womb, where they are not even differentiated beings, let alone isolated. For Freud, the desire for the mystical experience, so celebrated in religions, is nothing more than the desire every human being has to return to the womb, to a sense of undifferentiated connectedness. It is characterised by the complete opposite of the quest for maturity, it is in fact regression. It is therefore highly ironic that this experience should be seen as the pinnacle of spiritual development.*

Dossett, Lawson, Owen and Pearce, *Religion in Contemporary Society for AS Students,* UWIC Press, (2009)

Others have commented that the characteristics of mystical experiences bear remarkable resemblances to the effects felt by those who use alcohol and drugs such as LSD, which can stimulate the brain into hallucinating and experiencing so-called alternative realities.

Grade boost

Many of the scholars and philosophers who present challenges to mystical experiences are also important for study in other areas of philosophy, particularly religious language and general religious experience. Being confident with their views here may help you grasp some of their other teachings that are studied in the A2 part of the course.

18 Give one naturalistic explanation for a mystical experience.

Evaluative issues

The following tables demonstrate typical responses to the debates surrounding the evaluative issues relating to mysticism. There is, inevitably, a certain degree of crossover in material that can be used to support or deny the propositions that can be made relating to the various debates; as such, the material presented here can be variously applied to all of the issues related to mysticism in the specification.

1: 'Mysticism is made irrelevant by the empirical world.' Assess this view.

Irrelevant

- We live in a world that is based on reason, logic and scientific enquiry
- Mysticism is often seen as 'navel gazing' by its opponents and has no clear end or purpose
- There is often a total lack of empirical evidence for mysticism
- Those who are mystics tend to live apart from society and are therefore of no real relevance or value to those living within it
- It has been claimed that some who claim to practise mysticism do so for deceptive purposes
- Psychology and scientific methods can offer alternative explanations to the sensations and experiences often felt by mystics
- There is often confusion over interpreting mystical experience due to the nature of mysticism, thereby devaluing any empirical worth

Relevant

- Mysticism can help to strengthen religious belief for both individuals and communities
- Mysticism increases individual and, sometimes, corporate spiritual understanding
- Many of the world's most significant religious traditions are founded on mystical experiences, e.g. prophetic dreams, angelic visions, etc.
- It challenges a superficial material understanding of the world
- Mystics often claim that it reveals truths undiscoverable through other means
- In several religious traditions seeking contact with the divine/transcendent is encouraged
- Mysticism can deepen faith and provide comfort to many as it can also promote understanding of peace and unity between religious traditions and religious communities

2: 'Religious belief and practice should never be affected by mysticism.' Assess this view.

Should never be affected

- Religious practices are open to all, whereas mysticism can be seen to be exclusive and open only to a few
- The select nature of mysticism can be seen to open a debate about the cohesive/divisive nature of mystical experience within religious practice
- Religious belief can be the result of rational enquiry (i.e. natural theology, etc.) therefore not appropriate/ suitable to combine this with a subjective 'mystical' experience
- As mystical experiences can be open to different interpretations, they are therefore not solely adequate for grounds of 'belief'

Should affect

- Individual experiences of prayer, worship, etc., can lead to mystical experiences and help to strengthen religious belief for both the individuals and communities concerned
- Mystics are often accorded higher status within religious traditions and sought after for their ability to communicate with the divine
- Many of the world's religious traditions are founded on mystical experiences
- Actively seeking contact with the divine/transcendent reality is encouraged in several religious traditions

3: 'Challenges to authenticity devalue mystical experiences.' Assess this view.

Devalue

- Empirical testing can produce evidence against mystical experiences
- Challenges often claim that mysticism is sometimes seen as 'navel gazing' with no clear end or purpose
- Psychological investigations can produce alternative explanations for the experiences of mystics and therefore undermine their religious and spiritual integrity
- There can be confusion over interpreting mystical experience which can lead to devaluation
- Some claim mystical experiences in order to promote selfish and harmful agendas – challenges to authenticity can expose these and therefore can increase scepticism about all mystical experiences

Do not devalue

- Teresa of Avila's conditions for authenticity support and enhance the mystical experience
- Wittgenstein: Whereof we cannot speak, thereof we should remain silent
- Swinburne's Principles of testimony and credulity
- Buber's 'I-It' and 'I-Thou' categories can be applied to mystical experiences reducing the validity of challenging authenticity on rational and scientific grounds
- Mystical experiences can remain valuable for the individual who experiences them and produce beneficial outcomes, despite any empirical doubts over authenticity

quickfire

(19) Give two objections to the relevance of mysticism in the empirical world.

(20) State two reasons why some would say that challenges to authenticity do not devalue mystical experiences.

Summary: Religious experience: Mysticism

We have identified the key points on the WJEC AS specification and, combined with the information in this topic, represented them as a diagram which shows the main things that you need to know. You may want to fill in further details to elaborate and personalise this content.

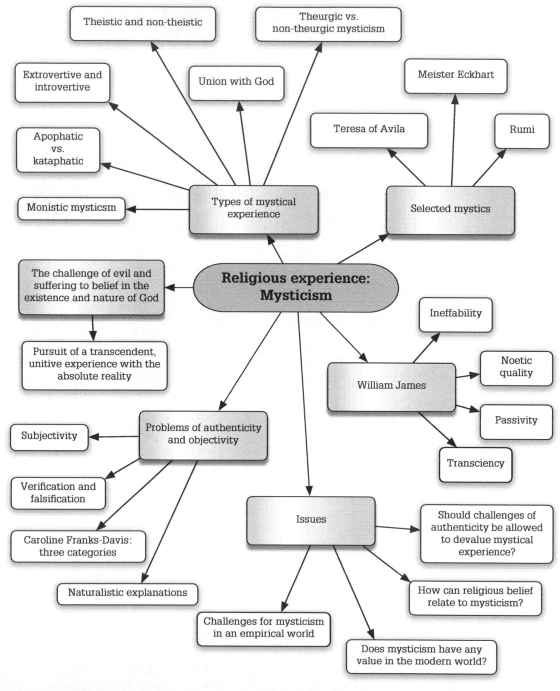

Theistic and non-theistic

Theurgic vs. non-theurgic mysticism

Extrovertive and introvertive

Union with God

Meister Eckhart

Apophatic vs. kataphatic

Teresa of Avila

Rumi

Monistic mysticsm

Types of mystical experience

Selected mystics

The challenge of evil and suffering to belief in the existence and nature of God

Religious experience: Mysticism

Pursuit of a transcendent, unitive experience with the absolute reality

Ineffability

William James

Noetic quality

Passivity

Subjectivity

Problems of authenticity and objectivity

Transciency

Verification and falsification

Issues

Should challenges of authenticity be allowed to devalue mystical experience?

Caroline Franks-Davis: three categories

Naturalistic explanations

How can religious belief relate to mysticism?

Challenges for mysticism in an empirical world

Does mysticism have any value in the modern world?

Unit 2
What is Ethics?

Consider the following:

If your best friend offered you a DVD full of pirated MP3s of your favourite band's songs, would you take it?

How would you make your decision?

You make many decisions like the one above on a daily basis. What you are doing on each occasion is making an ethical decision.

The word 'ethics' is derived from a Greek word '*ethikos*' which means 'character' or 'custom', so the term **'ethics'** refers to how you would normally behave. Another word which is often used in ethical debates is the term 'morality', which is derived from the Latin word '*moralis*' and is concerned with defining which actions are right and which are wrong, rather than the character of the person.

In modern society people often use these two terms to refer to the same thing – therefore the term 'ethics' has come to mean the study of the moral choices people make and the way in which they attempt to justify them. Almost every aspect of your life involves some form of moral or ethical thought.

When deciding how to make an ethical decision people often focus on one or more elements of an ethical action:

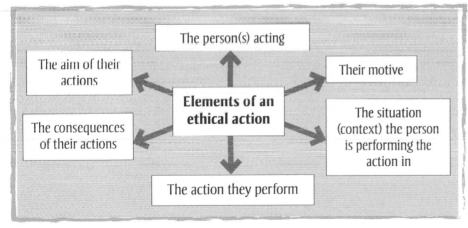

Some ethical theories focus on the consequences of an action; they are called consequentialist theories. So using the example above, if the only consequence of accepting the DVD was that I enjoyed the music, then a consequentialist would say this action was good. However, if there were other consequences such as I end up being prosecuted for receiving pirated music, then they would say the action was wrong. As we will discover, other ethical theories also tend to focus on one or more of the elements of an ethical action.

Key term

Ethics = the study of the moral choices people make and the way in which they attempt to justify them.

Grade boost

Once you've studied the three ethical theories in this book, devise a table which tells you which elements of an ethical action each theory focuses on.

Grade boost

Religious ethics holds a special place within ethics as a whole and has been contributed to by various thinkers of many different religious backgrounds.

In order to gain a greater understanding of how the religious and non religious ethical theories we study fit into the various periods of history, draw a timeline and add the following people/ethical theories to your timeline :

- Aquinas – Natural Law
- Bentham – Act Utilitarianism
- Mill's form of Utilitarianism (later referred to by some as Rule Utilitarianism)
- Fletcher's Situation Ethics.

5: Natural Law

The unit on Aquinas' Natural Law requires you to focus your revision on the main features of the theory. You should be able to explain why many regard Natural Law as being 'absolutist' and 'deontological', and demonstrate the relationship that Aquinas said existed between the four levels/types of law. It important that you can explain the importance for Aquinas of human rationality, its link to the final purpose for humans, the primary precepts and the relationship between the primary and secondary precepts. Furthermore, you will be required to explain the types of virtues within Natural Law and why they are an important feature of the theory. You need to know the difference between interior/exterior acts and real/apparent goods and be able to demonstrate how these ideas are linked to the concept of sin. You will be expected to provide examples of how to apply Natural Law, which may be drawn from the issues listed in the Applied Ethics section or from other issues you have studied. You should also be able to explain to what extent Natural Law is compatible with the traditional teaching of one major world religion. Finally, you should be able to evaluate the issues that arise out of studying Natural Law.

Revision checklist

Tick column 1 when you have completed brief revision notes.
Tick column 2 when you think you have a good grasp of the topic.
Tick column 3 during final revision when you feel you have mastery of the topic.

			1	2	3
What is the historical background to Natural Law?	p77	Rationality, efficient/final causes			
	p77	Everything has a purpose, cardinal virtues			
What type of theory is this?	p78	Absolutist, deontological			
How does Natural Law fit into Aquinas' hierarchical structure of laws?	p78	Four types of law			
What is the purpose of theory?	p79	Using rationality to fulfil our final purpose through the primary/secondary precepts			
What are the virtues and why are they important?	p81	Cardinal virtues			
	p82	Theological virtues			
How does Aquinas distinguish between an act's 'motive' and the actual act?	p83	Interior acts			
	p83	Exterior acts			
	p83	The principle of double effect			
Why did Aquinas identify two types of goods?	p84	Real and apparent goods			
To what extent is Natural Law compatible with the ethical teaching of one major world religion?	p85	Natural Law and its compatibility or not with Christian ethical teaching			
What are the main issues related to Natural Law?	p87	Strengths and weaknesses of Natural Law			
	p88	Does Natural Law provide an adequate basis for moral decision making?			
	p89	Could Natural Law's absolutist approach promote injustice and/or morally wrong behaviour?			
	p90	To what extent can Natural Law as an absolutist and deontological theory work in today's society?			
	p91	How far is Natural Law compatible with a religious approach to moral decision making?			

The historical background: Aristotle

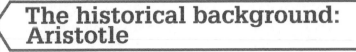

How did   influence   ?

How was a 13th-century Italian monk influenced by a 4th-century BCE Greek philosopher?

Aquinas was born (c.1224 CE) into a Europe that was emerging from the 'Dark Ages' (a period of intellectual 'darkness' caused by the decline of the Roman Empire). At this time, the Church was becoming increasingly challenged as more and more people began to question its claims to absolute authority. It was at around this time that the Crusaders were bringing back new religious and intellectual ideas from the Holy Land (which included the work of Aristotle translated into Arabic). Aquinas studied Aristotle's works at the University of Naples at the age of 14 and he was greatly influenced by what he read.

In particular Aquinas agreed with Aristotle that **rationality** (the ability to reason) was a key element of human existence. He also realised that if the truths of the teachings of both the Bible and Christianity could be shown to be based on reason and not just faith, then Aquinas could help defend the faith against rising challenges. Aquinas also used many of Aristotle's terms in his Natural Law theory, e.g. he supported Aristotle's idea of there being 'efficient' and 'final' causes.

For example, let's consider efficient and final causes using the example of this revision book: the 'efficient' cause (the agent which brings about the final cause) are the revision notes within this book which (hopefully!) will lead to the final cause (the final aim or purpose of something, or the end product) which will be AS students getting better grades in their exam.

Aquinas agreed with Aristotle that everything in the world had a purpose, but unlike Aristotle he argued that this purpose was given to it by God. Aquinas borrowed Aristotle's idea of cultivating the cardinal virtues in order to develop fully as a human. He put this thinking into his Natural Law theory which we will look at in more detail later.

Key Term
Rationality = the ability to think logically, or the ability to reason.

Key Figure

Thomas Aquinas was a 13th-century Dominican priest (1224–1274) generally regarded as the most influential philosopher/theologian within the Roman Catholic Church. His works include *Summa Theologica* and *Summa Contra Gentiles*. He developed the ethical theory known as Natural Law or Natural Moral Law.

See also p9.

Grade boost

Only include this background information on Aquinas' Natural Law if it is relevant to the question, e.g. in a question which states 'Explain Aquinas' Natural Law theory' you could *briefly* explain how Aquinas developed Aristotle's ideas. This information would not be needed, however, in a question like 'Explain why some religious believers accept Aquinas' Natural Law whilst others reject it.'

quickfire

① What did Aquinas say was a key element of human existence?

Key Terms

Absolutist = the belief that there are universal moral norms which apply to all situations.

Legalistic = the idea that one must obey a religious law in order to gain eternal life.

Deontological = derived from the Greek 'deon', meaning 'obligation' or 'duty'. The morality of an action is based on a human's duty to abide by a rule or series of rules regardless of the consequences or the situation the action is performed in.

Grade boost

Make sure that you are able to spell and define the terms absolutist and deontological. It is also important that you can explain the four types of law and how they are related to each other.

quickfire

② What were the four types of law identified by Aquinas?

PP

Aquinas' Natural Law: an absolutist, legalistic, deontological theory

Aquinas' Natural Law theory is often referred to as being **absolutist**, **deontological** and **legalistic**, but what do these key terms mean?

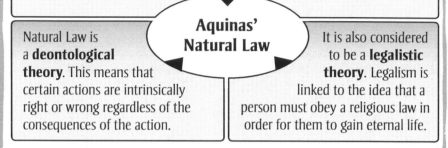

Aquinas' theory is considered by some to be an **absolutist theory** (although others will argue differently!). An absolutist believes that there are universal moral norms which apply in all situations and at all times.

Natural Law is a **deontological theory**. This means that certain actions are intrinsically right or wrong regardless of the consequences of the action.

Aquinas' Natural Law

It is also considered to be a **legalistic theory**. Legalism is linked to the idea that a person must obey a religious law in order for them to gain eternal life.

Aquinas believed in laws which were universal (applicable at all times and in all places) and eternal (everlasting) laws. He identified four types of law, which he said were inter-related.

Eternal law:
God creates everything and his will and wisdom is revealed to us through:

Divine law:
the sacred text and the teachings of the Church, which are made known in:

Natural law:
the innate human ability to know what is naturally right. From which:

Human law
develops, e.g. the law found within a society – its legal systems.

Aquinas' Natural Law – the four types of law

The importance of rationality in Natural Law

As mentioned earlier, Aquinas agreed with Aristotle in the belief that what makes humans unique is their ability to reason. Reason, he believed, was God's gift to humanity. He said that humankind's God-given purpose could be identified through the application of reason. 'The moral life is the life according to reason' (Aquinas in *Summa Theologica*). Reason is the means by which we can identify our final cause and then choose to follow it or not. For example, the efficient cause of sex is sexual attraction, but the final cause of sex (if we examine the complementarity of the female and male sexual organs) using our ability to reason, must be procreation.

Humankind's nature and final purpose

Aquinas believed that there is an 'ideal' universal uniform human nature which all humans can potentially achieve. Aquinas stated that humans should 'do good and avoid evil'. He did not believe that people deliberately chose to be evil. All people (religious or not) can know what is right and what is wrong using our ability to reason. As St Paul says in Romans Chapter 2v14 'the requirements of the law are written on their hearts, their consciences also bearing witness'.

He believed that it should be the ultimate goal or final purpose of every human to re-establish a 'right' relationship with God and by doing so gain eternal life with God in heaven. He stated that humans need to re-establish this 'right' relationship with God because it was broken by Adam and Eve. It was their act of 'original' sin, when they disobeyed God in the Garden of Eden, that broke this 'right' relationship.

How do the primary precepts help humans achieve their final purpose?

Whether or not acts lead us towards God depends upon whether the action fits the purpose that humans were made for. If the action helps us to fulfil that purpose then it is good. The **primary precepts** help us to identify what are our God-given purposes in life, and therefore they identify which acts are 'good'. If we fulfil these purposes, they will bring us closer to God and our ultimate goal of re-establishing a 'right' relationship with God. By doing so we may gain eternal life with God in heaven.

Key Term

Primary precepts = humans have five main purposes (given by God) outlined in Aquinas' Natural Law theory.

Grade boost

When explaining a secondary precept it would be better to state the primary precept AND THEN state that this secondary precept derives from a primary precept. For example, from the primary precept 'reproduction' we can derive the secondary precept 'no contraception' as this would go against the primary precept. Also don't forget to mention that the secondary precepts are more flexible (NOT absolutist) and can be broken in extreme circumstances.

Key Term

Secondary precepts = these are rules derived from the primary precepts. However, the secondary precepts have to be interpreted in the context of the situation, and there is some flexibility in extreme cases and these rules can be broken.

quickfire

③ What are the five primary precepts of Natural Law?

④ How do the primary precepts achieve humanity's final purpose?

⑤ What is a secondary precept?

⑥ How do the secondary precepts help humans to achieve their ultimate purpose?

Primary precepts — what are they? How do they help us?

Aquinas believed there were five main purposes or primary precepts of human existence:

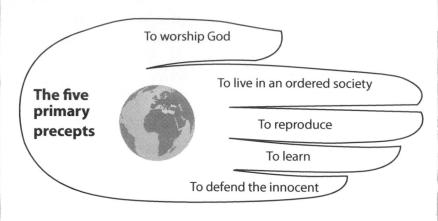

Aquinas' Natural Law – The primary precepts

Reason tells us that these precepts are what humans are here to do and therefore the primary precepts identify which acts are 'good'. (This is also supported by Biblical evidence such as Genesis Chapters 1 & 2.)

What are secondary precepts?

Aquinas also outlined **secondary precepts**, which were rules that help people to work out or know what they should or shouldn't do because they either uphold or fail to uphold the primary precepts. Aquinas deduces the secondary precepts from the primary ones, e.g. from the primary precept 'to defend the innocent' you could deduce by the use of reason that acts such as abortion and euthanasia are wrong. Another example, the principle 'to live in an ordered society' leads to rules such as 'return property to those from whom it was stolen'.

Are the secondary precepts absolutist?

However, the secondary precepts have to be interpreted in the context of the situation and there is some flexibility in extreme cases. For example, if the secondary precept 'do not steal' comes from the primary precept 'to live in an ordered society', what if someone has a gun and intends to kill others with it? In this case stealing the gun (although breaking a secondary precept) would be the rational thing to do as in this particular situation doing so would fulfil the primary precept of 'living in an ordered society'.

The cardinal and theological virtues: their significance in Natural Law

What is a virtue?

The word '**virtue**' comes from the Greek word '*areté*' which means 'excellence' in terms of personal qualities of character.

Why did Aquinas think that that developing certain virtues was important?

Aquinas said that there is a link between happiness and virtuous behaviour and that reason can guide people in developing the right virtues. The virtues are important because they represent the human qualities that reason suggests help us to live a moral life and to fulfil our true human nature. This in turn will lead us to achieving life in heaven with God.

The four cardinal virtues

Aquinas outlined four human qualities which he believed are necessary to form the basis of a moral life. These virtues can be found in the writings of Aristotle. They are known as the **cardinal virtues** because the Latin term '*cardo*' means 'hinge' – they are of fundamental importance. The four virtues are **prudence, justice, fortitude and temperance**.

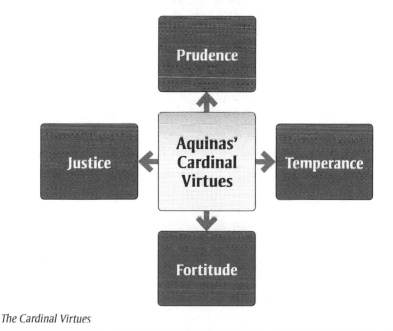

The Cardinal Virtues

Key Terms

Virtue = 'excellence' in terms of personal qualities of character.

Prudence = the ability to judge between actions with regard to appropriate actions at a given time.

Justice = this helps us to balance our interests with the rights and interests of others.

Fortitude = this is sometimes referred to as courage. It means to possess the ability to confront fear and uncertainty in order to achieve one's goal.

Temperance = to be able to practise self-control or restraint in order to be considered honourable.

quickfire

⑦ Why are certain virtues important to Aquinas?

⑧ What are the cardinal virtues?

Key Terms

Faith = belief in God, in the truth of God's revelation and in obedience to God.

Hope = an expectation of and desire of receiving eternal life in heaven with God.

Charity = selfless, unconditional and voluntary loving; kindness for others in response to God's love.

quickfire

⑨ What are the theological virtues?

Grade boost

Make sure you understand the importance of the virtues within Natural Law, not just what the virtues are.

The theological virtues

In addition to this, Aquinas referred to three revealed virtues of **faith, hope** and **charity.** They are referred to as the **revealed virtues** as they were disclosed through Scripture (St Paul in 1 Corinthians 13). They are also often called the **theological virtues** because they are directed to the divine being (Greek word *theos*), God. Christian theology teaches that these virtues differ from the cardinal virtues in that they cannot be obtained by human effort. A person can only receive them by their being infused through divine grace.

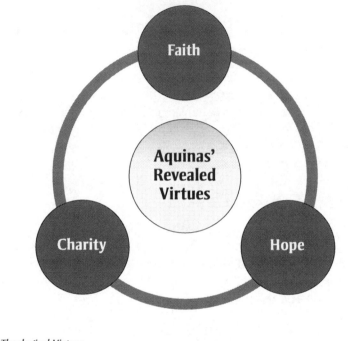

The Theological Virtues

Interior and exterior acts

Aquinas distinguished between '**interior**' and '**exterior**' acts:

- The interior act is the intention or motive behind the act, which must be good (e.g., giving to charity because you want to help others).
- The exterior act is the external act you can see, which must also be good (e.g., giving to charity).

People must perform a good exterior act AND do so with the right intention (interior act) if they wish to glorify God.

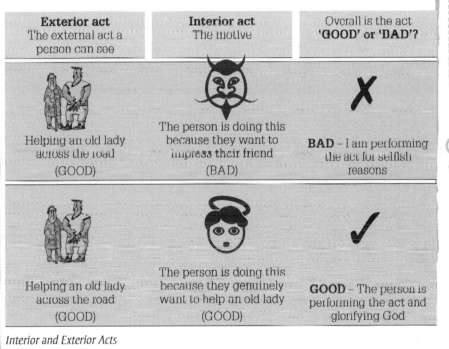

Exterior act The external act a person can see	Interior act The motive	Overall is the act **'GOOD' or 'BAD'?**
Helping an old lady across the road (GOOD)	The person is doing this because they want to impress their friend (BAD)	**BAD** – I am performing the act for selfish reasons
Helping an old lady across the road (GOOD)	The person is doing this because they genuinely want to help an old lady (GOOD)	**GOOD** – The person is performing the act and glorifying God

Interior and Exterior Acts

The principle of double effect

Aquinas stated that even if a good act which has an intended good effect has secondary bad consequences, it is still right to carry out that act. This is known as the principle of double effect. What is important is your intention when performing the act and you cannot be held responsible for any unintended consequences of an act. For example, a doctor had to perform a hysterectomy (because there was no other choice) to remove a cancerous uterus from a pregnant woman in order to save the woman's life. This act also led to the death of the foetus, but this would still be acceptable, as the original intention was to save the woman's life and killing the foetus was an unintended by-product of the action.

Key Terms

Interior act = is one's motive/intention for performing an act.

Exterior act = is the actual act itself which one can see.

Grade boost

Don't confuse interior/exterior acts with each other and also don't confuse both of these terms with real and apparent goods. Remember for an act to be truly good BOTH the interior AND exterior act must be good.

quickfire

(10) What is the difference between an interior and exterior act?

Key Terms

Real good = is a characteristic that will help people to become closer to the ideal human nature that God had planned for people.

Apparent good = is a vice or sin that takes people further away from the ideal human nature that God had planned for them.

Grade boost

Don't confuse 'real' and 'apparent' goods and also don't confuse both of these terms with 'interior' and 'exterior' acts.

⑪ Why did Aquinas say people should develop 'real' goods?

Real and apparent goods

Aquinas promoted the idea that there are certain cardinal and theological virtues that allow people to achieve the ideal human nature. He stated, however, that humans often sin or fall short of God's intentions because they confuse an **apparent good** with a **real good**.

Real good	Apparent good
A characteristic that will help people to become closer to the ideal human nature that God had planned for them.	A vice or sin that takes people further away from the ideal human nature that God had planned for them.

E.g. one could develop that virtue of 'charity' and helping others by being a sociable person (without chemically altering one's personality).	E.g., if someone needs to take drugs or alcohol in order to become more sociable and to develop the virtue of 'charity', then this is wrong.

Real and apparent goods

Aquinas believed that human nature was essentially good, and that no one intentionally pursues evil, but rather their use of reason is misguided. He recognised that not everyone clearly perceives what is good, e.g. some people do not have a guilty conscience about making false accusations or about stealing. This is because their desires and emotions override their rational sense of right and wrong and their ability to think virtuously. They fail to pay attention to what their ability to reason would tell them is virtuous behaviour.

The degree to which Natural Law is compatible with the traditional ethical teaching of one major world religion

As the majority of candidates answer this question from a Christian perspective this is how this question will be addressed here. However, many similar arguments could be equally applied to Judaism or Islam, for example.

Remember in order to achieve the higher levels of response, you would need to **develop** the brief points given below:

This is not an exhaustive list of points that could be used here. Any valid points that are supported by reasoning and evidence would deserve credit in an exam.

Grade boost

If used as an AO1 question it simply requires the facts unlike the AO2 exemplar question on p.88 which does require a judgement. It does NOT require any analysis or evaluation.

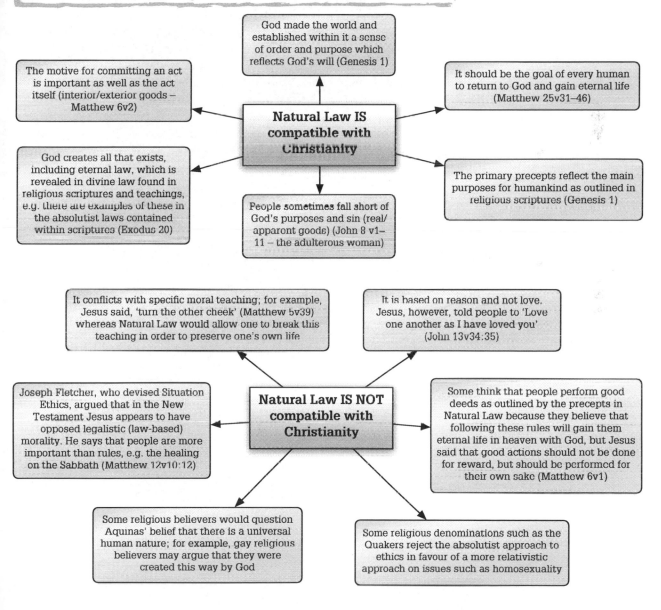

God made the world and established within it a sense of order and purpose which reflects God's will (Genesis 1)

The motive for committing an act is important as well as the act itself (interior/exterior goods – Matthew 6v2)

It should be the goal of every human to return to God and gain eternal life (Matthew 25v31–46)

God creates all that exists, including eternal law, which is revealed in divine law found in religious scriptures and teachings, e.g. there are examples of these in the absolutist laws contained within scriptures (Exodus 20)

Natural Law IS compatible with Christianity

The primary precepts reflect the main purposes for humankind as outlined in religious scriptures (Genesis 1)

People sometimes fall short of God's purposes and sin (real/apparent goods) (John 8 v1–11 – the adulterous woman)

It conflicts with specific moral teaching; for example, Jesus said, 'turn the other cheek' (Matthew 5v39) whereas Natural Law would allow one to break this teaching in order to preserve one's own life

It is based on reason and not love. Jesus, however, told people to 'Love one another as I have loved you' (John 13v34:35)

Joseph Fletcher, who devised Situation Ethics, argued that in the New Testament Jesus appears to have opposed legalistic (law-based) morality. He says that people are more important than rules, e.g. the healing on the Sabbath (Matthew 12v10:12)

Natural Law IS NOT compatible with Christianity

Some think that people perform good deeds as outlined by the precepts in Natural Law because they believe that following these rules will gain them eternal life in heaven with God, but Jesus said that good actions should not be done for reward, but should be performed for their own sake (Matthew 6v1)

Some religious believers would question Aquinas' belief that there is a universal human nature; for example, gay religious believers may argue that they were created this way by God

Some religious denominations such as the Quakers reject the absolutist approach to ethics in favour of a more relativistic approach on issues such as homosexuality

Key terms

Adequate = satisfactory for a particular purpose.

Incompatible = not able to work together with something else.

Injustice = treatment of people with inequality and unfairness, both generally and before the law.

Grade boost

Read the question carefully. It is the QUALITY of your arguments that will help you to achieve the higher levels and not the QUANTITY of your arguments. Don't forget what is being assessed in the AO2 type questions is your ability to evaluate and analyse.

Evaluative issues

Many candidates make common errors when addressing the AO2 type questions on Natural Law. The three main errors are:

- They answer every part (b) (AO2) question as a 'strengths and weaknesses' of Natural Law question, which is only one of the possible questions that could be set.
- They simply 'list' points that agree or disagree with the statement with little or no analysis or evaluation (which is what is being assessed here).
- They fail to give a conclusion.

Over the next few pages are some examples of the arguments that could be used to address the issues identified by the specification. The arguments given here are not an exhaustive list and any relevant arguments will be credited. Some of the same arguments can be used to answer different questions, but you need to select these arguments carefully. Some students choose to present their arguments and counter arguments in the same paragraph others prefer to deal with these issues in separate paragraphs. Use whichever style you prefer, but make sure you consider the important points mentioned underneath the given issue.

1: Assess the strengths and weakness of Natural Law.

Strengths

- One strength of Natural Law is that, being **absolutist and deontological,** it provides clear-cut rules, e.g. abortion is wrong as it breaks the primary precept to reproduce. As Robert Bowie states in his book *Ethical Studies*, '*It enables people to establish common rules in order to structure communities.*'

- A strength of Natural Law is that **it is based upon human ability to reason and does not rely on unpredictable consequences or emotions**. As a result it is universally applicable. It therefore applies to all people at all times and in all places. As Mel Thompson states in his book *An introduction to Philosophy and Ethics (Second edition)*, '*Feelings can change, but the issue of right and wrong remains fixed.*'

- For many religious believers, a strength of Natural Law is it **creates a link between the creator, our creation and our purpose**. As Robert Bowie states in his book *Philosophy of Religion and Religious Ethics*, '*Natural law directs people to their final destiny. It is the divine law, God's law as opposed to human law.*'

- Another strength of Natural Law is that **it is simple to follow as it assumes that there is an ideal and universal human nature all humans need to do is strive towards this state**. As Peter Cole and Richard Gray state in their book *Religious Studies for AS Students*, '*Being human means acting in line with our true nature, when we follow our natural inclinations.*' So, for Aquinas, homosexuality is unnatural because the natural human state is to be heterosexual.

Weaknesses

- However, this means that **Natural Law fails to consider the situation people find themselves in or the consequences of an action**. For example, it does not allow abortion even in the case of rape. Joseph Fletcher, who developed Situation Ethics, also rejected this legalistic approach as it does not allow people any moral autonomy.

- However, **not all rational people agree with Natural Law and not everyone bases their moral choices on reason**. As Mel Thompson says in his book *Ethical Theory (Third edition)*, '*One could argue that most moral choices are made as the result of unconscious promptings that are based on needs laid down in infancy, rather than a logical assessment of the final goal of human life.*' Theories such as Situation Ethics and Utilitarianism would argue that the consequences are an important aspect which must be considered as they have an effect on people.

- However, a **non-believer would have no desire to follow a system of ethics based upon a belief in a creator God and fulfilling God's will**. As Patrick J Clarke states in his book *Examining Philosophy and Ethics*, '*If mankind has no religious destiny, it could be argued that the idea of following a natural law ethic ultimately makes no sense.*'

- **Many people would question the idea that there is a universal human nature**. As Robert Bowie states in his book *Philosophy of Religion and Religious Ethics*, '*... the idea that there is a single or fixed human nature is simplistic and seems to fly in the face of increasing diversity and the changeable nature of personal identity (such as homosexuality, transexuality, and so on)*'.

2: 'Natural Law provides an adequate basis for making moral decisions.' Assess this view.

You should try to consider each of the following points when developing your arguments and a conclusion:

- Have you supported your arguments using reasoning and/or evidence?
- Is the point raised strong/convincing?
- Does this response dispose of the argument?
- Is the issue evenly balanced, or is there one view which is clearly more convincing/correct or proven?

Strengths

- Some agree with the statement as it **prescribes laws which derive from God and are unchanging and eternal**. They are therefore appropriate for any culture or time. For example, abortion is generally wrong as it goes against the primary precept 'to defend the innocent'. As Joe Jenkins states in his book *Ethics and Religion (Second edition)*, *'each person is born with a particular purpose to fulfil in his or her life and human nature was created by God'*.

- Others agree with the statement because it **provides clear-cut laws**, e.g. stealing is wrong as it goes against the precept 'to live in an ordered society'. As Robert Bowie states in his book *Philosophy of Religion and Ethics*, *'It gives clear unambiguous answers to moral questions in times of moral uncertainty.'*

- Some religious believers may also agree with the statement as **the Natural Law approach appears to be supported by religious texts**. For example, the primary precepts agree with the purpose of human life as outlined in Genesis chapter 1, where it states that humans should reproduce.

- **The Roman Catholic Church would argue that Natural Law has provided an adequate basis for making moral decisions for over seven hundred years.** It forms the basis of their moral teaching. It gives due place to God-given conscience/reason in ethical decision making. Pope Benedict in an address to the German Parliament in September 2011 said that Christianity *'has pointed to nature and reason as the true sources of law – and to harmony of objective and subjective reason, which naturally presupposes that both spheres are rooted in the creative reason of God'*.

Weaknesses

- However, James Rachels in his book *The Elements of Moral Philosophy (Fourth edition)* also states that *'**the theory of Natural Law has gone of out of fashion**…. The world as described by Galileo, Newton and Darwin has no place for "facts" about right or wrong. Their explanations of natural phenomena make no reference to values or purposes.'*

- The problem with such an approach is that it **fails to consider several other factors in any moral action such as the individual, the culture, the individual's situation or the consequences**. A follower of Situation Ethics would argue that sometimes stealing is the right thing to do, e.g. stealing to feed a starving child, as this brings about loving consequences.

- However, G. E. Moore stated **Aquinas committed a 'naturalistic fallacy' by deriving an 'ought' from an 'is'**. He said what 'is' the case and what 'ought' to be the case are logically different. For example, sex does sometimes lead to reproduction, but it does not mean that this is the only reason to have sex.

- **Atheists, however, would dispute the claim that God-given reason and nature provide us with the source of law**. As Mel Thompson states in his book *Ethical Theory (Third edition)*, if one comes to the conclusion based on observation such as innocent suffering that the world *'is unlikely to be the product of an omnipotent or loving creator then the natural law argument loses its foundation'*.

3: 'Natural Law's absolutist approach promotes injustice/morally wrong behaviour.' Assess this view.

You should try to consider each of the following points when developing your arguments and a conclusion:
- Have you supported your arguments using reasoning and/or evidence?
- Is the point raised strong/convincing?
- Does this response dispose of the argument?
- Is the issue evenly balanced, or is there one view which is clearly more convincing/correct or proven?

Agree

- It promotes injustice as **it fails to recognise that some acts, e.g. sex, can have more than one purpose and as a result discriminates against those who perform an act without fulfilling its purpose,** e.g. a married couple simply having sex for pleasure. As G. E. Moore stated, Aquinas committed a 'naturalistic fallacy' by deriving an 'ought' from an 'is'. As Joe Jenkins states in his book *Ethics and Religion (Second Edition)* '*but, is what is the case and ought to be the case logically different? For example, sex does produce babies, but this does not necessarily mean that people ought to have sex only for this purpose.*'

- It promotes morally wrong behaviour/injustice because **it does not consider the individual or the situation in which an act is performed**. For example, not allowing abortion even in the case of pregnancy as a result of rape. Act Utilitarianism and Situation Ethics would consider both these elements of an action.

- **Being old fashioned and based purely on reason, it promotes injustice and morally wrong behaviour because it does not consider the consequences of an action**, e.g. it states that divorce is wrong because it breaks the primary precept 'to live in an ordered society' despite the fact that this may harm a couple and their families. Consequentialist theories such as Act Utilitarianism and Situation Ethics would consider the consequences which are ultimately what have an effect upon others.

Disagree

- It promotes justice and morally right behaviour as it **provides clear-cut views on what is right or wrong,** e.g. abortion is wrong as it breaks the primary precept to reproduce. As Robert Bowie states in his book *Ethical Studies (Second edition),* '*It enables people to establish common rules in order to structure communities*'.

- Many would argue that Natural Law **promotes both justice and moral behaviour by advocating through the primary precepts basic human rights such as the right to life, the right to education and the right live in an ordered society.** As Peter Vardy and Paul Grosch argue in their book *The Puzzle of Ethics,* '*At the end of the Second World War, Nazi war criminals were tried at Nuremburg according to what were claimed to be universal moral laws which were closely modelled on natural law thinking.*'

- However, you cannot accurately predict the consequences of an action. At least by **being based upon a human's ability to reason Natural Law promotes justice as it is discoverable by anyone religious or not. It is therefore universal and not limited to any one culture or religion**. As Mel Thompson says in his book *Ethical Theory (Third edition),* '*if everything is created for a purpose, human reason, in examining that purpose is able to judge how to in order to conform to that purpose*'.

4: 'Natural Law as an absolutist/deontological theory cannot work in today's society' Assess this view.

You should try to consider each of the following points when developing your arguments and a conclusion:
- Have you supported your arguments using reasoning and/or evidence?
- Is the point raised strong/convincing?
- Does this response dispose of the argument?
- Is the issue evenly balanced, or is there one view which is clearly more convincing/correct or proven?

Agree

- **Atheists would dispute the claim that God-given reason and nature provide us with the source of law.** As Mel Thompson states in his book *Ethical Theory (Third edition)*, if one comes to the conclusion based on observation such as innocent suffering that the world *'is unlikely to be the product of an omnipotent or loving creator then the natural law argument loses its foundation'*.

- James Rachels in his book *The Elements of Moral Philosophy (Fourth edition)* also states that *'the theory of Natural Law has gone out of fashion.... The world as described by Galileo, Newton and Darwin has no place for "facts" about right or wrong. Their explanations of natural phenomena make no reference to values or purposes.'* **Perhaps no absolutist laws exist and there are no 'right' and 'wrong' actions as defined by a deontological approach**.

- The problem with an absolutist and deontological approach is that it **fails to consider several other factors in any moral action such as the individual, the culture, the individual's situation or the consequences**. A follower of Situation Ethics would argue that sometimes stealing is the right thing to do, e.g. stealing to feed a starving child, as this brings about loving consequences. A Utilitarian would also allow this if it leads to the 'greatest happiness for the greatest number'.

- **Many people prefer to adopt relativistic/ consequentialist theories such as Situation Ethics or Utilitarianism which give them a greater sense of moral autonomy** rather than Natural Law's absolutist/ deontological approach. For example, abortion is almost always wrong in Natural Law, but an Act Utilitarian would allow this if it leads to the greatest happiness for the greatest number.

Disagree

- **It is the basis of Roman Catholic moral teaching and has been for several centuries**, e.g. *Humanae Vitae,* 1968. Pope Benedict in an address to the German Parliament in September 2011 said that Christianity *'has pointed to nature and reason as the true sources of law – and to harmony of objective and subjective reason, which naturally presupposes that both spheres are rooted in the creative reason of God'*.

- Others disagree with the statement because **it provides clear-cut laws** e.g. stealing is wrong as it goes against the precept 'to live in an ordered society'. As Robert Bowie states in his book *Philosophy of Religion and Ethics,* '*It gives clear unambiguous answers to moral questions in times of moral uncertainty*'.

- **It cannot be out of date as it prescribes laws which derive from God and are unchanging and eternal.** They are therefore appropriate for any culture or time. For example, abortion is generally wrong as it goes against the primary precept 'to defend the innocent'. As Joe Jenkins states in his book *Ethics and Religion (Second edition),* '*each person is born with a particular purpose to fulfil in his or her life and human nature was created by God*'.

- Many would argue that Natural Law's absolutist and deontological approach **forms the basis of the United Nations Declaration of Human Rights. Through the promotion of (the majority of) the primary precepts, humans have recognised basic human rights such as the right to life, the right to education and the right live in an ordered society.**

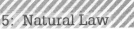

5: 'Natural Law is incompatible with a religious approach to moral decision making' Assess this view.

You should try to consider each of the following points when developing your arguments and a conclusion:

- Have you supported your arguments using reasoning and/or evidence?
- Is the point raised strong/convincing?
- Does this response dispose of the argument?
- Is the issue evenly balanced, or is there one view which is clearly more convincing/correct or proven?

(The arguments given here refer to Christianity, but arguments using any one major world religion would be acceptable.)

Agree

- **Jesus' teachings appear to contradict some of Natural Law's primary precepts**, e.g. you have the right to protect yourself from the primary precept 'to defend the innocent'. He stated (Matthew 5v39), 'If someone strikes you on the right cheek, turn to him the other also'.

- In the **New Testament, Jesus appears to oppose legalistic (law-based) morality**. He appears to have adopted a form of 'personalism' (Situation Ethics). He says that people are more important than rules, e.g. the healing on the Sabbath (Matthew 12v9–13).

- **Natural Law appears to override 'free-will', which is an important feature of many of the major world religions**. Natural Law's legalistic approach leaves little room for personal autonomy. Joseph Fletcher, the founder of Situation Ethics, argued that people should have the freedom to make their own moral choices using agape love as a guide.

- **It is based on reason and not love and so appears to go against Jesus' teaching** in John 13v34 'Love one another. As I have loved you …' Some Christian denominations such as the Quakers would oppose the use of Natural Law and based upon quotations such as the one above, might prefer to make their moral decisions using Situation Ethics. For example, they would allow sex before marriage as an expression of selfless love even if it did break the primary precept of 'reproduction' as the couple may have no intention of reproducing.

Disagree

- **By following Natural Law you are fulfilling God's will** according to many sacred texts, e.g. purpose of sex is procreation as stated in the Bible (Genesis 1).

- **It is compatible with religious absolute morality – the 'divine' laws found within most major world religions** (e.g., Exodus 20). For example, 'do not murder' upholds the primary precept 'to live in an ordered society'. As Patrick J Clarke states in his book *Examining Philosophy and Ethics*, '*An extra dimension to Aquinas' theory was his identification of natural law with divine law. What was right or wrong in regard to nature and its laws was also right or wrong in the eyes of God.*'

- **It gives due place to God-given conscience and reason in ethical decision making**. As Mel Thompson says in his book *Ethical Theory (Third edition)*, '*if everything is created for a purpose, human reason, in examining that purpose is able to judge how to in order to conform to that purpose*'.

- **It is the basis of Roman Catholic moral teaching and has been for several centuries** e.g. *Humanae Vitae*, 1968. Pope Benedict in an address to the German Parliament in September 2011 said that Christianity '*has pointed to nature and reason as the true sources of law – and to harmony of objective and subjective reason, which naturally presupposes that both spheres are rooted in the creative reason of God*'.

Summary: Natural Law

We have identified the key points on the WJEC AS specification and, combined with the information in this chapter, summarised them in the diagram below. You may want to fill in further details to elaborate and personalise this content.

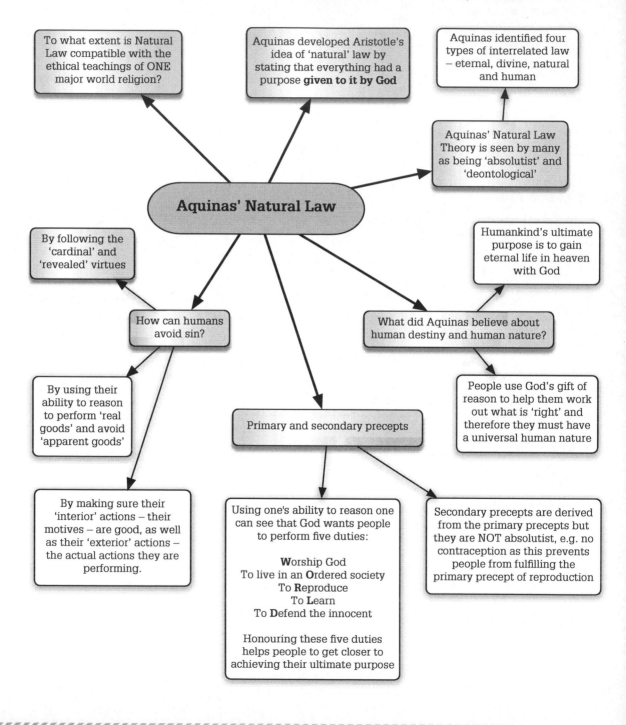

To what extent is Natural Law compatible with the ethical teachings of ONE major world religion?

Aquinas developed Aristotle's idea of 'natural' law by stating that everything had a purpose **given to it by God**

Aquinas identified four types of interrelated law – eternal, divine, natural and human

Aquinas' Natural Law Theory is seen by many as being 'absolutist' and 'deontological'

Aquinas' Natural Law

By following the 'cardinal' and 'revealed' virtues

How can humans avoid sin?

Humankind's ultimate purpose is to gain eternal life in heaven with God

What did Aquinas believe about human destiny and human nature?

By using their ability to reason to perform 'real goods' and avoid 'apparent goods'

Primary and secondary precepts

People use God's gift of reason to help them work out what is 'right' and therefore they must have a universal human nature

By making sure their 'interior' actions – their motives – are good, as well as their 'exterior' actions – the actual actions they are performing.

Using one's ability to reason one can see that God wants people to perform five duties:

Worship God
To live in an **O**rdered society
To **R**eproduce
To **L**earn
To **D**efend the innocent

Honouring these five duties helps people to get closer to achieving their ultimate purpose

Secondary precepts are derived from the primary precepts but they are NOT absolutist, e.g. no contraception as this prevents people from fulfilling the primary precept of reproduction

6: Situation Ethics

The unit on Situation Ethics requires you to focus your revision on the main features of the theory. You should be able to explain why many regard Situation Ethics as being a 'relativistic', 'teleological' and 'consequentialist' theory. You must be able to demonstrate why Fletcher rejected other types of ethical approaches and claimed that his theory was the 'middle way'. You should be able to explain the concept of 'agape' as well as the four working and six fundamental principles within his theory. It is important that you can explain the significance of the biblical evidence which is used to support this theory. You will be expected to provide examples of how to apply Situation Ethics, which may be drawn from the issues listed in the Applied Ethics section or from other issues you have studied. You should also be able to explain to what extent Situation Ethics is compatible with the traditional teaching of one major world religion. Finally, you should be able to evaluate the issues that arise out of studying Situation Ethics.

Revision checklist

Tick column 1 when you have completed brief revision notes.
Tick column 2 when you think you have a good grasp of the topic.
Tick column 3 during final revision when you feel you have mastery of the topic.

			1	2	3
What type of theory is this?	p94	A relativistic, teleological and consequential theory			
Why did Fletcher reject other types of ethical approaches?	p95	Antinomianism			
	p95	Legalism			
	p95	Situation Ethics is the 'middle way'			
Which concept is Situation Ethics based on? What are Situation Ethics' main principles?	p96	Agape			
	p96	The four working and six fundamental principles			
	p97	An application of the ten principles of Situation Ethics			
The biblical evidence used to support Situation Ethics?	p98	John 15v13			
	p98	Galatians 5v14			
	p98	Mark 2v27			
	p98	John 5v1–16			
	p98	Matthew 22v37–39			
	p98	Luke 6v27			
To what extent is Situation Ethics compatible with the ethical teaching of one major world religion?	p99	Situation Ethics and its compatibility or not with Christian ethical teaching			
What are the main issues related to Situation Ethics?	p101	Strengths and weaknesses of Situation Ethics			
	p102	Does 'agape' provide an adequate basis for moral decision making?			
	p103	Could the principles of Situation Ethics promote injustice and/or morally wrong behaviour?			
	p104	To what extent can Situation Ethics as a relativistic and teleological theory work in today's society?			
	p105	How far is Situation Ethics compatible with a religious approach to moral decision making?			

Situation Ethics: a relativistic, consequentialist and teleological theory

Key Terms

Relativistic = this means there are no universal moral norms or rules and that each situation has to be looked at independently because each situation is different.

Consequentialist = people should make moral judgements based on the outcome or the consequences of an action.

Teleological = concerned with the end purpose or goal of an action – in this case the goal should always be 'self-sacrificing love'.

Grade boost

Make sure that you are able to spell and define the terms relativistic, consequentialist and teleological. Weaker candidates also often confuse the meanings of the terms 'consequentialist' and 'teleological'.

quickfire

① Who developed the theory known as Situation Ethics?

② What type of love is the guiding principle of Situation Ethics and what does it mean?

In 1966 Joseph Fletcher published his book *Situation Ethics: The New Morality*. His theory was based on one guiding principle – agape. This is the Christian principle of selfless love. Agape is one of the Greek words for love used in the New Testament. It is the word used to describe God's love for humanity and the love that Christians should show towards God and other people. Situation Ethics is also referred to as relativistic, consequentialist and teleological theory.

> Joseph Fletcher's theory is considered to be a **relativistic theory**. This means there are no universal moral norms or rules and that each situation has to be looked at independently because each situation is different.

> It is also considered to be a **consequential theory**. This means that moral judgements – whether something is right or wrong – should be based on the outcome or the consequences of an action – in this case does it bring the most loving outcome?

> **Situation Ethics**

> **Situation Ethics is a teleological theory**. This means that it is concerned with the end purpose or goal of an action – in this case the goal should always be 'self-sacrificing love'.

Situation Ethics: a relativistic, consequential and teleological theory

Key Figure

Joseph Fletcher was an American professor (1905–1991) who formalised the theory known as Situation Ethics in his book *Situation Ethics: The New Morality* (1966). He was a leading academic involved in topics ranging from abortion to cloning. He was ordained as a priest, but later identified himself as an atheist. He stated that we should always use the principle of love or agape (selfless love) and apply it to each unique situation.

Why did Fletcher reject both antinomianism and legalism?

Fletcher claimed that most moral theories adopted either an antinomian or a legalistic approach to ethics. He argued that neither of these approaches works.

Antinomianism and why Fletcher rejected it

Antinomianism literally means 'against law'. A situationist attitude based on the idea that people are under no obligation to obey the laws of ethics or morality as presented by religious authorities. The situation will provide the solution which can be found through intuition/use of a person's conscience. Fletcher rejected this as he said with no guiding principles there could well be moral chaos.

Legalism and why Fletcher rejected it

Legalism is an attitude that exalts laws above all other considerations, e.g. Natural Law. Fletcher rejected this approach as he said it gave people no choice but to follow the rules.

Fletcher referred to Situation Ethics as the 'middle way' between both these approaches. It has no rules, but only one guiding principle the application of agape – the love which Jesus commanded in the New Testament.

Key terms

Antinomianism = literally means 'against law'. A situationist attitude based on the idea that people are under no obligation to obey the laws of ethics or morality as presented by religious authorities. The situation will provide the solution which can be found through intuition/use of a person's conscience.

Legalism = an attitude that exalts laws above all other considerations.

Grade boost

Don't forget to explain what the terms 'antinomianism' and 'legalism' mean BUT also why Fletcher rejected both of these approaches to ethics, if that is what the exam question requires.

quickfire

③ What is antinomianism?

④ Why did Fletcher reject antinomianism?

⑤ What is 'legalism'?

⑥ Why did Fletcher reject the 'legalistic' approach to ethics?

Key Quotes

Fletcher on antinomianism:

... it is literally unprincipled, purely ad hoc and casual. They follow no forecastable course from one situation to another. They are exactly anarchic i.e. without a rule.

Fletcher on legalism:

... with this approach one enters into every decision making process encumbered with a whole apparatus of prefabricated rules and regulations.

Situation Ethics. A New Morality

Agape = selfless love – giving love constantly and unconditionally, regardless of the actions of the loved one.

Four working principles = personalism, positivism, pragmatism and relativism. The first of the two sets of principles within Situation Ethics which are used to determine if any action is loving.

Six fundamental principles = the second of the two sets of guiding principles of Situation Ethics devised by Fletcher in order to determine what the most loving action in any given situation would be. (See the diagram to the right.)

Grade boost

The most misunderstood/ misquoted/misspelt principles are 'positivism', 'only one thing is *intrinsically* good; namely, love: nothing else at all' and 'A *loving* end justifies the means'. Make sure you learn them and are able to explain what they mean.

quickfire

⑦ What are the four working principles?

⑧ What does the term 'positivism' mean?

⑨ One of the six fundamental principles is 'only one thing is intrinsically good; namely, love: nothing else at all'. What does 'intrinsically' mean?

⑩ Another of the six fundamental principles is 'A loving end justifies the means'. Explain this principle.

Agape, and the four working and six fundamental principles of Situation Ethics

Situation Ethics is based on one principle: acting out of '**agape**'. 'Agape' is defined as 'selfless love which is given constantly and unconditionally, regardless of the actions of the loved one'. Situation Ethics has often been referred to as 'Christian utilitarianism' because it aims to achieve the greatest love for the greatest number. This, however, led to the issue of 'How do you ensure the most loving outcome is achieved?' Fletcher came up with ten principles that he believed could guide people and help them achieve 'agape' love in any situation.

Pragmatism – The proposed course of action must work (be practical) and be motivated by love.	**Positivism** – Agape provides justification not proof for an ethical decision. People must accept that acting in the most loving way is the right thing to do.

The Four Working Principles

Personalism – The desire to put people, not laws, first. The Christian is committed to love people, not rules or laws.	**Relativism** – The right response will depend upon each unique situation. People must respond with 'agape' love to each situation. A supporter of Situation Ethics avoids words like 'never' or 'always' as they believe that circumstances can always throw up exceptions.

Situation Ethics: the four working principles

'The ruling norm of any Christian decision is love, nothing else.' – as St Paul said in 1 Corinthians 13, love is the basis of Christian decision making.	'Only one thing is intrinsically good; namely, love: nothing else at all.' – Nothing is good in and of itself except for love. Intrinsically means 'belonging naturally to or essential to'.	'Love and justice are the same, for justice is love distributed, nothing else.' Justice is love at work in the community.

The Six Fundamental Principles

'Love wills the good of others, regardless of feelings.' People should show love to all, even their enemies, as agape is selfless love.	'Love's decisions are made situationally, not prescriptively.' People have autonomy – the freedom to make their own decisions, but they must use this freedom responsibly and apply love to each situation.	'A loving end justifies the means.' One must achieve a loving end and one can perform any action in order to achieve this.

Situation Ethics: the six fundamental principles

An example of the application of Situation Ethics

Students should be encouraged to use examples from the Applied Ethics section and also to find new examples of their own. Religious Studies text books, journals, national newspapers and national TV news items are good sources of information.

Scenario: Two conjoined twins have been born by Caesarean section. They are joined at the head and if they remain joined then they have approximately only a 25% chance of survival.

A follower of Situation Ethics might assess the situation as follows (under exam conditions it is unlikely you will have time to assess the situation using all ten principles of Situation Ethics, so be selective):

Working principle: Pragmatism	It is practically possible to separate the twins and there is likely to be a loving outcome because when the operation has ended at least one of them will have a greater chance of survival.
Working principle: Relativism	The course of action taken is dependent on the situation as conjoined twins are not always joined at the head. Each case would be assessed differently. A situationist would not say you should 'always' or 'never' separate conjoined twins.
Working principle: Personalism	The medical team's desire to save the children is person-centred. Fletcher would have argued that they should perform this operation even if it breaks the law as it is the most loving thing to do.
Fundamental principle: Love and justice are the same, for justice is love distributed, nothing else	By attempting to save both the children, even if one child dies, they have acted out of love and therefore fairly ensured justice has been served.
Fundamental principle: A loving end justifies the means	By achieving a loving outcome and saving at least one of the children then the act of performing the operation and risking both their lives will have been justifiable.
Fundamental principle: Love wills the good of others, regardless of feelings	Even if the father of the children is the person who murdered the surgeon's mother, the surgeon should still act in a loving way towards the children and their father. As Fletcher said we should show love to all, even our enemies. Christian love is unconditional. Love wills the good of others.

The biblical evidence used to support Situation Ethics

Key Term

Biblical = in or relating to the Bible.

Grade boost

Don't just list biblical passages that could be linked to Situation Ethics, explain how they could be linked to the various elements of Situation Ethics. It is important that you develop any points made and not just give a brief description if you wish to be awarded a higher level for your answer.

Key Quote

William Temple (Archbishop of Canterbury 1942–44) stated in an essay entitled *Mens creatrix*, '*There is only one ultimate and invariable duty, and its formula is "Thou shalt love thy neighbour as thyself". How to do this is another question, but this is the whole of moral duty.*'

Students should also find the verses given below in a Bible and read them in their original context, preferably with the help of a **biblical** commentary. There are numerous biblical passages which may be referred to, and here are just some of those that could be used to address this issue:

John 15v13

In which Jesus states , '*No one has greater love than this, to lay down one's life for one's friends.*'

This appears to support the concept of 'agape' love.

Galatians 5v14

'*For the whole law is fulfilled in one word, You shall love your neighbour as yourself.*' This appears to support one of Fletcher's six fundamental principles 'The ruling norm of any Christian decision is love, nothing else.'

Mark 2v27

'*The Sabbath was made for man, not man for the Sabbath.*' – Some claim that Jesus adopted a relativistic approach to ethics, for example he attacked the Pharisees' insistence on following the Torah or Jewish Law. This links to Fletcher's four working principles – relativism.

John 5v1–16

Jesus put people first, he broke Sabbath laws to heal on the Sabbath – he healed the paralysed man on the Sabbath.

This links to Fletcher's four working principles – personalism.

Matthew 22v37–39

'*Love your neighbour as yourself.*' – Jesus stated that love is the highest principle above the Law.

One of Fletcher's six fundamental principles states 'The ruling norm of any Christian decision is love, nothing else.'

Luke 6v27

Jesus stated that you should '*Love your enemies, do good to those who hate you.*'

One of Fletcher's six fundamental principles states 'Love wills the good of others regardless of others.'

The Biblical evidence for Situation Ethics

To what extent is Situation Ethics compatible with the traditional teaching of one major world religion?

Remember in order to achieve the higher levels of response you would need to develop the brief points given below.

As the majority of candidates answer this question from a Christian perspective, this is how the question will be addressed here. However, many similar arguments could be equally applied to Judaism or Islam, for example.

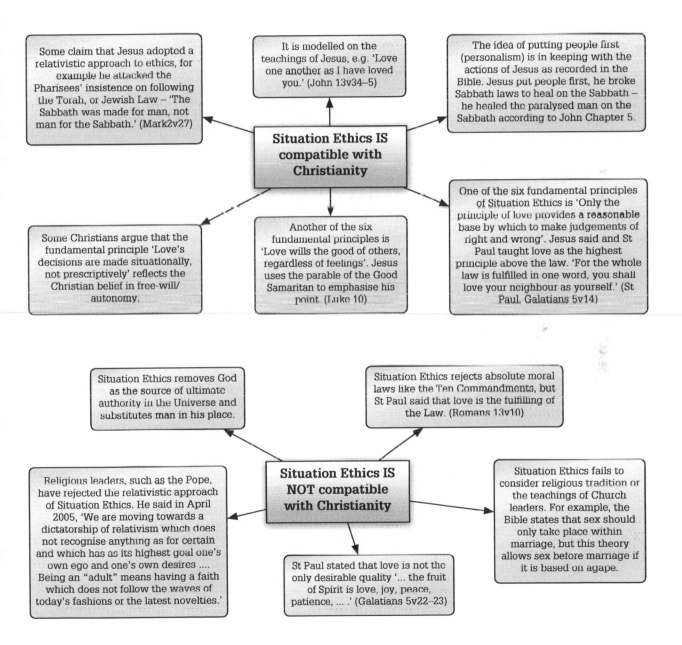

Some claim that Jesus adopted a relativistic approach to ethics, for example he attacked the Pharisees' insistence on following the Torah, or Jewish Law – 'The Sabbath was made for man, not man for the Sabbath.' (Mark 2v27)

It is modelled on the teachings of Jesus, e.g. 'Love one another as I have loved you.' (John 13v34–5)

The idea of putting people first (personalism) is in keeping with the actions of Jesus as recorded in the Bible. Jesus put people first, he broke Sabbath laws to heal on the Sabbath – he healed the paralysed man on the Sabbath according to John Chapter 5.

Situation Ethics IS compatible with Christianity

Some Christians argue that the fundamental principle 'Love's decisions are made situationally, not prescriptively' reflects the Christian belief in free-will/autonomy.

Another of the six fundamental principles is 'Love wills the good of others, regardless of feelings'. Jesus uses the parable of the Good Samaritan to emphasise his point. (Luke 10)

One of the six fundamental principles of Situation Ethics is 'Only the principle of love provides a reasonable base by which to make judgements of right and wrong'. Jesus said and St Paul taught love as the highest principle above the law. 'For the whole law is fulfilled in one word, you shall love your neighbour as yourself.' (St Paul, Galatians 5v14)

Situation Ethics removes God as the source of ultimate authority in the Universe and substitutes man in his place.

Situation Ethics rejects absolute moral laws like the Ten Commandments, but St Paul said that love is the fulfilling of the Law. (Romans 13v10)

Situation Ethics IS NOT compatible with Christianity

Religious leaders, such as the Pope, have rejected the relativistic approach of Situation Ethics. He said in April 2005, 'We are moving towards a dictatorship of relativism which does not recognise anything as for certain and which has as its highest goal one's own ego and one's own desires .... Being an "adult" means having a faith which does not follow the waves of today's fashions or the latest novelties.'

Situation Ethics fails to consider religious tradition or the teachings of Church leaders. For example, the Bible states that sex should only take place within marriage, but this theory allows sex before marriage if it is based on agape.

St Paul stated that love is not the only desirable quality '... the fruit of Spirit is love, joy, peace, patience, ...' (Galatians 5v22–23)

Key terms

Adequate = satisfactory for a particular purpose.

Compatible = able to work together with something else.

Injustice = treatment of people with inequality and unfairness, both generally and before the law.

Relativistic = this means there are no universal moral norms or rules and that each situation has to be looked at independently because each situation is different.

Teleological = concerned with the end purpose or goal of an action – in this case the goal should always be 'self-sacrificing love'.

Situation Ethics: evaluative issues

Many candidates make common errors when addressing the AO2 type questions on Situation Ethics. The three main errors are:

- They answer every part (b) (AO2) question as a 'strengths and weaknesses' of Situation Ethics question, which is only one of the possible questions that could be set.
- They simply 'list' points that agree or disagree with the statement with little or no evaluation or analysis (which is what is being assessed here).
- They fail to give a conclusion.

Over the next few pages are some examples of the arguments that could be used to address the issues identified by the specification. The arguments given here are not an exhaustive list and any relevant arguments will be credited. Some of the same arguments can be used to answer different questions, but you need to select these arguments carefully. Some students choose to present their arguments and counter arguments in the same paragraph others prefer to deal with these issues in separate paragraphs. Use whichever style you prefer, but make sure you consider the important points mentioned underneath the given issue.

Grade boost

Read the question carefully. It is the QUALITY of your arguments that will help you to achieve the higher levels and not the QUANTITY of your arguments. Don't forget what is being assessed in the AO2 type questions is your ability to evaluate and analyse.

1: Assess the strengths and weaknesses of Situation Ethics

You should try to consider each of the following points when developing your arguments and a conclusion:

- Have you supported your arguments using reasoning and/or evidence?
- Is the point raised strong/convincing?
- Does this response dispose of the argument?
- Is the issue evenly balanced, or is there one view which is clearly more convincing/correct or proven?

Strengths

- Situation Ethics as a relativistic theory is flexible and practical. **It takes into account the situation a person is faced with and can help make decisions in situations where, from a legalistic view all options are wrong**. For example, to lie in a particular situation in order to save a life. As Mel Thompson states in his book *An Introduction to Philosophy and Ethics (Second Edition)*, 'It allows individuals to make up their own minds about what is right or wrong in a particular situation.'

- Situation Ethics **allows people the individual freedom to make decisions for themselves** (on issues such as contraception, abortion, euthanasia, etc.) which many people nowadays prefer to the prescriptive/legalistic approach. As Mel Thompson states in his book *An Introduction to Philosophy and Ethics (Second edition)*, 'It allows individuals to make up their own minds about what is right or wrong in any particular situation.'

- **Agape involves 'selfless' love – putting others first, which should ensure fairness and justice**. As Sarah K. Tyler and Gordon Reid state in their book *Advanced Religious Studies (Second edition)*, 'Love seeks the well-being of others, even if the course of action is not one of preference.'

- Due to Fletcher's use of the fundamental principle 'A loving end justifies the means', **people would have to consider the likely consequences of their actions before they take them** and it is only the consequences that have a real effect on human well-being.

- The idea of **putting people before rules 'personalism' appears to be in keeping with the actions of Jesus as recorded in the Bible** – Healing the paralysed man, John Chapter 5.

Weaknesses

- **Many people argue we need rules to avoid issues such as moral chaos**. As J. Macquarrie states in *A Dictionary of Christian Ethics*, '… it seems to be assumed that somehow one intuits what is right in a situation from the situation itself. Even if some people have this remarkable gift of insight, there are stages on the way to moral maturity, and a great many people need the guidance of rules and generalisations which the community has built up from experience.'

- **Situation Ethics gives so much freedom to the individual it is difficult to decide what action to take**. As Bowie states in his book *Ethical Studies (Second edition)*, 'How can individuals safely decide what is the most loving action?' This is because 'love' is a subjective concept.

- **Agape love is too subjective a concept to be used practically, as humans are prone to making mistakes or being influenced by selfishness rather than love**. As Edwin Williams wrote in an article entitled *Situation Ethics: The New Morality*, 'Love left to itself … can easily turn into the licence of permissiveness'. In others words people could claim to perform any act out of love when really they are doing as they please.

- **People cannot accurately predict the consequences of their actions**. As Peter Vardy and Paul Grosch state in *The Puzzle of Ethics*, 'It is not easy to determine the consequences of actions and this the situationist needs to do'. A person might think it loving in the short term to allow their pregnant teenage daughter to have an abortion; however, you cannot be sure that in the long term this will not cause her great distress and ultimately lead to unloving consequences.

- Cardinal Ratzinger (now Pope Benedict,) in April 2005 stated 'We are moving towards a dictatorship of relativism which does not recognise anything as for certain and which has as its highest goal one's own ego and one's own desires …. Being an "Adult" means having a faith which does not follow the waves of today's fashions or the latest novelties.' This idea appears to reflect the teachings of **St Paul who said that love is the fulfilling of the law** – Romans 13v10 and not doing what we consider to be loving.

2: 'Situation Ethics provides an adequate basis for making moral decisions.' Assess this view

You should try to consider each of the following points when developing your arguments and a conclusion:
- Have you supported your arguments using reasoning and/or evidence?
- Is the point raised strong/convincing?
- Does this response dispose of the argument?
- Is the issue evenly balanced, or is there one view which is clearly more convincing/correct or proven?

Agree

- **Each situation is considered differently unlike absolutist theories where a person has to follow rules**. An abortion may be allowed according to Situation Ethics if the abortion was an act of selfless love, whereas in Natural Law this would not be allowed as it goes against the primary precept of reproduction. As Mel Thompson states in his book *An Introduction to Philosophy and Ethics (Second Edition)*, *'It allows individuals to make up their own minds about what is right or wrong in a particular situation.'*

- **The use of Situation Ethics would encourage people to act selflessly and put other people first**. Fletcher would also argue that acting in such a way would ensure justice, as one of the six fundamental principles states '**love is justice distributed**'.

- As Situation Ethics is a consequentialist theory so **one must consider any possible consequences before acting**. This makes people consider the impact of their actions on others before taking them. Fletcher would argue that acting in such a way would ensure the outcome is loving as a 'loving end justifies the means'.

- If people used Situation Ethics as a basis for moral decision making they should act in a loving way to all as one of the six fundamental principles states '**love wills the good of others, regardless of feelings**'. There would be no room for prejudice or discrimination. People should treat a stranger in the same way as they treat a member of their family.

Disagree

- In 1952 Pope Pius XII described **situationist approaches to ethics as** *'an individualistic and subjective appeal to concrete circumstances of actions to justify decisions in opposition to the natural law of God's revealed will'*. In other words it was **a failed attempt by humans to try and excuse the fact that their actions were against God's will**.

- **'Love' is subjective – what one person considers to be a selflessly loving act another person may not**. Some people may argue that euthanasia is an act of selfless love whilst others might argue it is the opposite. As Bowie states in his book *Ethical Studies (Second edition)*, *'How can individuals safely decide what is the most loving action?'*

- **People cannot accurately predict the consequences of their actions**. As Joe Jenkins states in his book *Ethics and Religion (Second edition)*, that Situation Ethics assumes that humans are *'able always to predict what the most "loving" course of action is…Yet who is able to foretell the consequences of such acts and so determine, in advance, what is the most "loving" thing to do.'*

- **Agape love is too subjective a concept to be used practically as humans are prone to making mistakes or being influenced by selfishness rather than love**. As Joe Jenkins states in his book *Ethics and Religion (Second edition)*, *'often people interpret situations according to their own point of view and there is the danger that people claiming to act in "the name of love" may in fact be acting from selfish motives'*. People have emotional bonds and duties which link them to individuals and these will undoubtedly influence the decisions they make.

3: 'The principles of Situation Ethics promote injustice and/or morally wrong behaviour.' Assess this view.

You should try to consider each of the following points when developing your arguments and a conclusion:
- Have you supported your arguments using reasoning and/or evidence?
- Is the point raised strong/convincing?
- Does this response dispose of the argument?
- Is the issue evenly balanced, or is there one view which is clearly more convincing/correct or proven?

Agree

- **Someone could claim to be acting out of love and could perform acts such as murder or adultery whilst really acting in a selfish, unfair and unjust way** (on those who suffer as a result). As Edwin Williams wrote in an article entitled *Situation Ethics: The New Morality*, *'Love left to itself ... can easily turn to into the licence of permissiveness'*. In other words people could claim to perform any act out of love when really they are doing as they please.

- **People are unlikely to act in the same way to a stranger as they are to a member of their family – they have emotional ties to them which will undoubtedly influence their decisions and cause them to act unjustly.** As Joe Jenkins states in his book *Ethics and Religion (Second edition)*, *'often people interpret situations according to their own point of view and there is the danger that people claiming to act in "the name of love" may in fact be acting from selfish motives'*.

- Religious believers may argue that **God should decide what is fair and just, God is the ultimate source of authority and not humans who often make wrong decisions because of their sinful nature.**

- **Although the intention may have been to act in loving, fair and just way, the consequences of an act are not always loving or predictable.** As Joe Jenkins states in his book *Ethics and Religion (Second edition)*, that Situation Ethics assumes that humans are *'able always to predict what the most "loving" course of action is .... Yet who is able to foretell the consequences of such acts and so determine, in advance, what is the most "loving" thing to do.'*

Disagree

- The use of **Situation Ethics would encourage people to act selflessly and put other people first**. Fletcher would also argue that acting in such a way would ensure justice, as one of the six fundamental principles states '**love is justice distributed**'. As Peter Vardy and Paul Grosch state in *The Puzzle of Ethics*, *'Justice is – or should be – working out the most loving thing to do taking the interests of all those in the community into account.'*

- If people followed the fundamental principle '**Love wills the good of others, regardless of feelings**' there would be no place for prejudice and discrimination (as Jesus demonstrated in the Parable of the Good Samaritan – Luke Chapter 10). As Sarah K. Tyler and Gordon Reid state in their book *Advanced Religious Studies (Second edition)*, *'Love seeks the well-being of others, even if the course of action is not one of preference.'*

- **It promotes justice as each situation is considered differently unlike absolutist theories where a person has to follow rules**. An abortion may be allowed according to Situation Ethics if the abortion was an act of selfless love, whereas in Natural Law this would not be allowed as it goes against the primary precept of reproduction. As Mel Thompson states in his book *An Introduction to Philosophy and Ethics (Second Edition)*, *'It allows individuals to make up their own minds about what is right or wrong in a particular situation'*.

- Due to Fletcher's use of the fundamental principle 'A loving end justifies the means', **people would have to consider the likely consequences of their actions and determine if they would be fair before they take them** and it is only the consequences that have a real effect on human well-being.

4: 'Situation Ethics as a relativistic and teleological theory works well in society.' Assess this view.

You should try to consider each of the following points when developing your arguments and a conclusion:

- Have you supported your arguments using reasoning and/or evidence?
- Is the point raised strong/convincing?
- Does this response dispose of the argument?
- Is the issue evenly balanced, or is there one view which is clearly more convincing/correct or proven?

Agree

- Situation Ethics as a relativistic theory is flexible and practical. **It takes into account the situation a person is faced with and can help make decisions in situations where, from a legalistic view, all options are wrong**. For example, to lie in a particular situation in order to save a life. As Mel Thompson states in his book *An Introduction to Philosophy and Ethics (Second Edition)*, *'It allows individuals to make up their own minds about what is right or wrong in a particular situation.'*

- **Being a teleological theory** (one of the fundamental principles being 'A loving end justifies the means') **it ensures people consider the likely outcome of their actions before they take them** – they have to try to ensure as best as they can that the outcome is loving.

- Situation Ethics **being a relativistic theory allows people the individual freedom to make decisions for themselves** (on issues such as contraception, abortion, euthanasia, etc.) which many people nowadays prefer to the prescriptive/legalistic approach. As Mel Thompson states in his book *An Introduction to Philosophy and Ethics (Second edition)*, *'It allows individuals to make up their own minds about what is right or wrong in any particular situation.'*

- **As a teleological theory it is pragmatic and realistic – concentrating on the outcome of an action**. For example, in the case of conjoined twins it might well allow an operation to at least try and save one of the children as the intended outcome is a loving one.

Disagree

- **Many people argue we need rules to avoid issues such as moral chaos**. As J. Macquarrie states in *A Dictionary of Christian Ethics*, *'… it seems to be assumed that somehow one intuits what is right in a situation from the situation itself. Even if some people have this remarkable gift of insight, there are stages on the way to moral maturity and a great many people need the guidance of rules and generalisations which the community has built up from experience.'*

- **People cannot accurately predict the outcome of their actions**. A person might think it loving in the short term to allow their teenage son to sleep with his girlfriend when she stays the night; however, you cannot be sure that in the long term this will not cause her great distress, e.g. an unwanted pregnancy and ultimately not result in a loving outcome.

- **Situation Ethics gives so much freedom to the individual it is difficult to decide what action to take**. As Bowie states in his book *Ethical Studies (Second edition)*, *'How can individuals safely decide what is the most loving action?'* This is because 'love' is a subjective concept.

- **Being a teleological theory it will allow any action, but other theories such as Natural Law would argue that some actions are intrinsically wrong**. As Sarah K. Tyler and Gordon Reid, state in their book *Advanced Religious Studies (Second edition)*, *'The theory justifies adultery, murder and even genocide in the interests of love. Surely Fletcher is guilty of calling good what is in reality evil?'*

5. 'Situation Ethics is compatible with a religious approach to moral decision making.' Assess this view.

You should try to consider each of the following points when developing your arguments and a conclusion:

- Have you supported your arguments using reasoning and/or evidence?
- Is the point raised strong/convincing?
- Does this response dispose of the argument?
- Is the issue evenly balanced, or is there one view which is clearly more convincing/correct or proven?

(The arguments given here refer to Christianity, but arguments using any one major world religion would be acceptable.)

Agree

- **It is modelled on 'altruistic' love which is a major feature of many religions.** For example Jesus' command to 'love one another as I have loved you' (Luke Chapter 10). As William Temple (Archbishop of Canterbury 1942–44) stated in an essay entitled *Mens creatrix*, *'There is only one ultimate and invariable duty, and its formula is "Thou shalt love thy neighbour as thyself". How to do this is another question, but this is the whole of moral duty.'*

- **The idea of putting people first 'personalism' is in keeping with the actions of Jesus** as recorded in the Bible – healing the paralysed man, John Chapter 5. As Joe Jenkins states in his book *Ethics and Religion (Second edition)*, *'Situation Ethics appears to be more in line with Jesus' teachings whereby love is more important than law.'*

- Some Christians argue that the fundamental principle **'Love's decisions are made situationally, not prescriptively' reflects the Christian belief in free-will/ autonomy**. J.A.T. Robinson said in his book *Honest to God*, that *'Dr Fletcher's book is the only ethic for the man "come of age"'*. He was suggesting that Fletcher's ethics allows humankind moral autonomy.

- One of the six fundamental principles of Situation Ethics is 'Only the principle of love provides a reasonable base by which to make judgements of right and wrong'. **Jesus and St Paul appear to have taught that love as the highest principle above the law,** e.g. 'For the whole law is fulfilled in one word, you shall love your neighbour as yourself' (St Paul, Galatians 5v14).

- **It is used by some liberal religious believers to make moral decisions** (e.g., by some Quakers) on issues such as sex before marriage **by considering the most loving outcome.**

Disagree

- It rejects absolute moral laws like the Ten Commandments, but **St Paul said that love is the fulfilling of the Law** – Romans 13v10.

- **The 'rules' Jesus broke were more like religious conventions (such as Sabbath observance) rather than moral laws**. As Patrick J Clarke states in his book *Examining Philosophy and Ethics*, *'At no time did Jesus set aside a significant moral law, such as those contained in the Decalogue, in order to help someone.'*

- In 1952 Pope Pius XII described **situationist approaches to ethics** as *'an individualistic and subjective appeal to concrete circumstances of actions to justify decisions in opposition to the natural law of God's revealed will'*. In other words **a failed attempt by humans to try and excuse the fact that their actions had gone against God's will**.

- **St Paul stated that love is not the only desirable quality '... the fruit of Spirit is love, joy, peace, patience ...'** (Galatians 5v22–23).

- Cardinal Ratzinger (now Pope Benedict) in April 2005 stated, *'We are moving towards a dictatorship of relativism which does not recognise anything as for certain and which has as its highest goal one's own ego and one's own desires .... Being an "Adult" means having a faith which does not follow the waves of today's fashions or the latest novelties.'*

Summary: Situation Ethics

We have identified the key points on the WJEC AS specification and combined with the information in this chapter, summarised them in the diagram below. You may want to fill in further details to elaborate and personalise this content.

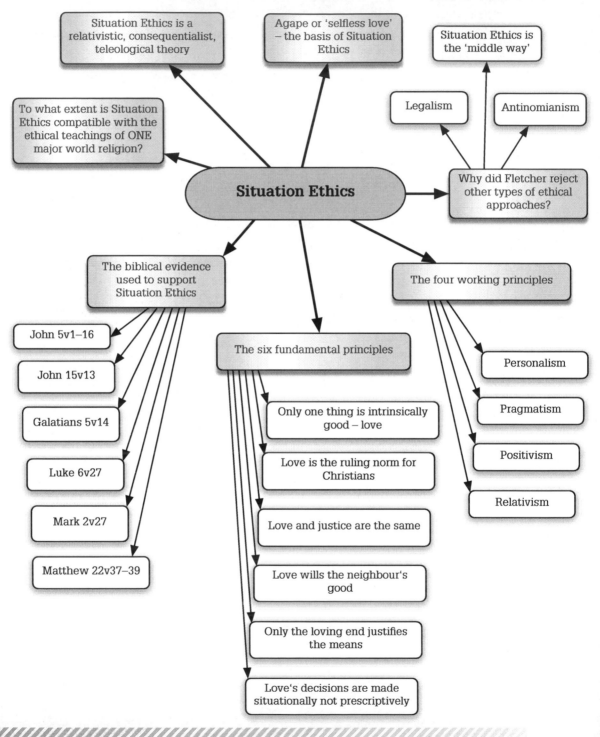

Situation Ethics is a relativistic, consequentialist, teleological theory

Agape or 'selfless love' – the basis of Situation Ethics

Situation Ethics is the 'middle way'

To what extent is Situation Ethics compatible with the ethical teachings of ONE major world religion?

Legalism

Antinomianism

Situation Ethics

Why did Fletcher reject other types of ethical approaches?

The biblical evidence used to support Situation Ethics

The four working principles

John 5v1–16

John 15v13

Galatians 5v14

Luke 6v27

Mark 2v27

Matthew 22v37–39

The six fundamental principles

Only one thing is intrinsically good – love

Love is the ruling norm for Christians

Love and justice are the same

Love wills the neighbour's good

Only the loving end justifies the means

Love's decisions are made situationally not prescriptively

Personalism

Pragmatism

Positivism

Relativism

7: Utilitarianism

The unit on Utilitarianism requires you to focus your revision on the main features of the theory. You should be able to explain why many regard Bentham's Act Utilitarianism as being a 'relativistic', 'teleological' and 'consequentialist' theory. You should be able to define Act Utilitarianism. You must be able to explain the principle of utility, the hedonic calculus and Bentham's focus on the quantity of happiness. You will be required to explain how Mill differed from Bentham and focussed on the quality of happiness using 'higher' and 'lower' pleasures. Furthermore you need to explain the basis for Rule Utilitarianism (rules which fulfil the principle of utility based on past experience) and how this developed into Weak and Strong Rule Utilitarianism. You will be expected to provide examples of how to apply Bentham and Mill's versions of Utilitarianism, which may be drawn from the issues listed in the Applied Ethics section or from other issues you have studied. You should also be able to explain to what extent Utilitarianism is compatible with the traditional teaching of one major world religion. Finally, you should be able to evaluate the issues that arise out of studying Utilitarianism.

Revision checklist

Tick column 1 when you have completed brief revision notes.
Tick column 2 when you think you have a good grasp of the topic.
Tick column 3 during final revision when you feel you have mastery of the topic.

			1	2	3
What type of theory is Act Utilitarianism?	p108	A relativistic, teleological and consequential theory			
	p108	Defining Act Utilitarianism			
What principle is Act Utilitarianism based on?	p109	What was Bentham concerned about measuring?			
	p100	What did he devise to measure happiness?			
	p109	The principle of utility			
	p109	The quantity of happiness			
	p110	An application of the hedonic calculus			
Mill's Utilitarianism	p111	Quality of pleasure			
	p111	Higher and lower pleasures			
Rule Utilitarianism	p112	Fulfilling the principle of utility using rules based on past experience			
	p112	Weak Rule and Strong Rule Utilitarianism			
To what extent is Utilitarianism compatible with the ethical teaching of one major world religion?	p113	Utilitarianism and its compatibility or not with Christian ethical teaching			
What are the main evaluative issues related to Utilitarianism?	p115	Strengths and weaknesses of Utilitarianism			
	p116	Does 'happiness' provide an adequate basis for moral decision making?			
	p117	Could Utilitarianism's use of the principle of utility/the hedonic calculus promote injustice and/or morally wrong behaviour?			
	p118	To what extent can Utilitarianism as a relativistic and teleological theory work in today's society?			
	p119	How far is Utilitarianism compatible with a religious approach to moral decision making?			

Key Terms

Act Utilitarianism = a form of Utilitarianism associated with Bentham that treats each moral situation as unique and applies the hedonic calculus to each 'act' to see if it fulfils the 'principle of utility'. Any action is right if it produces 'the greatest happiness for the greatest number'.

Relativistic = means there are no universal moral norms or rules and that each situation has to be looked at independently because each situation is different.

Consequentialist = people should make moral judgements based on the outcome or the consequences of an action.

Teleological = concerned with the end purpose or goal of an action – in this case the goal should always be 'happiness'.

Grade boost

Make sure that you are able to spell and define the terms relativistic, consequentialist and teleological. Weaker candidates also often confuse the meanings of the terms consequentialist and teleological.

quickfire

① Who developed the theory known as Act Utilitarianism?

② Define the term Act Utilitarianism.

Bentham's Act Utilitarianism: a relativistic, consequentialist and teleological theory

Jeremy Bentham was a philosopher, economist and social reformer. He developed the theory known as **Act Utilitarianism** in his book *An Introduction to the Principle of Morals and Legislation* (1789) and he believed our main aim in life was to achieve 'happiness' and avoid 'pain'. As he stated in his book: *'Nature has placed mankind under the governance of two sovereign masters, pain and pleasure.'*

Jeremy Bentham (1748–1832)

> Jeremy Bentham's theory is considered to be a **relativistic theory**. This means there are no universal moral norms or rules and that each situation has to be looked at independently because each situation is different.

> It is also considered to be a **consequentialist theory**. This means that moral judgements – whether something is right or wrong – should be based on the outcome or the consequences of an action. In this case does it lead to the 'greatest happiness for the greatest number'?

Act Utilitarianism

> Act Utilitarianism is a **teleological theory**. This means that it is concerned with the end purpose or goal of an action – in this case the goal should always be 'happiness'.

Act Utilitarianism – a relativistic, consequentialist and teleological theory

Key Figure

Jeremy Bentham was very much concerned with the social conditions of his day, becoming particularly involved with both hospitals and prisons. He also believed in women's right to vote and the decriminalisation of homosexuality. He developed the theory known as Act Utilitarianism. He believed that people should aim to achieve happiness and avoid pain. He introduced the 'principle of utility'. This states that an action is right if it produces 'the greatest happiness for the greatest number'. He also devised the hedonic calculus as a means of measuring happiness.

Utilitarianism: the principle of utility, the hedonic calculus, its seven criteria and how it measures the quantity of happiness

Once Bentham had established happiness as the basis for his ethic, he then defined its main principle which was the **principle of utility** or 'usefulness'. This principle states that we should aim to achieve 'the greatest happiness for the greatest number'.

> 'By the principle of utility is meant that principle which approves or disapproves of every action whatsoever, according to the tendency which appears to have to augment or diminish the happiness of the party whose interest is in question…I say of every action whatsoever….'
>
> Jeremy Bentham, *An Introduction to the Principles of Morals and Legislation* (1789)

His version of Utilitarianism is referred to as 'Act' Utilitarianism because it states that the principle of utility should be applied to every act performed in each unique situation. Any act is justifiable if it produces 'the greatest happiness for the greatest number'.

He also devised the 'hedonic calculus' as a means of measuring happiness. It was given this name because the word *hedone* means 'pleasure' in Greek.

= Happiness

- Intensity
- Duration +
- Certainty +
- Extent +
- Remoteness +
- Richness +
- Purity +

Intensity
How strong is the happiness?

Duration
How long does the happiness last for?

Certainty
How sure can you be that the act will produce happiness?

Extent
How many people will receive happiness?

Remoteness
How close (in terms of time) is the happiness?

Richness
How likely is this happiness to lead to further happiness?

Purity
How free from pain is this act?

Utilitarianism: the hedonic calculus

Bentham was concerned with maximising the quantity of happiness; he was not concerned about prioritising which forms of happiness were superior to others. Bentham wrote in *The Rationale of Reward*: 'Prejudice apart, the game of push-pin is of equal value with the arts and sciences of music and poetry.' Bentham's position was that all pleasures are of equal value.

Key term
Principle of utility = Bentham's guiding principle for Act Utilitarianism – 'the greatest happiness for the greatest number'

Grade boost
Good candidates can define both Act Utilitarianism and the principle of utility. They also know what the hedonic calculus is and can explain (if needed in an 'explain Act Utilitarianism' type question) each of its seven criteria.

quickfire

③ What is the principle of utility?

④ What does the Greek term 'hedone' mean?

⑤ What is the hedonic calculus?

⑥ Name the seven parts of the hedonic calculus.

◄ A mnemonic to help you remember the initial letters of the hedonic calculus is 'In Dark Corners Emily Reads Rugby Programmes'.

An example of the application of the hedonic calculus

A young couple have recently discovered that they are about to have a baby. They live in a small house with a garage. In order to make room for the baby, the garage will need to be converted into a room at an approximate price of £10,000. The builder, however, has offered to do the work for £2,000 less if they pay cash – as he will not declare the work and therefore not pay tax. Using the Hedonic calculus we can consider the situation and decide what the couple should do:

Hedonic calculus Criteria	Don't pay tax	Pay tax
Intensity	The couple will gain strong happiness in saving £2000 at a time when they will need it. (+)	Unless others find out about their tax avoidance, there is unlikely to be any strong pain felt by others. (–)
Duration	The money they save will only bring them happiness for a few months until it has been spent. (–)	If they pay the full amount, the revenue raised by the government through taxing the builder's earnings might be used towards education or healthcare and so any happiness gained is likely to last longer, e.g. the money might be used to restore the sight of someone with cataracts. (+)
Certainty	Initially the saving will bring happiness to the couple, but if they have the conversion done on a 'cash in hand basis', do they have any guarantee on this conversion? If there are any problems with the conversion then the happiness this brings will also be short lived. Also, if their deception is discovered, they might end up having to pay the tax and a fine. (–)	Even if the government received the tax from the builder, is it likely to be spent wisely? It might be wasted as part of a failed attempt to update NHS IT systems. (–)
Extent	Happiness gained by the couple, their child, the builder and possibly their friends and family through use of garage conversion or the way the builder's tax saving is spent. (–)	If the government received the tax from the builder it might end up paying for a new whiteboard in a comprehensive school, which over the years brings happiness to thousands of pupils. (+)
Remoteness	The couple will receive immediate happiness upon paying the builder less and the builder will receive immediate happiness paying less tax. (+)	Any pain which comes about if the deception is discovered will only come about later. (–)
Richness	The child and its parents will receive happiness from using their new room for many years to come. The builder might treat his family to a holiday with the money he saved by not paying tax. (–)	If the government received the tax from the builder, they might use it to improve the education system and this will in turn lead to smarter adults who can in turn make their children smarter. (+)
Purity	The couple and the builder might experience some pain knowing they have avoided paying tax. They might also fear being caught and fined. If their deception is discovered, their local community will experience pain knowing that they have had to pay the tax for similar work to be done. (–)	The couple and the builder will not have a guilty conscience and will not fear being prosecuted. (+)

Key

+ = predicted positive outcome when weighed against the other option

– = predicted negative outcome when weighed against the other option

Overall the hedonic calculus appears to show the couple should pay the extra £2,000 as there are more positive criteria in favour of this. However, the example also shows how reliant on 'prediction' Act Utilitarianism is and that if a person favours a certain outcome, they could manipulate their predictions in order to justify the outcome they wanted.

Mill's Utilitarianism: higher and lower pleasures and the quality of happiness

John Stuart Mill's form of Utilitarianism was very different from that of Bentham's in two main ways. Firstly, he believed that the quality of pleasure an act produced was more important than the quantity of pleasure.

Mill agreed with Bentham's idea of the principle of utility 'the greatest happiness for the greatest number', but like many others saw a major flaw in Bentham's version of Utilitarianism. It was concerned entirely with the quantity of the happiness an act produced. Mill was concerned that one person's unhappiness could be entirely overlooked if the majority were happy.

For example, after a spate of murders an innocent man is arrested and about to be sentenced to death (despite the authorities knowing he is innocent). The public are happy because they think the murderer has been caught, but the innocent man is in great pain. According to Bentham the man could be executed if his death fulfils the principle of utility.

As a result of this flaw, Mill shifted the focus in his version of Utilitarianism from the quantity of happiness/pleasure to the quality of the pleasure. He recognised that some pleasures were superior to others and developed a system of '**higher**' and '**lower**' **pleasures**.

What made humans unique was their capacity to achieve the higher pleasures. As Mill stated:

> '*It is better to be a human being dissatisfied than a pig satisfied; better to be Socrates dissatisfied than a fool satisfied.*'
>
> *Utilitarianism* (1863)

Key Figure

John Stuart Mill was a British philosopher, political economist, civil servant and Member of Parliament. Bentham was his mentor and a close family friend. He was an influential liberal thinker and developed Bentham's version of Utilitarianism. He focussed more on the 'quality' of pleasure rather than the 'quantity' of pleasure. Retrospectively some scholars have credited him as introducing Rule Utilitarianism.

Mill's higher pleasures

According to Mill, intellectual pleasures help humans to develop their intellect.

Albert Einstein became famous for scientific discoveries – he achieved 'higher' pleasures by using his intellect.

Mill's lower pleasures

'Lower' pleasures are inferior pleasures of the body – physical pleasures such as sex and eating. Eating a cheese burger might (if you like this type of thing!) fulfil a 'lower' pleasure – and satisfy someone's bodily needs by preventing them from becoming hungry.

Mill did, however, recognise that people must first achieve the lower pleasures – they need to eat, sleep, etc., before they can aim for the higher pleasures.

Key terms

Higher pleasure = pleasures of the intellect or mind are 'higher' and superior, e.g. reading philosophy or poetry.

Lower pleasure = inferior pleasures of the body — physical pleasures such as sex and eating.

Grade boost

Good candidates recognise that Mill focussed on the 'quality of pleasure'. They can also define and give examples of 'higher' and 'lower' pleasures as well as explaining why 'higher' pleasures are the superior form of pleasure.

John Stuart Mill (1806–1873, who wrote Utilitarianism in 1863)

quickfire

⑦ What did J.S. Mill think was more important that the quantity of pleasure?

⑧ Define the terms 'higher pleasure' and 'lower pleasure'.

Key terms

Rule Utilitarianism = a view associated with John Stuart Mill. Rule Utilitarians believe that by using the 'principle of utility' – the greatest happiness for the greatest number – one can draw up general rules, based on past experiences, which would help to keep this principle.

Strong Rule Utilitarianism = a strong rule utilitarian believes that any rules formulated and established through the application of the 'principle of utility' should never be broken as they guarantee happiness for society.

Weak Rule Utilitarianism = a 'weak rule' utilitarian tries to allow for the fact that in extreme cases the rule created using the 'principle of utility' needs to be broken in order to achieve the greatest happiness for the greatest number.

Grade boost

Good candidates can define Rule Utilitarianism and demonstrate their understanding by giving examples. They are also able to explain the difference between 'Strong' and 'Weak' Rule Utilitarianism.

quickfire

⑨ What question would a Rule Utilitarian ask with regards to happiness?

⑩ When would a Weak Rule Utilitarian allow the rules to be broken?

Rule Utilitarianism: rules which fulfil the 'principle of utility' based on past experience

Unlike Bentham, who was an Act Utilitarian, Mill appears to have been a **Rule Utilitarian** (although different scholars do argue over whether this is the case). This was a term Mill himself would probably not have used, but it has been used subsequently to describe his version of Utilitarianism. There appears to be evidence in his writings to support this claim. For example, in his book *Utilitarianism* first published in 1863, he states:

> 'There is no case of moral obligation in which some secondary principle is not involved' and
>
> 'All action is for the sake of some end, and rules of action, it seems natural to suppose, must take their whole character and colour from the end to which they are subservient.'

Rule Utilitarians believe that by using the principle of utility, 'the greatest happiness for the greatest number', you can draw up general rules based on past experience, which would help you to keep this principle without having to assess each situation.

A Rule Utilitarian would ask: 'Which general rules promote the greatest happiness?' Mill himself mentioned some 'rules' for Utilitarianism in his book *On Liberty* (1865). He said we should not lie or cause injury to others. Other rules could include 'do not steal' or 'do not murder'.

Strong and Weak Rule Utilitarianism

In modern times two types of Rule Utilitarianism have been identified.

A **'strong rule' utilitarian** believes that any rules created using the 'principle of utility' should never be broken. This is because the rules were made in order to promote happiness.

A **'weak rule' utilitarian** tries to allow for the fact that in extreme cases the rule created using the 'principle of utility' needs to be broken in order to achieve the greatest happiness. For example, the rule 'do not kill' might have be broken by someone during World War II if they had the opportunity to kill Hitler, as this would have fulfilled the 'principle of utility'.

Mill has been described by some scholars as a 'Weak Rule' Utilitarian.

To what extent is Utilitarianism compatible with the traditional teaching of one major world religion?

As the majority of candidates answer this question from a Christian perspective, this is how the question will be addressed here. However, many similar arguments could be equally applied to Judaism or Islam, for example.

Remember in order to achieve the higher levels of response, you would need to develop the brief points given below.

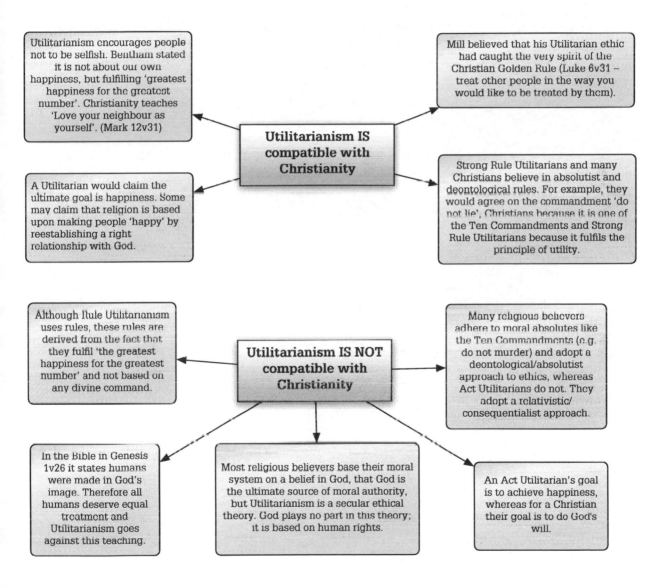

Utilitarianism encourages people not to be selfish. Bentham stated it is not about our own happiness, but fulfilling 'greatest happiness for the greatest number'. Christianity teaches 'Love your neighbour as yourself'. (Mark 12v31)

Mill believed that his Utilitarian ethic had caught the very spirit of the Christian Golden Rule (Luke 6v31 – treat other people in the way you would like to be treated by them).

Utilitarianism IS compatible with Christianity

A Utilitarian would claim the ultimate goal is happiness. Some may claim that religion is based upon making people 'happy' by reestablishing a right relationship with God.

Strong Rule Utilitarians and many Christians believe in absolutist and deontological rules. For example, they would agree on the commandment 'do not lie', Christians because it is one of the Ten Commandments and Strong Rule Utilitarians because it fulfils the principle of utility.

Although Rule Utilitarianism uses rules, these rules are derived from the fact that they fulfil 'the greatest happiness for the greatest number' and not based on any divine command.

Utilitarianism IS NOT compatible with Christianity

Many religious believers adhere to moral absolutes like the Ten Commandments (e.g. do not murder) and adopt a deontological/absolutist approach to ethics, whereas Act Utilitarians do not. They adopt a relativistic/consequentialist approach.

In the Bible in Genesis 1v26 it states humans were made in God's image. Therefore all humans deserve equal treatment and Utilitarianism goes against this teaching.

Most religious believers base their moral system on a belief in God, that God is the ultimate source of moral authority, but Utilitarianism is a secular ethical theory. God plays no part in this theory; it is based on human rights.

An Act Utilitarian's goal is to achieve happiness, whereas for a Christian their goal is to do God's will.

Key Terms

Adequate = satisfactory for a particular purpose.

Compatible = able to work together with something else.

Injustice = treatment of people with inequality and unfairness, both generally and before the law.

Relativistic = there are no universal moral norms or rules and each situation has to be looked at independently because each situation is different.

Teleological = it is concerned with the end purpose or goal of an action – in this case the goal should always be achieving 'happiness'.

Evaluative issues

Many candidates make common errors when addressing the AO2 type questions on Utilitarianism. The three main errors are:

- They answer every part (b) (AO2) question as a 'strengths and weaknesses' of Utilitarianism question, which is only one of the possible questions that could be set.
- They simply 'list' points that agree or disagree with the statement with little or no evaluation or analysis (which is what is being assessed here).
- They confuse Act Utilitarianism with Rule Utilitarianism and subsequently any arguments used are incorrect.
- They fail to give a conclusion.

Over the next few pages are some examples of the arguments that could be used to address the issues identified by the specification. The arguments given here are not an exhaustive list and any relevant arguments will be credited. Some of the same arguments can be used to answer different questions, but you need to select these arguments carefully.

Grade boost

Read the question carefully. It is the QUALITY of your arguments that will help you to achieve the higher levels and not the QUANTITY of your arguments. Don't forget what is being assessed in the AO2 type questions is your ability to evaluate and analyse.

1: Assess the strengths and weaknesses of Utilitarianism.

You should try to consider each of the following points when developing your arguments and a conclusion:
- Have you supported your arguments using reasoning and/or evidence?
- Is the point raised strong/convincing?
- Does this response dispose of the argument?
- Is the issue evenly balanced, or is there one view which is clearly more convincing/correct or proven?

Strengths

- **Act Utilitarianism is pragmatic and concentrates on the effects of an action.** As Sarah K. Tyler and Gordon Reid state in their book *Religious Studies AS & A2*, *'Consequences have real effects on people and should therefore be the basis of evaluating actions, irrespective of previous precedents.'*

- **For many people 'happiness' is an important aspect of decision making as it is their main aim in life.** As Patrick J. Clarke states in his book *Examining Philosophy and Ethics*, *'... supporters of the utility principle say that its truth is self-evident. If the promotion of happiness and the lessening of pain is what we all value, then all human actions should have these aims and effects.'*

- **The theory treats everyone the same – no one gets special treatment due to their emotional or social attachments.** A Utilitarian would argue that the use of the 'principle of utility' has led to great social reform in the UK. As Patrick J. Clarke states in his book *Examining Philosophy and Ethics*, *'The principle of utility has probably provided the greatest impetus to modern social reforms in the UK, such as the Divorce and Abortion Acts of 1969.'*

- **Act Utilitarianism appears to be simple to follow. Just aim to achieve the 'greatest happiness for the greatest number'.** As Mel Thompson states in his book *An introduction to Philosophy and Ethics (Second Edition)*, *'It is straightforward and based on clear principle.'*

- **Bentham has provided humans with a means of calculating the 'greatest happiness for the greatest number' using the hedonic calculus.** As James Rachels in his book *The Elements of Moral Philosophy (Fourth edition)* states, *'Bentham went so far as to produce a hedonic calculus by which the utility value of an action could be empirically judged. Good actions are capable of producing a balance of pleasure over pain.'*

Weaknesses

- **Act Utilitarianism relies upon a human's ability to predict the consequences of an action which are impossible.** As Cain Rolleston states in his book *Utilitarianism in Focus*, *'It is often hard to know what consequences will result from an action and many consequences are either unforeseen, unintended or both.'*

- **Some would argue that Bentham has committed the 'naturalistic fallacy' by deriving an 'ought' from an 'is'.** Saying happiness 'is' good is not the same as saying happiness 'ought' to be good. As James Rachels in his book *The Elements of Moral Philosophy (Fourth edition)* states, *'Happiness is not something that is recognized as good for its own sake, with other things desired as only a means of bringing it about. Instead happiness is a response to the attainment of things that we recognize as good, independently in their own right. We think that friendships is a good thing, and so having friends makes us happy.'*

- **Utilitarianism fails to consider that we have certain duties or obligations towards others,** e.g. a mother's duty to protect her child. As James Rachels in his book *The Elements of Moral Philosophy (Fourth edition)* states, *'In practice, none of us is willing to treat all people as equals, for it would require that we abandon our special relationships with friends and family.'*

- **Happiness is subjective – people have different ideas about what constitutes 'pleasure'.** What is one person's pleasure is another person's idea of pain, so the theory cannot be applied consistently. As Robert Bowie states in his book *Ethical Studies (Second edition)*, *'If human beings don't have the same idea of what gives them pain or pleasure, then the premise on which utilitarianism is built is severely weakened.'*

- **Using the hedonic calculus to calculate the 'greatest happiness for the greatest number' is impractical.** As Noel Stewart wrote in his article 'Act and Rule Utilitarianism: the basics' in the November 2011 edition of the journal *Dialogue*, *'It cannot cope with emergency situations .... Imagine you've been mugged ... and in need of urgent hospital treatment. Just then Bentham turns up with his hedonic calculus, not ready to help but ready to do some number crunching using its seven factors .... By the time Bentham finishes asking you ... you'll probably be dead.'*

2: 'Utilitarianism provides an adequate basis for making moral decisions.' Assess this view

You should try to consider each of the following points when developing your arguments and a conclusion:
- Have you supported your arguments using reasoning and/or evidence?
- Is the point raised strong/convincing?
- Does this response dispose of the argument?
- Is the issue evenly balanced, or is there one view which is clearly more convincing/correct or proven?

Agree

- **Aiming for the 'greatest happiness for the greatest number' discourages selfish behaviour.** As Cain Rolleston states in his book *Utilitarianism in Focus*, Utilitarianism *'can require considerable self-sacrifice in the general interest and this altruism is often considered and essential aspect of a serious moral system'.*

- **Using happiness as a basis for decision making allows humans to adopt a flexible, relativistic approach to each situation.** As Noel Stewart in his article Act and Rule Utilitarianism: the basics in the November 2011 edition of the journal *Dialogue*, said that the flexibility of Utilitarianism *'can be a seen as a strength in many situations. There are no rigid rules which lay down one single course of action no matter what.'*

- **You can argue that many of the major social reforms in the UK such as democracy and the healthcare system are based on Utilitarian principles.** You can only please some of the people some of the time so you aim to achieve the 'greatest happiness for the greatest number' As Patrick J. Clarke states in his book *Examining Philosophy and Ethics,* *'The principle of utility has probably provided the greatest impetus to modern social reforms in the UK, such as the Divorce and Abortion Acts of 1969.'*

- **For many people 'happiness' is an important aspect of decision making as it is their main aim in life.** As Robert Bowie states in his book *Ethical Studies (Second edition)*, *'It seems reasonable to link morality with the pursuit of happiness and the avoidance of pain and misery, and this connection would receive popular support.'*

- **Bentham and Mill both devised ways of measuring the happiness an action produces using the hedonic calculus or the concept of higher and lower pleasures.** As James Rachels in his book *The Elements of Moral Philosophy (Fourth edition)* states, *'Bentham went so far as to produce a hedonic calculus by which the utility value of an action could be empirically judged. Good actions are capable of producing a balance of pleasure over pain.'*

Disagree

- **Aiming for 'greatest happiness for the greatest number' often means a minority are allowed to suffer.** As Cain Rolleston states in his book *Utilitarianism in Focus*, *'There appears to be no automatic reason, for example, why utility could not lead to the total destruction of a minority group in society if it would bring greater pleasure to the majority, or indeed the killing of an innocent man to appease an angry mob.'*

- **When basing decisions solely on happiness, people ignore other important factors such as love, God's will, etc.** As Sarah K. Tyler and Gordon Reid state in their book *Advanced Religious Studies (Second edition)*, *'Happiness may be seen to be a dubious benefit to some religious believers – different from joy, peace, loving kindness, patience and charity which are gifts of the Spirit.'*

- **It fails to acknowledge the idea of human rights for all citizens. Bentham rejected the idea of human rights.** In *Anarchical Fallacies* (1824) he referred to natural rights as *'simple nonsense, natural and imprescriptible rights, rhetorical nonsense – nonsense upon stilts'*. This could therefore lead to considerable abuses of humans in order to fulfil the principle of utility, e.g. allowing slavery.

- **Utilitarianism does not provided a good basis for making moral decisions as what some people consider to be happiness others consider to be pain.** Happiness is subjective. What is one person's pleasure is another person's idea of pain, so the theory cannot be applied consistently. As Robert Bowie states in his book *Ethical Studies (Second edition)*, *'If human beings don't have the same idea of what gives them pain or pleasure, then the premise on which utilitarianism is built is severely weakened.'*

- **Using the hedonic calculus to calculate the 'greatest happiness for the greatest number' is impractical.** As Noel Stewart wrote in his article Act and Rule Utilitarianism: the basics in the November 2011 edition of the journal *Dialogue*, *'It cannot cope with emergency situations .... Imagine you've been mugged ... and in need of urgent hospital treatment. Just then Bentham turns up with his hedonic calculus, not ready to help but ready to do some number crunching using its seven factors .... By the time Bentham finishes asking you ... you'll probably be dead.'*

3: Assess how far utilitarianism promotes injustice and/or morally wrong behaviour.

You should try to consider each of the following points when developing your arguments and a conclusion:
- Have you supported your arguments using reasoning and/or evidence?
- Is the point raised strong/convincing?
- Does this response dispose of the argument?
- Is the issue evenly balanced, or is there one view which is clearly more convincing/correct or proven?

Agree

- **Many religions believe in moral absolutes and claim that certain actions are always morally wrong** such as 'Do not kill' – and are based on rules given by God. They claim that God's rules ensure justice, whereas Act Utilitarians simply look at the consequences of each act to determine whether the act is good or bad.

- **As happiness is subjective, two similar situations could be treated differently as people have different ideas of what happiness is.** This could lead to injustice for those involved. As Robert Bowie states in his book *Ethical Studies (Second edition)*, *'If human beings don't have the same idea of what gives them pain or pleasure, then the premise on which utilitarianism is built is severely weakened.'*

- **Act Utilitarianism allows a minority to suffer as long as the majority are happy.** It could justify acts such as the torture or death of an innocent person as long as it fulfilled 'the greatest happiness for the greatest number'. As Cain Rolleston states in his book *Utilitarianism in Focus*, *'There appears to be no automatic reason, for example , why utility could not lead to the total destruction of a minority group in society if it would bring greater pleasure to the majority, or indeed the killing of an innocent man to appease an angry mob.'*

- **As it is a consequentialist theory the intended outcome is not guaranteed and so people may end up being treated unfairly.** As Cain Rolleston states in his book *Utilitarianism in Focus*, *'It is often hard to know what consequences will result from an action and many consequences are either unforeseen, unintended or both.'*

- **Even Rule Utilitarianism can be unjust as its rules could lead to an unfair distribution of happiness in society or may lead to extreme punishments in the pursuit of the principle of utility.** For example, as Cain Rolleston states in his book *Utilitarianism in Focus*, *'Public execution for minor crimes may serve the general good by acting as an effective deterrent to others.'* Rule Utilitarianism could therefore formulate the rule that 'all shoplifters should be executed' even if it was their first offence.

Disagree

- **Act Utilitarianism takes the situation into account when making an ethical decision and therefore is more just than absolutist theories which simply prevent people from performing certain actions.** As Noel Stewart in his article Act and Rule Utilitarianism: the basics in the November 2011 edition of the journal *Dialogue*, said that the flexibility of Utilitarianism *'can be seen as a strength in many situations. There are no rigid rules which lay down one single course of action no matter what.'*

- **In Act Utilitarianism the use of the hedonic calculus ensures that everyone's happiness is considered when making an ethical decision,** so it is just. As James Rachels in his book *The Elements of Moral Philosophy (Fourth edition)* states, *'Bentham went so far as to produce a hedonic calculus by which the utility value of an action could be empirically judged. Good actions are capable of producing a balance of pleasure over pain.'*

- **In its initial assessment of the situation Utilitarianism considers everyone as equal and everyone has an equal say.** As Mel Thompson states in his book *An Introduction to Philosophy and Ethics (Second Edition)*, *'It is easy to demonstrate that Utilitarianism is fair, since its basic principles are widely accepted.'*

- **By considering the consequences of each action, Act Utilitarianism makes people consider how their actions affect others.** As Sarah K. Tyler and Gordon Reid state in their book *Religious Studies AS & A2*, *'Consequences have real effects on people and should therefore be the basis of evaluating actions, irrespective of previous precedents.'*

- **Rule Utilitarianism provides rules which are based on the principle of utility and ensure that similar actions are treated the same way**, e.g. do not murder. As Noel Stewart in his article Act and Rule Utilitarianism: the basics in the November 2011 edition of the journal *Dialogue*, said, Rule Utilitarianism *'won't create an unhappy or immoral society precisely because only rules that are moral maximisers of happiness will get picked'.*

4: 'Utilitarianism as a relativistic and teleological theory works well in society.' Assess this view

You should try to consider each of the following points when developing your arguments and a conclusion:
- Have you supported your arguments using reasoning and/or evidence?
- Is the point raised strong/convincing?
- Does this response dispose of the argument?
- Is the issue evenly balanced, or is there one view which is clearly more convincing/correct or proven?

Agree

- **Act Utilitarianism is pragmatic and concentrates on the effects of an action**. As Sarah K. Tyler and Gordon Reid state in their book *Religious Studies AS & A2*, *'Consequences have real effects on people and should therefore be the basis of evaluating actions, irrespective of previous precedents.'*

- **In Act Utilitarianism the use of the hedonic calculus helps to ensure that the outcome should fulfil the 'principle of utility'**. As James Rachels in his book *The Elements of Moral Philosophy (Fourth edition)* states, *'Bentham went so far as to produce a hedonic calculus by which the utility value of an action could be empirically judged. Good actions are capable of producing a balance of pleasure over pain.'*

- **Act Utilitarianism being a relativistic theory allows humans to adopt a flexible, approach to each situation**. As Noel Stewart in his article Act and Rule Utilitarianism: the basics in the November 2011 edition of the journal *Dialogue*, said that the flexibility of Utilitarianism *'can be a seen as a strength in many situations. There are no rigid rules which lay down one single course of action no matter what.'*

- **By considering the intended outcome and therefore the consequences of each action Act Utilitarianism makes people consider how their actions affect others**. As Sarah K. Tyler and Gordon Reid state in their book *Religious Studies AS & A2*, *'Consequences have real effects on people and should therefore be the basis of evaluating actions, irrespective of previous precedents.'*

Disagree

- **Many religions believe that a lack of moral absolutes will lead to chaos**. Rules such as 'Do not kill' are given to humans by God. Some acts are intrinsically bad even if they do lead to 'the greatest happiness for the greatest number'.

- **It gives no credit for a person's motivation when acting but focusses entirely on the outcome of an action.** As Sarah K. Tyler and Gordon Reid state in their book *Advanced Religious Studies*, *'The theory gives no credit for motivation. Not every action done out of good will is going to result in good consequences.'*

- **Utilitarianism does not work because what some people think will bring about a 'happy' outcome in a situation others will consider as bringing a painful one**. For example, allowing smoking in public places – some thinks this brings happiness others do not. Happiness is subjective. What is one person's pleasure is another person's idea of pain, so the theory cannot be applied consistently. As Robert Bowie states in his book *Ethical Studies (Second edition)*, *'If human beings don't have the same idea of what gives them pain or pleasure, then the premise on which utilitarianism is built is severely weakened.'*

- **As it is a consequentialist theory, the intended outcome (happiness) is not guaranteed and so people may end up being treated unfairly**. As Cain Rolleston states in his book *Utilitarianism in Focus*, *'It is often hard to know what consequences will result from an action and many consequences are either unforeseen, unintended or both.'*

5. 'Utilitarianism is compatible with a religious approach to moral decision making.' Assess this view

You should try to consider each of the following points when developing your arguments and a conclusion:
- Have you supported your arguments using reasoning and/or evidence?
- Is the point raised strong/convincing?
- Does this response dispose of the argument?
- Is the issue evenly balanced, or is there one view which is clearly more convincing/correct or proven?

(The arguments given here refer to Christianity, but arguments using any one major world religion would be acceptable)

Agree

- **Some people would argue that Jesus' self-sacrifice, death on the cross and resurrection are an example of the principle of utility** – he died to give others happiness through eternal life.

- **A Utilitarian would claim the ultimate goal is happiness; some may claim that religion is based upon making people happy by enabling them to develop a relationship with God.**

- **Mill believed that his utilitarian ethic had caught the very spirit of the Christian Golden Rule** (Matthew 7v12) – treat people as you would like to be treated. As Patrick J. Clarke states in his book *Examining Philosophy and Ethics*, *'Defenders of Utilitarianism often point to the prominent utilitarian strand in the teaching of the Bible, particularly the teachings of Jesus. The heart of Jesus' teaching was the love of God expressed through the love of neighbour.'*

- **Strong Rule Utilitarians and many Christians believe in absolutist and deontological rules**. For example, they would agree on the 'do not lie'. Christians, because it is the Ten Commandments, and Strong Rule Utilitarians, because it fulfils the principle of utility.

- **Act Utilitarians and some Christians (e.g. Anglicans) may agree on certain issues, e.g. divorce – if one partner in a married couple commits adultery**, then for the other partner's sake and for their children, it may be better (less painful) for all concerned if they divorce.

Disagree

- **In John 18v14 it is states that Caiaphas advised the Jews that it was better for one man to die for the good of the people. Jesus was prepared to offer his own life as an act of agape love for others, whereas Caiaphas wanted to sacrifice Jesus for the greater good**. As Joe Jenkins says states in his book *Ethics and Religion (Second edition)*, *'Jesus and Caiaphas act from totally different ethical principles.'*

- Most world religions believe that people will gain happiness by following God's will/ teachings, etc. God is the ultimate source of authority and it is not up to individuals to decide what 'happiness' should be.

- **Religious believers would not accept the fact that under both Act and Rule Utilitarianism a minority might be allowed to suffer for the majority** as this fails to uphold Jesus' Golden rule. As Joe Jenkins says states in his book *Ethics and Religion (Second edition)*, *'For Utilitarians love is subordinate to justice, whereas for Christians, selfless love (agape) is at the heart of all ethical behaviour.'* Agape love does not consider what is best for the collective good, but cares about every individual. It does not sacrifice the few for the sake of the majority.

- **The reason Christians follow the Ten Commandments is not because of any utilitarian benefits but because they are considered to be divine laws** – from God. As Patrick J. Clarke states in his book *Examining Philosophy and Ethics*, *'… laws such as the Ten Commandments are charters of human rights, designed to protect the interests and well-being of all of us, in all circumstances. This shows that if the Bible is a charter of utilitarian benefits for others, it is so by a different route and only by way of secondary effect. In the first place comes the primacy of God on which everything else depends. Thus to invoke the Bible in support of utilitarianism is an over simplification …'*

- **However according to Natural Law's deontological approach adopted by the Roman Catholic Church, some actions are intrinsically right or wrong** (like divorce as it breaks the primary precept 'to live in an ordered society'). This is not a consequentialist approach and the means do not justify the end. Whereas Act Utilitarians simply look at the consequences of each act to determine whether the act is good or bad.

Summary: Utilitarianism

We have identified the key points on the WJEC AS specification and, combined with the information in this chapter, summarised them in the diagram below. You may want to fill in further details to elaborate and personalise this content.

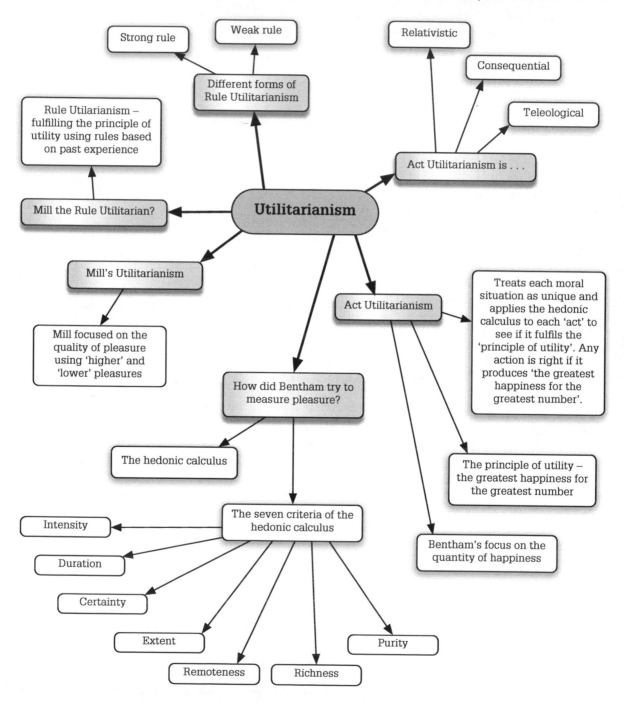

Strong rule

Weak rule

Relativistic

Consequential

Teleological

Different forms of Rule Utilitarianism

Rule Utilarianism – fulfilling the principle of utility using rules based on past experience

Act Utilitarianism is . . .

Mill the Rule Utilitarian?

Utilitarianism

Treats each moral situation as unique and applies the hedonic calculus to each 'act' to see if it fulfils the 'principle of utility'. Any action is right if it produces 'the greatest happiness for the greatest number'.

Mill's Utilitarianism

Act Utilitarianism

Mill focused on the quality of pleasure using 'higher' and 'lower' pleasures

How did Bentham try to measure pleasure?

The principle of utility – the greatest happiness for the greatest number

The hedonic calculus

The seven criteria of the hedonic calculus

Bentham's focus on the quantity of happiness

Intensity

Duration

Certainty

Extent

Purity

Remoteness

Richness

8: Applied Ethics

The unit on Applied Ethics requires you to focus your revision on the ethical teaching of ONE major world religion on the three areas identified:

- Sexual orientation (Is it a choice? Should all forms of sexuality be allowed to be expressed through sex?).
- Sex outside marriage (including heterosexual sex, gay and lesbian sex and adultery).
- Marriage – its purposes (including sex within marriage) and the morality of gay and lesbian marriages and civil partnerships.

Where appropriate you should be aware of diversity of ethical attitude and behaviour within the religion you have studied. For example, whereas most Christians share the same view on issues such as adultery (that it is wrong and sinful) not all Christians have the same view of gay and lesbian sex. Different denominations have differing views on this issue and even individuals within a denomination might not agree with the official view of the denomination to which they belong.

You need to be able to explain the religious principles involved in response to the issues identified and should understand how such ethics are based on religious authority (sacred texts, leaders, tradition, conscience and reason). You also need to be able to demonstrate your understanding of how religious concepts (such as God as creator, the sanctity of marriage, agape love, responsibility to God, and sin) affect moral principles, and be aware of the importance for many of absolutist rules, general principles and priorities of doctrine over reasons/feelings/circumstances. Finally, you should be able to evaluate the issues that arise out of this area of the specification.

As the majority of candidates attempt this section from a Christian viewpoint this is the religion that will be referred to in the examples given in this section, although any major world religion could be referred to in order to address any question set in the exam.

Revision checklist

Tick column 1 when you have completed brief revision notes.
Tick column 2 when you think you have a good grasp of the topic.
Tick column 3 during final revision when you feel you have mastery of the topic.

The ethical teaching of ONE major religion on:			1	2	3
Sexual orientation	p123	Is sexual orientation a choice?			
	p123	Should all forms of sexuality be allowed to be expressed through sex?			
Sex outside marriage	p126	Heterosexual sex, gay and lesbian sex, and adultery			
Marriage	p131	The purpose of marriage and sex within marriage; gay and lesbian marriage and civil partnerships			
Evaluative issues	p136	Below are some examples of the evaluative issues which could arise: ■ 'In today's society religious responses to sex outside marriage are no longer adequate.' ■ 'In today's society a relativistic approach should be adopted towards the issues of gay/lesbian marriage and civil partnerships.' ■ 'Decreasing marriage rates do not harm society.' ■ 'Traditional religious attitudes towards adultery are unfair.' Any of the three identified areas (sexual orientation, sex outside marriage or marriage) could be used with any of the four types of evaluative question in this section.			

How to plan answers for questions in the Applied Ethics part of the exam

When answering questions in the Applied Ethics section, you should refer to the teaching of only ONE major world religion.

However, it is important to note that, where appropriate, you should be aware of diversity of ethical attitude and behaviour within the religion you have studied.

For example, whereas most Christians share the same view on adultery (that it is wrong and sinful) not all Christians have the same view of gay and lesbian sex. Different denominations have differing views on this issue and even individuals within a denomination might not agree with the official view of the denomination to which they belong.

As the majority of candidates attempt this section from a Christian viewpoint, this is the religion that will be referred to in the examples given in this section. However, any major world religion could be referred to in order to address any question set in the exam.

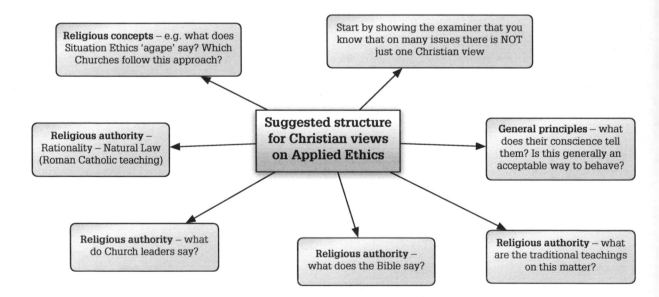

Religious concepts – e.g. what does Situation Ethics 'agape' say? Which Churches follow this approach?

Start by showing the examiner that you know that on many issues there is NOT just one Christian view

Religious authority – Rationality – Natural Law (Roman Catholic teaching)

Suggested structure for Christian views on Applied Ethics

General principles – what does their conscience tell them? Is this generally an acceptable way to behave?

Religious authority – what do Church leaders say?

Religious authority – what does the Bible say?

Religious authority – what are the traditional teachings on this matter?

The ethical teaching of one major world religion on sexual orientation

General principles

There are various Christian perspectives on human sexuality and sexual difference and in Genesis Chapter 1 sexual difference is recognised as a feature of all species including humans; it is viewed as being God-made and good. Christianity highly values marriage and family life and approves of sexual intercourse within marriage. Traditionally, Christianity has tended to regard heterosexuality as the only legitimate orientation, sex as being permissible only within marriage and heterosexual marriage as the only form of marriage allowed. In some Christian traditions, lifelong virginity has been applauded as admirable, and required of Catholic priests, monks and nuns. Attitudes towards all of these issues have changed markedly in recent decades and are highly controversial within churches today. For example, some Christians see homosexual orientation as a 'lifestyle' choice that goes against God's will. Others see this as a 'natural' state, as according to Genesis Chapter 1 humans are all made in God's image.

One Roman Catholic view

Religious authority: tradition

Heterosexual **sexual orientation** is considered to be the traditional norm within most branches of Christianity, but not all. This is based mainly on God's command to reproduce found in Genesis 1v28 and the promotion of heterosexual relationships in Genesis 2v24.

However, there is also a great diversity of opinion on the issue of homosexuality within Christianity and sometimes even within a particular denomination within Christianity. Christians in general do not discriminate against people on the basis of their sexual orientation alone. If, however, they act upon their sexual orientation and perform homosexual acts then many **denominations** (although not all) regard them as sinful.

The Roman Catholic Church does not consider homosexual/lesbian orientation to be a **sin** in itself. Orientation of this type is said to be 'disordered' in the sense that they tempt one to do something that *is* sinful (i.e., perform a homosexual act).

Religious authority: In both Natural Law (one of the primary precepts being 'reproduction') and in the Bible (Genesis 1v28) it states that heterosexual orientation leads to the fulfilment of God's command for humans to reproduce.

Key terms

Denomination = a recognised branch of the Christian Church.

Sexual orientation = a pattern of romantic, emotional and/or sexual attraction to men, women, or both genders.

Sin = an act, word or deed which goes against a religious law given by God.

Tradition = the passing on of religious beliefs, concepts and attitudes from generation to generation.

Grade boost

Try not to stereotype different groups of religious believers; for example, not all Catholics agree with the official teachings of their Church and not all Protestants are 'liberal' Christians. Make it clear to the examiner that you are aware of any diversity which exists within a religion or even denomination. For example, not all Catholics hold the view that homosexual orientation is a 'disordered' one. Support the points you are attempting to make with evidence.

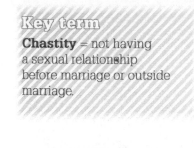

Key term

Chastity = not having a sexual relationship before marriage or outside marriage.

① What is the traditional Christian view of sexual orientation?

② Does the Roman Catholic Church teach that homosexual orientation is a sin?

③ Do all Quakers believe that homosexual orientation is acceptable?

Religious authority: teaching

The Catechism of the Roman Catholic Church states that:

> *The number of men and women who have deep-seated homosexual tendencies is not negligible. This inclination, which is objectively disordered, constitutes for most of them a trial. They must be accepted with respect, compassion, and sensitivity. Every sign of unjust discrimination in their regard should be avoided. These persons are called to fulfil God's will in their lives and, if they are Christians, to unite to the sacrifice of the Lord's Cross the difficulties they may encounter from their condition.*
>
> Catechism of the Catholic Church, 2nd edition, paragraph 2358

For those who do experience gay sexual attractions, the Catholic Church offers the following advice:

> *Homosexual persons are called to chastity. By the virtues of self-mastery that teach them inner freedom, at times by the support of disinterested friendship, by prayer and sacramental grace, they can and should gradually and resolutely approach Christian perfection.*
>
> Catechism of the Catholic Church, 2nd edition, paragraph 2359

Different Catholic views

After the election of Pope Benedict XVI, the Congregation for Catholic Education issued an instruction prohibiting any individuals who 'present deep-seated homosexual tendencies or support the so-called "gay culture", or any individuals having had such "tendencies" within the past three years, from entry to seminary, and from joining the priesthood'.

Religious authority: Natural Law/the Bible – alternative views.

Some gay/lesbian Roman Catholics would use Natural Law to claim that God their Divine Creator (**religious concept**) has created them in his image (Genesis 1v27) and for them their homosexual orientation is their 'natural' state.

They might argue therefore that to deny them the right to express their sexuality is morally wrong.

Religious Authority: leaders/teaching

There is no direct comment from Jesus on this issue, but some people have pointed out that Jesus showed his approval of heterosexual marriage (Mark 10v6–8) – therefore implying that this is the intended norm and not homosexuality.

Quaker views

The views of Quakers around the world towards homosexual orientation also range from acceptance to non-acceptance.

One Quaker view

In the UK some Quakers agree with the view expressed below:

Religious authority: teachings

> *Quakers were one of the first churches to talk openly about sexuality .... We feel that the quality and depth of feeling between two people is the most important part of a loving relationship, not their gender or sexual orientation.*
>
> Statement in a *Britain Yearly Meeting.*

The book *Towards a Quaker view of Sex* (1963) forms one of the first Quaker statements regarding sexuality, and includes affirmation that gender or sexual orientation are unimportant in a judgement of an intimate relationship and that the true criterion is the presence of agape or 'selfless love' (**religious concept**). Adopting the view later developed by Joseph Fletcher in his ethical theory known as Situation Ethics.

A different Quaker view

However, in 2007, in a message delivered as the devotional by Andrew Kurima, clerk of Uganda Yearly Meeting, he quoted Romans 1:18–32 (**Religious authority – the Bible**), saying that homosexuals and even those who support them are worthy of death. Although in his later letter of apology he said that he was referring to spiritual death.

Key terms

Gay sex = sexual activity between men.

Lesbian sex = sexual activity between women.

Adultery = sexual intercourse between a married person and another person who is not his or her spouse.

Chastity = not having a sexual relationship before marriage or outside marriage.

Absolutist morality = the idea that certain actions are always good or evil regardless of the situation.

Complementarity = the belief that the female and male sex organs are designed to be used together to fulfil their purpose of reproduction.

Grade boost

Remember unless the question specifically states a particular form of sex outside marriage then you can refer to all or one of the following issues: heterosexual sex before marriage, gay or lesbian sex or adultery. Also remember you are attempting a Religious Studies exam and not a General Studies exam. The examiner is expecting to see 'religious' content. Give evidence to support the points you make.

The ethical teaching of one major world religion on sex outside marriage

It is important to note that candidates could approach this question by referring to one or more of the following issues: **sex between unmarried partners**, **gay** and **lesbian sex** or **adultery**.

Sex between unmarried (heterosexual) partners

General principles

Christians believe that marriage is the appropriate relationship for sex, therefore they think that sex outside marriage is harmful. It cannot build the special relationship that marriage can and does not provide a secure situation for a child born outside marriage. It can also lead to sexual disease, unwanted pregnancy and people being used as sex objects, which would be wrong, as every human is created in God's image and therefore deserves to be respected.

Some Christian views

Religious authority: tradition

Christian views on sex have been heavily influenced by the Jewish tradition out of which the religion was born. Christians in general believe that sex is a sacred gift from God only to be used within marriage. Heterosexual sex is seen as having three main purposes: to create children, to bring a married couple together in physical union and to strengthen the bond between them. In modern times it has been recognised that it has a further purpose to create pleasure (although this was condemned by Early Church leaders such as St Augustine as being sinful).

Religious authority: Bible

> *A man will leave his mother and father and be united to his wife, and the two will become one flesh.* Genesis 2v24

This means that a couple should only become 'one flesh', (i.e. have sex) within marriage.

Religious authority: leaders

Jesus re-affirmed the sanctity of sex within marriage in Matthew 19v5 stating that God the Creator (**religious concept**) intended a man and a woman to become 'one flesh'.

St Paul stated in 1 Corinthians 6v18–19:

> *Flee from sexual immorality. All other sins a person commits are outside the body, but whoever sins sexually, sins against their own body. Do you not know that your bodies are temples of the Holy Spirit, who is in you, whom you have received from God?*

St Paul believed that sex outside marriage devalues the sanctity and sacrament of marriage and the marriage vows. It is regarded as a sin. He advocated **chastity** for those who were not married.

Religious authority: rationality – Natural Law

Whilst Natural Law promotes sex for reproduction (a primary precept) this is only within marriage. Sex outside marriage can lead to pregnancy and STIs both of which would break the primary precept of 'an ordered society': pregnancy as it would mean a child not being brought up in a stable environment and STIs as they would cause disruption to society. Sex outside marriage could also lead to abortion, which would break the primary precepts 'to reproduce' and 'to live in an ordered society'.

> Every sexual act must be within the framework of marriage.
>
> Catholic Truth Society (An absolutist morality)

Other Christian views

Religious concepts: Situation Ethics – agape

Situation Ethics, an ethic used by some Christians as it based on Jesus' idea of 'selfless love' (agape), would not condemn sex outside marriage. One of the four working principles within the theory is 'relativism'. This principle rejects ideas such as 'never' or 'always' and considers each situation as unique. Situation Ethics would condemn someone who had sex with a stranger they picked up in a nightclub to fulfil their sexual desires (as this would be the wrong type of love – 'eros' – sexual love or lust). It would not condemn someone who had sex outside marriage as an act of selfless love for their partner. Many Quakers in the UK also adopt this view. For example, they see sex as gift from God and their focus is on the way in which it is used in human relationships. Sex itself is neither good nor bad.

> Sexual activity is essentially neither good nor evil; it is a normal biological activity which, like most other human activities, can be indulged in destructively or creatively.
>
> Towards a Quaker View of Sex (1963)

> No relationship can be a right one which makes use of another person through selfish desire.
>
> Advices (1964)

Gay and lesbian sex

There are varying views within the different Christian denominations about these issues. Even within a denomination such as the Church in Wales there exists a great diversity of opinion.

General principles

As Christians believe that marriage is the appropriate relationship for sex, they think that gay or lesbian sex is harmful. Whilst some Christian denominations do not see homosexual orientation as a sin, they do see homosexual sexual acts as sinful. Homosexual sex cannot take place within the sanctity of marriage as gay/lesbian marriages cannot yet take place within the UK, though there are government proposals (in 2012) to make this legal. Homosexual sex can also lead to sexual disease or people using others as sex objects, which would be wrong as every human is created in God's image and is worthy of respect.

Some Christian views

Religious authority: tradition

Due to the traditional Christian view that heterosexual sex within marriage is the 'norm' many Christians see both gay and lesbian sex as a sin.

Religious authority: Bible

Many Christians believe the main purpose of sex is to create children and to bring those in marriage together in a physical union. So, homosexual sex is a sin as it cannot take place within marriage or create a child.

> *So God created mankind in his own image, in the image of God he created them;*
> *male and female he created them. God blessed them and said to them, 'Be fruitful*
> *and increase in number' …* Genesis 1v27–28
>
> *For this reason a man will leave his father and mother and be united to his wife,*
> *and they will become one flesh.* Genesis 2v24

Other passages which condemn homosexual sex include:

> *You shall not lie with man as you would with a woman: it is an abomination.* Leviticus 18v22

Romans 1v24–27 talks about people engaged in homosexual and lesbian sex receiving 'due penalty' or punishment for their sins.

Religious authority: leaders

Jesus made no specific pronouncement about gay or lesbian sex, but he reaffirmed the sanctity of sex within heterosexual marriage in Matthew 19v5 stating that **God the Creator (religious concept)** intended a man and a woman to become 'one flesh' – which many would say is what he considered to be the 'norm'.

St Paul states in 1 Corinthians 6v9:

> *Or do you not know that wrongdoers will not inherit the kingdom of God? Do not be deceived:*
> *neither the sexually immoral nor idolaters nor adulterers nor men who have sex with men.*

Religious authority: rationality – Natural Law

According to Natural Law all homosexual sex is wrong as the main purpose of sex is to create children (a primary precept) and there is no possibility of such acts creating children. Natural Law is an absolutist morality and therefore its views on homosexuality will never change.

> *Tradition has always declared that 'homosexual acts are intrinsically*
> *disordered'. They are contrary to the natural law. They close the sexual act*
> *to the gift of life … under no circumstances can they be approved.*
>
> *Catechism of the Roman Catholic Church* 1994

Aquinas' Natural Law theory allows or condemns actions depending on whether they fulfil their purpose. Sex that doesn't involve procreation (a primary precept) is unnatural and wrong. The Roman Catholic Church maintains that homosexual acts don't proceed from a genuine affective and sexual complementarity.

Other Christian views

Religious concepts: Situation Ethics – agape

Situation Ethics, an ethic used by some Christians as it based on Jesus' idea of 'selfless love' (agape), would not condemn sex outside marriage. One of the four working principles within the theory is 'relativism'. This principle rejects ideas such as 'never' or 'always' and considers each situation as unique. Quakers in the UK also adopt this view. For example, they see sex as gift from God and their focus is on the way in which it is used in human relationships. Gay or lesbian sex itself is neither good nor bad.

> *Sexual activity is essentially neither good nor evil, it is a normal biological activity which, like most other human activities, can be indulged in destructively or creatively.*
>
> *Towards a Quaker view of sex, 1963*

> *No relationship can be a right one which makes use of another person through selfish desire.*
>
> *Advices, 1964*

Gareth Moore, in his book *The Body in Context: Sex and Catholicism* (1992), says that while Christians are happy to follow the law set out in Leviticus, which says that it's immoral for a man to lie with a man, they do not follow the requirement in Leviticus 19:19 that forbids the wearing of garments made of two kinds of material. He argues that we are simply selecting passages that attack minorities that we don't like (Moore, *The Body in Context: Sex and Catholicism* 1992, pp. 184–186).

Rev. Peter J. Gomes, the former Plummer Professor of Christian Morals at Harvard, stated in his book *The Good Book: Reading the Bible With Mind and Heart,* HarperCollins (1996),

> *The biblical writers never contemplated a form of homosexuality in which loving, monogamous and faithful persons sought to live out the implications of the Gospel with as much fidelity to it as any heterosexual believer.*

He meant that the forms of homosexuality that the New Testament writers were condemning were forms of prostitution or perversion and not Christian, committed and loving relationships.

Adultery

General principles

Adultery can lead to a breakdown in trust in a relationship and ultimately to divorce. It can also lead to the breakup of the family unit and this in turn has a negative effect on society. University of Utah researcher Nicholas H. Wolfinger, in his book *Understanding the Divorce Cycle: The Children of Divorce in Their Own Marriages* (Cambridge University Press, 2005) suggested that those who come from a family where the parents have been divorced are more likely to get divorced themselves. He gave the following information — if one spouse comes from divorced parents, the couple may be up to twice as likely to divorce. Spouses who are both children of divorced parents are three times more likely to divorce as couples who both come from intact families. His research was based on the American National Survey of Families and Households, which included detailed information on family background for 13,000 people, and the General Social Survey, which surveyed 20,000 people over a 30-year period.

Some Christian views

Religious authority: tradition

Many Christian denominations see marriage as a sacrament. It is divinely ordained by God, and adultery breaks this sacrament. Adultery is against the moral law of all the major world religions because it breaks the marriage vows, which include the promise to stay faithful until death, and it is a sign of promiscuity and lust.

Religious authority: Bible

Adultery is condemned several times in the Bible. For example,

If a man is found sleeping with another man's wife, both the man who slept with her and the woman must die. You must purge the evil from Israel.

Deuteronomy 22v22

It is also condemned in the Ten Commandments:

You shall not commit adultery

Exodus 20v14

Religious authority: leaders
Jesus stated:

*You have heard that it was said, 'You shall not commit adultery.'
But I tell you that anyone who looks at a woman lustfully has already committed adultery with her in his heart.*

Matthew 5v28

He condemned not only the act of adultery but even lustful thoughts towards others. He also stated that adultery was grounds for divorce:

Moses permitted you to divorce your wives because your hearts were hard. But it was not this way from the beginning. I tell you that anyone who divorces his wife, except for sexual immorality, and marries another woman commits adultery.

Matthew 19v8–9

St Paul stated:

Or do you not know that wrongdoers will not inherit the kingdom of God? Do not be deceived: Neither the sexually immoral nor idolaters nor adulterers nor men who have sex with men.

Corinthians 1v9

Religious authority: rationality – Natural Law
Natural Law condemns adultery. One of the five primary precepts of Natural Law is that humans should aim to live 'in an ordered society'. Catholics would argue that adultery could lead to divorce and this in turn leads to the breakdown of the family unit and in turn to the breakdown of an ordered society. One could also argue that adultery breaks the 'To learn/educate children' precept as it sets a bad example for future generations.

Other Christian views

Religious concepts: Situation Ethics – agape
Situation Ethics, an ethic used by some Christians as it based on Jesus' idea of 'selfless love' (agape) would not condemn adultery outright. One of the four working principles within the theory is 'relativism'. This principle rejects ideas such as 'never' or 'always' and considers each situation as unique.

Joseph Fletcher gave an example of when adultery would be acceptable in his book *Situation Ethics – A New Morality* (1966).

A German woman called Mrs Bergmeier was separated from her family at the Battle of the Bulge and she was imprisoned in the Ukraine. There were only two reasons the Russians would release her: 1) severe medical treatment or 2) pregnancy. She slept with a Russian soldier in order to become pregnant. She became pregnant, was released and united with her family. Fletcher claimed that this was a loving act, the religious law against adultery being overridden by the fact that she acted out of selfless love for her family.

 **quickfire**

④ What are four of the main purposes of sex for Christians?

⑤ When condemning sex outside marriage how did St Paul describe the human body?

⑥ Quakers do not define sex outside marriage as wrong, but state that the rightness or wrongness of each act depends on what?

⑦ Traditionally why have Christians condemned gay or lesbian sex?

⑧ What does Leviticus 18v22 say about gay sex?

⑨ What point did the Rev. Peter J. Gomes make about the Bible's condemnation of gay sex?

⑩ What does Deuteronomy 22v22 say about adultery?

⑪ Jesus did not only condemn the act of adultery. What else did he condemn?

⑫ What two primary precepts does adultery break?

Marriage: the purposes of marriage and sex within marriage

General principles

Marriage provides the basis for a '**nuclear**' **family** which consists of a father, a mother and children. This in turn provides the basic building blocks of a society. It is within the family unit that children learn to become good citizens, develop their sense of morality and where they learn about the importance of relationships. Sex within marriage provides an outlet for sexual desire, helps the couple develop their relationship, prevents unwanted pregnancies, abortions and stops the spread of STIs.

Religious tradition

In Christianity marriage is seen as part of God's intended design and **purpose**. Marriage has several purposes including:

- To provide a relationship between the married couple that reflects God's relationship with humanity (Ephesians 5);
- To creates a loving, spiritual bond between a man and a woman (Genesis 2);
- To create a life-long commitment between one man and one woman (Matthew 19);
- To create a new stable social unit in which children may be nurtured (Ephesians 6).

Sex within marriage also has several purposes including:

- To express faithful intimacy to one's partner (1 Corinthians 6);
- To provide an outlet for sexual desire which when fulfilled will allow the couple to focus on their spiritual duties (1 Corinthians 7);
- To create a physical bond between a couple (Genesis 1);
- To fulfil God's command to reproduce (Genesis 1).

Religious authority: teachings

These beliefs are reflected in Christian teachings, e.g. the Presbyterian Church of Wales states in its *Handbook of Order and Rules January 2010*:

Marriage is a holy estate instituted by God. It is based on natural tendencies and needs, and it is an expression of the Divine intention in our creation, to realise moral and spiritual ends.

In the Church of England's *Marriage: A teaching document* (1999) it states,

Marriage is a pattern that God has given in creation, deeply rooted in our social instincts, through which a man and a woman may learn love together over the course of their lives .... Sexual intercourse, as an expression of faithful intimacy, properly belongs within marriage exclusively ...

Key terms

'**Nuclear**' **family** = a traditional family unit, which includes a father, a mother and children.

Marriage = the formal and legal union of a man and a woman by which they become husband and wife.

Purpose = the reason for something's existence.

Grade boost

Support the points you are attempting to make with evidence. Do not simply 'list' what happens in a Christian wedding. You can, however, select relevant parts of the service to support the points you are trying to make. For example, the vow 'as long as we both shall live' reflects the traditional teaching of the Church that marriage should be a lifelong commitment.

For example, in the Church in Wales marriage service you have the taking of vows (i.e., 'as long as we both shall live' – promising to be faithful), the giving of rings (a symbol of eternal love) and the proclamation (the creation of a spiritual bond declared by the priest). Many Christian churches (e.g., Roman Catholic, Anglican, Orthodox, etc.) regard marriage as a sacrament.

Religious authority: Bible

In Genesis 2v24 it states:

> *For this reason a man will leave his father and mother and be united to his wife, and they will become one flesh.*

This implies that it was **God the Creator's (religious concept)** plan for every man and woman to marry and then begin a sexual relationship.

Religious authority: religious leaders

Jesus also expressed the belief given in Genesis 2v24 that heterosexual marriage is part of God's intended design and purpose (Matthew 19v4–6).

St Paul stated that Christian marriage stresses that each spouse's body belongs to the other spouse and to them both jointly (1 Corinthians 7v4). He believed our body is a gift given to us by God – sex within marriage allows us to express God's love for others.

Religious authority: rationality – Natural Law

Marriage and sex within marriage fulfils four of five primary precepts:

To worship God: humans are worshipping God by fulfilling his commands in the Bible to marry.

To reproduce: one of the main purposes of marriage.

To live in an ordered society: having children within marriage creates a family unit, which provides order for society.

To learn: as a family unit provides children with an environment in which they can learn to become good citizens, develop their sense of morality and where they learn about the importance of relationships.

quickfire

⑬ Give two of the main purposes of marriage.

⑭ Give two of the main purposes of sex within marriage.

⑮ Give one example of how a Christian marriage service reflects Christian teaching on marriage.

⑯ What did Jesus say about marriage?

⑰ Give one example of how marriage and sex within marriage fulfil the precepts of Natural Law.

Gay and lesbian marriage and civil partnerships

General principles

It is important to note that the views of individuals and the collective stance of the Churches they belong to on these issues are not necessarily the same.

Civil partnerships and **gay/lesbian marriages** are not supported by some Christians because they believe they cannot fulfil one of the main purposes of a marriage which is reproduction. They also cannot provide a traditional 'nuclear' family unit, which many argue is the basis of society. However, other Christians would argue that reproduction is only one of the purposes of marriage and that other purposes (such as creating a loving bond between two people) can be fulfilled within a civil partnership or gay/lesbian marriage. They may also argue that a gay or lesbian partnership/marriage may actually provide a more loving/ stable environment for children than some heterosexual marriages.

Some Christians are more supportive of civil partnerships than the notion of gay/lesbian marriage for a number of reason including:

- A same sex couple living in civil partnership are not necessarily involved in a sexual relationship and so their relationship may not be contrary to the teachings of the Church.
- For many Christians, marriage by definition can only take place between a man and a woman. They would argue that there is biblical evidence to support this, e.g. Matthew 19v4–6.

Christian views of same-sex marriage and civil partnerships

Diversity exists within Christianity and even within denominations on these issues.

Some Christian views

Religious authority: traditional teachings

Generally, Christians traditionally see marriage as a sacred event which should only take place between a man and a woman.

For **Roman Catholics**, marriage only between a baptised man and woman is considered to be a sacrament. This means it is a visible sign of the grace that God gives them to help them live their lives here and now so as to be able to join him in eternity.

The **Church of England** through the House of Bishops issued a pastoral statement on Civil Partnerships in 2005, in which it stated:

> *Marriage, defined as a faithful, committed, permanent and legally sanctioned relationship between a man and a woman, is central to the stability and health of human society.*

Key terms

Civil partnerships = since December 2005 same-sex couples have had the ability to legally register their relationship as civil partners of each other. This allows them to have equal treatment to married couples in a wide range of legal matters, including taxation and nationality.

Gay/lesbian marriage = the formal and legal union of persons of the same sex.

Grade boost

Where available try to show the diversity that exists within the religion you have studied. Do not stereotype religious believers, e.g. by claiming that all Christians oppose civil partnerships or gay/lesbian marriage, or that all Quakers support civil partnerships or gay/lesbian marriage. Support the points you are attempting to make with evidence.

quickfire

⑱ Give one reason why some Christians are opposed to gay/lesbian marriages or civil partnerships.

⑲ Give one reason why other Christians support gay/lesbian marriage or civil partnerships.

⑳ Can you name two denominations which have supported the introduction of civil partnerships?

The statement did go on to recognise that civil partnerships in themselves may not be contrary to the teachings of the Church provided there is no sexual relationship between the couple within the partnership. The statement also said that clergy of the Church of England should not provide services of blessing for those who register a civil partnership. Some clergy have, however, openly defied this order and carried out blessing of civil partnerships within a church.

Similarly the Bishops of the Church in Wales agreed the following regarding civil partnerships in 'Civil Partnerships – December 2005, Revised March 2012':

> The Civil Partnership Act came into force in December 2005. As a result, two people of the same sex are able to acquire a new legal status by registering a civil partnership …. The Bishops of the Church in Wales cannot and do not wish to prevent what the law allows for Church members, both lay and clerical. The legislation leaves entirely open the nature of the commitment that members of a couple might choose to make to each other when forming a civil partnership, and is not predicated on the intention to engage in a sexual relationship. … In December 2011, provision was made for civil partnerships to be registered in religious premises if the denomination wishes to allow it. … Until such time as the Governing Body of the Church in Wales permits the use of Church in Wales buildings for such purposes, it is not possible for individual parochial church councils to apply to local authorities for authorisation for Church in Wales buildings to be used in this way.

The Bishops of the Church in Wales also agreed the following statement on marriage between same-sex couples in March 2012:

> We abide by the Christian doctrine of marriage as the union of one man with one woman freely entered into for life. We acknowledge that whilst issues of human sexuality are not resolved, there are couples living in other life-long committed relationships who deserve the welcome, pastoral care and support of the Church. We are committed to further listening, prayerful reflection and discernment regarding same-sex relationships.

Religious authority: the Bible

In Genesis 2v24 it states: '*For this reason a man will leave his father and mother and be united to his wife, and they will become one flesh.*' This implies that it was **God the Creator's (religious concept)** plan for every man and woman to marry and then begin a sexual relationship. There are no passages in the Bible which condone gay/lesbian marriage or civil partnerships.

Religious authority: leaders

Although there are no direct quotes from Jesus on this matter, some Christians would claim that Jesus spoke out clearly in favour of heterosexual marriage. **Jesus** re-affirmed the sanctity of heterosexual marriage in Matthew 19 stating that **God the Creator (religious concept)** intended a man and a woman to become 'one flesh'. This teaching implies that this is the 'norm' and gay/lesbian marriage or civil partnerships go against this teaching.

In January 2012, **Dr John Sentamu the Archbishop of York** (Church of England), speaking to the *Daily Telegraph* said:

> *Marriage is a relationship between a man and a woman, I don't think it is the role of the state to define what marriage is. It is set in tradition and history and you can't just [change it] overnight, no matter how powerful you are.*

The Archbishop of Wales, Dr Barry Morgan, however, stated in his presidential address to members of the Church in Wales' Governing Body in April 2012,

> *If the legislation to allow civil marriage is passed, I cannot see how we as a church, will be able to ignore the legality of the status of such partnerships and we ought not to want to do so.*

Religious authority: rationality – Natural Law

Natural Law would oppose gay/lesbian marriage and civil partnerships. Natural Law promotes heterosexual marriage and sex within marriage for reproduction (a primary precept). Failing to create a traditional 'nuclear' family would also lead to a disordered society and therefore break another primary precept – an ordered society.

Other Christian views

Situation Ethics, an ethical system used by some Christians as it is based on Jesus' idea of 'selfless love' (agape), would not condemn civil partnerships or gay/lesbian marriage outright. One of the four working principles within the theory is 'relativism'. This principle rejects ideas such as 'never' or 'always' and considers each situation as unique.

The views of Quakers toward civil partnerships and gay/lesbian marriage range from complete acceptance and celebration of same-sex marriage, to the view that homosexuality is abhorrent and sinful.

In a number of British meetings since 1994 there have been celebrations of same-sex relationships through an official meeting for commitment – a public act of worship something very like the traditional Quaker wedding. British Quakers also supported the introduction of the legal status of 'civil partnership' in the UK, and there is currently debate whether they should press for the legal right to put spiritual and legal union together as is the case for marriage. A report from the central body Quaker Life, found that nearly all meetings supported in principle celebration of same-sex commitments, and that a majority would support the legalisation of gay marriage.

The Methodist Church has stated in its document 'The Methodist Church Response to the consultation on Civil Partnerships on religious premises' (2011), '*The Methodist Conference has confirmed that, whilst there is no reason a Methodist cannot enter into a Civil Partnership, Methodist premises may not be used for blessing Civil Partnerships.*'

In July 2012, the United Reformed Church passed a resolution at its General Assembly allowing same-sex civil partnerships on its premises. It has also stated that it will conduct gay/lesbian marriages when it is legally allowed to do so. This view is also supported by many Unitarians.

Key terms

Adequate = satisfactory for a particular purpose.

Relativistic = this means there are no universal moral norms or rules and that each situation has to be looked at independently because each situation is different.

Secular = not having any connection with religion.

Unfair = not just or fair.

Grade boost

Read the question carefully. It is the QUALITY of your arguments that will help you to achieve the higher levels and not the QUANTITY of your arguments. Don't forget what is being assessed in the AO2 type questions is your ability to evaluate and analyse.

Evaluative issues

Many candidates make common errors when addressing the AO2 type questions on Applied Ethics. They make three main errors which are:

- They stereotype religious believers, e.g. claiming that all Protestants are 'liberal' thinkers.
- They simply 'list' points that agree or disagree with the statement with little or no evaluation or analysis (which is what is being assessed here).
- They fail to give a conclusion.

It is not possible to apply the various types of AO2 questions to all the issues identified in the Applied Ethics AO1 section (sexual orientation, sex outside marriage and marriage) in this revision material, but some examples have been given here. The arguments given are not an exhaustive list and any relevant arguments will be credited. Some of the same arguments can be used to answer different questions, but you need to select these arguments carefully.

1: 'In today's society religious responses to sex outside marriage are no longer adequate.' Assess this view

You should try to consider each of the following points when developing your arguments and a conclusion:

- Have you supported your arguments using reasoning and/or evidence?
- Is the point raised strong/convincing?
- Does this response dispose of the argument?
- Is the issue evenly balanced, or is there one view which is clearly more convincing/correct or proven?

Agree

- Four out of ten children are now born out of wedlock. **It does appear therefore that people no longer believe that sex should only take place within marriage or that marriage is the only environment in which to raise a child.** Many believe that cohabitation can provide a stable relationship both for sex and for children. As Andrew Goddard states in his book *A Pocket Guide to Ethical Issues*, '*It is important to realise that our culture's attitudes and practices in relation to sex and marriage have significantly changed in the course of a few generations.*'

- **A relativistic approach to sex outside marriage is adopted by some within society as they oppose the absolutist stance taken by some religious theories such as Natural Law and prefer to judge each situation independently.** Joseph Fletcher illustrated this point with his example of sacrificial adultery (Mrs Bergmeier). Many people would also see sex as being an acceptable expression of love for their partner.

- **A Utilitarian would also argue that any form of sex is acceptable provided it is in private, does not harm others and increases the participants' happiness and it should therefore be allowed.** People no longer see most forms of sex outside of marriage as wrong because they see sex simply 'for pleasure' as acceptable. This is in contrast to St Augustine's view that sex was an 'evil' which could only be acceptable if performed with the intention of creating offspring.

- **Since the 1960s the widespread use of contraception has taken away the fear of conception. Many people are also no longer afraid of others knowing they are in a sexual relationship outside of marriage (unless it is an adulterous one?) as much of society now accepts this as the norm.** As Andrew Goddard stated in his book *A Pocket Guide to Ethical Issues*, a 2005 UK study of 'lust' reported that ' ... *whereas in the 1950s 53% of women and 20% of men were married or engaged before having sexual intercourse, by the 1990s this had fallen to less than 1% for both men and women.*'

Disagree

- **Ensuring that sex only takes places within marriage usually means that any children created are brought up in a stable environment** whereas when sex takes place between unmarried partners many argue that this is less likely. This argument was supported by the UK government's Social Justice Strategy paper 2012, which stated that one in three cohabiting couples separate before a child's fifth birthday, compared with a figure of around one in ten married parents.

- **Some believers would argue that their responses to sex outside marriage are adequate. They would argue that sexual promiscuity outside of marriage in the last 50 years or so has had a direct negative effect on the traditional family unit and society in general** – STDs, rise in abortions, divorce due to adultery, etc. In March 2012, Pope Benedict XVI told a group of US bishops at the Vatican that '*It is in fact increasingly evident that a weakened appreciation of the indissolubility of the marriage covenant, and the widespread rejection of a responsible, mature sexual ethic grounded in the practice of chastity, have led to grave societal problems bearing an immense human and economic cost.*' (*Catholic Herald*)

- Peter Vardy in his book *The Puzzle of Sex*, states that those who have sex outside marriage simply for pleasure are '*effectively denying their intrinsic worth and treating each other (and allowing themselves to be treated) merely as an object, even if they are unaware of it at the time.... Religious people claim that they are persons of fundamental worth before God.*' **Waiting until you are married to have sex not only shows the level of commitment you are making to your marriage partner, but also that you recognise their intrinsic worth.** This idea is supported by 1 Corinthians 6v19–20.

- **Many religious believers prefer the prescriptive, absolutist/deontological approach to ethics (which comes from following a religion) to the relativistic approach, as they have clear-cut teachings to follow about sex with an unmarried partner.** They believe these teachings come from God, e.g. Matthew 19v4–6.

2: 'In today's society a relativistic approach should be adopted towards the issues of gay/lesbian marriage and civil partnerships.' Assess this view

You should try to consider each of the following points when developing your arguments and a conclusion:
- Have you supported your arguments using reasoning and/or evidence?
- Is the point raised strong/convincing?
- Does this response dispose of the argument?
- Is the issue evenly balanced, or is there one view which is clearly more convincing/correct or proven?

Agree

- **Today's 'relativistic' society is more accepting of these partnerships, and religious views are increasingly seen as out-of-date**. As Peter Vardy states in his book the *The Puzzle of Sex*, '*The Bible portrays homosexuality as a freely chosen activity – there is no suggestion of the idea that inclination towards a member of the same sex may be a matter of genetics or background or the nature of the individual concerned….The lack of awareness of modern knowledge about sexuality radically undermines the usefulness of the biblical material as a guide to conduct today.*' There appears to be evidence of homosexuality in other species so it is perfectly acceptable for such unions to be recognised by the law and by religions. **Also many people in today's society are atheists so a more relativistic approach to this issue based on love (Joseph Fletcher's Situation Ethics) or happiness (Bentham's Act Utilitarianism) is becoming more widely accepted.**

- **Religious views have generally failed to consider the situation the gay/lesbian couple find themselves in**, e.g. they may be in a long-term, loving relationships and wish to make a greater commitment. Adopting a relativistic approach to gay/lesbian marriage would allow people to consider the situation they are in.

- **A relativistic approach gives the individual the right to decide for themselves whether gay/lesbian marriage is right or wrong for them** based on their situation they find themselves in.

Disagree

- **Religious believers may argue that the moral chaos prevalent in society is caused by people abandoning traditional religious views and adopting a relativistic approach**. At present such unions are 'fashionable', but who knows if they will be in 20 years' time? Cardinal Ratzinger (now Pope Benedict) in April 2005 stated, '*We are moving towards a dictatorship of relativism which does not recognise anything as for certain and which has as its highest goal one's own ego and one's own desires … . Being an "Adult" means having a faith which does not follow the waves of today's fashions or the latest novelties.*'

- **There are still many religious believers in the world today who claim that religious views on this subject are still valid and relevant even if they are not fashionable**. For example, those who follow Natural Law would say that such unions are sinful and go against God's will. In March 2012, Pope Benedict XVI told a group of US bishops at the Vatican that he was aware of '*the powerful political and cultural currents seeking to alter the legal definition of marriage*' so that it would include same-sex couples. '*The Church's conscientious effort to resist this pressure calls for a reasoned defence of marriage as a natural institution … [which is] rooted in the complementarity of the sexes and oriented to procreation*', he said. '*Sexual differences cannot be dismissed as irrelevant to the definition of marriage*', the Pope said.

- **Religious believers would argue a relativistic approach could be corrupted by our selfishness**. Our views are flawed by our sinful nature. God (our Creator) should be the ultimate source of moral authority on such issues and not humankind. Several sacred texts state that 'marriage' should between a man and a woman, e.g. Matthew 19v4–6.

3: 'The move away from a traditional religious view that marriage is the ideal setting for a relationship is not harmful to society.' Assess this view

You should try to consider each of the following points when developing your arguments and a conclusion:

- Have you supported your arguments using reasoning and/or evidence?
- Is the point raised strong/convincing?
- Does this response dispose of the argument?
- Is the issue evenly balanced, or is there one view which is clearly more convincing/correct or proven?

Agree

- **The move away from traditional religious views towards marriage has been beneficial, some would claim, as it has allowed for the introduction of civil partnerships for gay and lesbian couples in 2005 and the possible introduction of gay/lesbian marriage in the UK in the near future.** People are no longer forced to comply with the traditional 'norm' within society of heterosexual marriage. As Sarah K. Tyler and Gordon Reid state in their book *Advanced Religious Studies (Second edition)*, the Civil Partnership act allowed '....same-sex couples to register their partnership legally in a civil ceremony. Civil Partnerships give to the partners the same legal rights as married couples over such matters as property, inheritance tax and pension benefits.'

- **Many of the population do not feel that not getting married is harmful to society as there is little difference or benefit socially or financially between living together and being married.** In fact it might be economically beneficial to cohabit rather than marry. As Andrew Goddard stated in his book *A Pocket Guide to Ethical Issues*, 'There are often very practical reasons for cohabitation, in particular the social and financial costs of developing a loving relationships whilst living apart and the costs of a wedding (the average cost of a wedding in the UK is now about £17,500).'

- **Some may argue that there is little evidence to suggest that cohabitation or a single lifestyle is damaging to society. In fact cohabitation may be beneficial as the couple get to know each other before making such a commitment.** Adrian Thatcher in his book *Living Together and Christian Ethics* (2002) claims that based on research in the UK more enter marriage from cohabitation than from a single state.

- **Many would argue that the move away from 'marriage as the ideal' is beneficial for society as it allows individuals the freedom to cohabit or to live a single lifestyle.** As Andrew Goddard stated in his book *A Pocket Guide to Ethical Issues*, 'Personal factors are also of vital importance as people make decisions, aware of their own situations and desire for well-being.'

Disagree

- **Some religious believers would argue that the move away from a traditional religious view that marriage is the ideal setting for a relationship is harmful, as marriage is seen as part of God's intended design (e.g., in Genesis) for humans.** As the Church in Wales' marriage service (2010) states 'Marriage is a way of life made holy by God, and blessed by the presence of Jesus in the marriage at Cana in Galilee, which all should uphold and honour.'

- **Some religious believers would argue that the move away from a traditional religious view that marriage is the ideal setting for a relationship is harmful because marriage publicly affirms the importance of love and provides the best option for couples to grow together in mutual support.** Also the decreasing popularity of marriage, some would argue, demonstrates a lack of lifetime commitment by partners. On its website the Church in Wales states that 'God not only loves us, but he promises he will always love us. Marriage is meant to be a reflection of that and is based on promises between a man and a woman – of lifelong commitment in love and faithfulness.'

- **The Centre for Policy Studies claims that there are strong links between marriage and family stability (2010) and that, although cohabitation is increasingly common, it is often short-lived. This leads to more family break-ups, which is bad for children and society.** Also the UK government's Social Justice Strategy paper 2012, stated that one in three cohabiting couples separate before a child's fifth birthday, compared with a figure of around one in ten married parents.

- **The Pope argues that the move away from a traditional religious view that marriage is the ideal setting for a relationship is harmful.** In March 2012, Pope Benedict XVI told a group of US bishops at the Vatican that 'It is in fact increasingly evident that a weakened appreciation of the indissolubility of the marriage covenant, and the widespread rejection of a responsible, mature sexual ethic grounded in the practice of chastity, have led to grave societal problems bearing an immense human and economic cost.' (Catholic Herald)

4: 'Traditional religious attitudes towards adultery are unfair.' Assess this view.

You should try to consider each of the following points when developing your arguments and a conclusion:
- Have you supported your arguments using reasoning and/or evidence?
- Is the point raised strong/convincing?
- Does this response dispose of the argument?
- Is the issue evenly balanced, or is there one view which is clearly more convincing/correct or proven?

Agree

- **Deontological religious principles are unfair as they fail to consider the consequences of not allowing adultery.** A Utilitarian, for example, would argue that provided the adultery is in private, does not harm others and increases the participants' happiness then it should be allowed. In the film *Indecent Proposal*, for example, a rich man offers a young man $1,000,000 to sleep with his beautiful wife. As long as all parties consented and the other conditions given above are met then a Utilitarian would claim that this act would lead to the 'greatest happiness for the greatest number'.

- **Absolutist religious principles fail to consider the situation that those who commit adultery may be in**, e.g. their marriage partner may be abusing them. Joseph Fletcher illustrated this point with his example of sacrificial adultery (Mrs Bergmeier). She committed adultery as a selfless act in order to be released from her prison camp.

- **Religious attitudes towards adultery are unfair because they fail to take into account the root cause of the adultery.** For example, the Catholic psychiatrist Jack Dominion stated in his book *The Church and the Sexual Revolution*, that '*Adultery can now be seen as a symptom in a marriage when the minimum needs of one or two people are not being met. This concept of the minimum needs evokes deep opposition from those who think only in terms of an abstract concept of the common good and ignore the reality of individual needs ... adultery is a cry for help arising from the depths of a tottering relationship. Adultery is either a cry for help or the sign of the death or non-existence of a relationship. Its significance has little to do with the enjoyment of an illicit pleasure outside the matrimonial bond ... the Christian response to adultery must be ... to examine the quality of a marriage: to find out whether a marriage really exists or not and if it does, however minimally, to help the couple in every way to restore their marital relationship.*' The traditional religious view of condemnation must be considered to be unfair therefore and be replaced with one of support.

- **Atheists would argue that religious views on adultery should not be applied to a mainly secular society.** Richard Dawkins in an article entitled '*Banishing the Green-Eyed Monster*' published in 2007, said that traditional religious attitudes towards adultery are unfair, '*what, actually, is wrong with loving more than one person? Why should you deny your loved one the pleasure of sexual encounters with others, if he or she is that way inclined? ... is it so very obvious that you can't love more than one person? ... why is erotic love the one exception that everybody instantly acknowledges without even thinking about it? Why can a woman not love two men at the same time, in their different ways? And why should the two – or their wives – begrudge her this?*'

Disagree

- **Deontological religious principles such as 'do not commit adultery' (Exodus 20v14) provide fair, clear-cut and God-given guidance on what is permissible or not for a religious believer.** God (our Creator) should be the ultimate source of moral authority on such issues and not humankind.

- **When they marry, partners make these vows to each other and before God, if they do not intend to keep these vows then they should not make such a commitment.** For example, when a couple get married in a Church in Wales' marriage service, they say: '*N, will you take N to be your wife? Will you love her, comfort her, honour and care for her, and, forsaking all others, be faithful to her as long as you both shall live?*'

- **Religious attitudes towards adultery are not unfair because marriage for many world religions is seen as part of God's intended design (e.g., in Genesis), with a divinely ordained purpose. Adultery is therefore a sin.** As Proverbs 6v32 states '*But a man who commits adultery has no sense; whoever does so destroys himself.*'

- **Marriage is a unique and exclusive bond by which a man and a woman unite themselves in love. It also creates a new social unit in which children may be nurtured. Adultery breaks this bond and could harm any children within the family unit.** Jesus stated that adultery was the only grounds for divorce – '*Moses permitted you to divorce your wives because your hearts were hard. But it was not this way from the beginning. I tell you that anyone who divorces his wife, except for sexual immorality, and marries another woman commits adultery.*' Matthew 19v8

Summary: Applied Ethics

We have identified the key points on the WJEC AS specification in the revision checklist and within the information in this chapter. In the diagram below you will find a suggested structure for answering an Applied Ethics question in the exam. You may want to fill in further details to elaborate and personalise this content by applying it to the various elements within the three areas identified – sexual orientation, sex outside marriage and marriage.

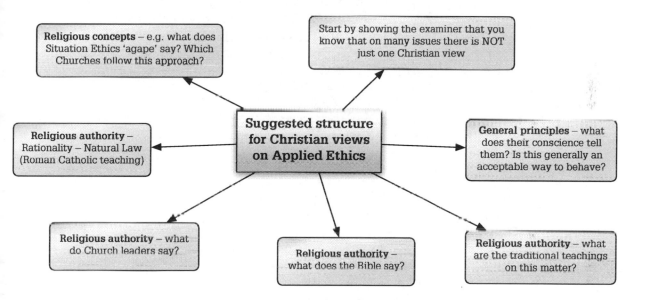

Religious concepts – e.g. what does Situation Ethics 'agape' say? Which Churches follow this approach?

Start by showing the examiner that you know that on many issues there is NOT just one Christian view

Religious authority – Rationality – Natural Law (Roman Catholic teaching)

Suggested structure for Christian views on Applied Ethics

General principles – what does their conscience tell them? Is this generally an acceptable way to behave?

Religious authority – what do Church leaders say?

Religious authority – what does the Bible say?

Religious authority – what are the traditional teachings on this matter?

Exam Practice and Technique

Exam practice and skills

How exam questions are set

WJEC AS Religious Studies aims to help students to:

- Acquire knowledge and understanding of the key concepts (for example, religious beliefs, teachings, doctrines, principles, ideas and theories), including how these are expressed in texts, writings and/or other forms and practices.

- Acquire knowledge and understanding of major issues and questions (for example, issues of commonality and diversity, the role of dialogue, methods of study, and relevance to contemporary society).

- Acquire knowledge and understanding of the contribution of significant people, traditions or movements.

- Acquire knowledge and understanding of religious language and terminology and to be able to use appropriate language and terminology in context.

- Acquire knowledge and understanding of the relationship between the area(s) of study and other aspects of human experience.

- Make connections between areas of study and in so doing develop a clearer understanding of the phenomena of religion.

- Acquire the ability to demonstrate higher order skills of analysis and evaluation in religious philosophical and ethical debates using reference to a range of ideas and concepts to argue a variety of standpoints.

Examination questions are written well in advance of the examination. They are written by the Principal Examiner responsible for the unit. A highly skilled academic then offers comments on the original submission for the principal to consider. Following this a committee of experienced examiners and teacher representatives discuss the quality of every question and changes are made to the questions until the committee agree that they are appropriate. The questions are written to reflect the substantive content and the success criteria as outlined in the specification.

How exam answers are marked

It is really important that candidates read the question carefully and interpret the specific demands of each question and produce relevant responses. It is not in the best interests of the examiners or candidates for questions to be unclear. In order to support candidates the WJEC has produced a list of 'trigger' words which are used to form part of each question. The 'trigger' words can be found on pages 92 and 93 of the Teachers Guidance 2009–2010 pdf file which can be downloaded from the WJEC AS RS section of the WJEC website: www.wjec.org.uk

- **Assessment Objective 1 (AO1) 60 out of 90 marks in an AS Module**

This is knowledge and understanding and it counts for 2/3 of the marks at AS.

Knowledge

You should be able to write accurately about something you know from your study of your chosen AS Religious Studies modules. You should be able to demonstrate knowledge of the topic required and select appropriate material to answer the question. You should be aware that only about half the AO1 marks in the examination are for factual knowledge, the rest are for understanding.

Understanding

It is important NOT to learn by rote and instead you should aim to achieve a deeper understanding of your chosen course(s). This should be demonstrated by clearly focussing your answer on the question being asked. Answers should also demonstrate an appropriate use of terminology. The use of evidence to support a particular point is an important feature of the success criteria and demonstrates clear understanding.

Grade boost AO1

Good candidates demonstrate four main characteristics in their AO1 essays:

1. Accuracy of information – facts, quotes from texts or scholars and relevancy of the response to the question set.

2. A concise introduction – avoiding regurgitating detailed background or irrelevant material.

3. Clarity in language, in structure (paragraphing – one point which is illustrated, elaborated or analysed) and in logical order.

4. Depth – demonstrated by relevant examples, scholarly references and clear explanation of the issue(s) covered.

Assessment Objective 2 (AO2) 30 out of 90 marks in an AS Module

This is analysis and evaluation and it counts for 1/3 of the marks at AS. Analysis and evaluation are often referred to as higher order skills, as they are deemed to be more sophisticated that the AO1 skills.

Analysis

Analysis is explaining in detail what something means or what a piece of evidence shows. Analysis also includes the ability to demonstrate your understanding by making connections between lines of debate and/or evidence and the question being asked. When you link your explanation to the question, you will achieve marks for analysis.

Evaluation

This is often regarded as the most demanding of the skills When you can demonstrate your understanding of the issue(s) and point out the strengths or weaknesses of an argument or piece of evidence, you will achieve marks for your evaluation.

Grade boost – AO2

Good candidates are expected to present more than one side of an issue and offer arguments for and against the issue. They often make good use of evidence, example and reasoning. They conclude with a critical analysis of both sides and a balanced and reasoned conclusion.

Exam performance advice and where students go wrong

Having learnt all of the information and revised thoroughly for the examination it all now comes down to the next 1¼ hours. Your examination performance is absolutely key to demonstrating to the examiner your knowledge, understanding and ability to evaluate relating to philosophy of religion and/or religion and ethics. We have provided hints throughout the first section of the book in the 'grade boost' sections and these focus on subject-specific issues. Here follows some general information that we believe will help you in your own performance. Some of these ideas may seem like common sense but year after year they represent the core performance indicators of the successful (and less successful) candidates.

Good examination candidates will

- Observe and obey trigger words (e.g. Explain, Outline, Describe, Assess)
- Have a good knowledge base
- Understand exam paper structure
- Follow examination rubric
- Be well prepared by teachers
- Make accurate use of terminology

What are good features of A level answers?

- Strong, focussed answers well supported with evidence from texts or scholars/schools of thought.
- Interesting and in-depth responses, entirely relevant to questions asked.
- Evidence of pertinent independent thought in responses – particularly in evaluation questions.

General issues

- Accurate spelling of key words
- Quotations to be accurate and relevant
- Awareness of variety of viewpoints
- Presentation legibility

Features of poor examination answers

- Examination rubric not followed
- Does not understand 'trigger' words
- Does not understand exam paper structure
- Poor knowledge/understanding of subject
- No use of specific terminology
- Irrelevance to the question asked

Where are the main shortcomings?

- Answers that lack relevance to the question
- Candidates that make unsubstantiated assertions
- Catch-all responses that do not take notice of the demands of the question
- Prepared answers to a question from a previous paper

Questions and answers

This part of the guide looks at student answers to examination-style questions through the eyes of an examiner. There is a selection of questions on topics in the AS specification with two sample answers – one of a high grade standard and one of a lower grade standard in each case. The examiner commentary is designed to show you how marks are gained and lost so that you understand what is required in your answers.

Your overall grade will depend on your total marks in the exam. You may be better prepared for some questions than for others so it is important that you work out where you can gain the most marks to get the best grade possible. The examiners will decide how many marks are needed for each grade by studying a selection of exam papers that have gained a particular number of marks, and it is common for these candidates to have gained their marks in different ways depending on the topics they have chosen.

Cosmological Argument

Teleological Argument

Evil and Suffering

Religious Experience: Mysticism

Natural Law

Situation Ethics

Utilitarianism

Applied Ethics

Cosmological Argument

1a Examine the cosmological argument for the existence of God.

(30 marks)

Seren's answer:

① The cosmological argument is an *a posteriori* argument based on the evidence that can be seen around us in the world. The word cosmological derives from the word cosmos meaning universe and argues that the world was created by a first cause.

② Aristotle was a Greek philosopher who supported the cosmological argument and believed that 'all things have the potential to change and become different in some way'. He believed that every object can go from its potential to actual but only with the addition of a third party. This third party, however, must already be in a state of actuality in order to fulfil the potential of other things. Aristotle used the example of the marble and the statue to explain his argument. He looked at how the marble went from its potential – a block of marble – to its actual – a beautiful statue – by the efficient cause – the sculptor, already in a state of actuality. Without the efficient cause, the marble remains unchanged.

③ St Thomas Aquinas created five ways from his book 'Summa Theologica' to prove God's existence. The first three of his five ways were in favour of the cosmological argument. The first way was the argument from change. Aquinas was greatly influenced by Aristotle and based his first way on what Aristotle had recognised. Aquinas also believed that things could go from their potential to actual by the addition of a third party and Aquinas called this the efficient cause. However, the efficient cause must be in a state of actuality before it can fulfil the potential of other things. Aquinas used a different example to Aristotle and used wood to hot example. The wood will go from its potential – a block of wood, to its actual – becoming hot – by the efficient cause of fire which is already in a state of actuality. Without fire, the wood would remain in its potential. Aquinas related this to the universe and believed that God changed objects from their potential to actual when creating the universe.

④ Aquinas' second way, the argument from cause, argues that everything has a first cause. He used the domino effect to explain this and looked at how the second domino will only fall if the first domino hits it. He believed that there was a law of cause and effect present everywhere in the universe and used the domino to represent the world being caused by the first cause. This first cause Aquinas believed was uncaused and caused the universe into existence. He believed that this first cause was God.

Examiner commentary:

① A clear introduction to the essay, stating the parameters upon which the cosmological argument is based.

② Discussing the classical formulation of the necessity for an efficient cause is a logical progression for the essay, although it might have worked better had it been part of the general discussion of Aquinas' First Way, where Aquinas uses it to support his own arguments of the need for a first 'unmoved' mover. The movement from potential to actual via an efficient cause is soundly explained and includes Aristotle's own example – this provides evidence of clear understanding.

③ Demonstrating further that Aquinas' First Way is based on Aristotle's own reasoning, this paragraph is a little less coherent than the previous one. However, there is reference to Aquinas' example of wood becoming hot and the all-important reference to how this idea relates to God, as the one responsible for bringing about the change from potential to actual in relation to the universe.

④ Attributing the domino example to Aquinas is inaccurate, but the concepts behind the example are accurate when it comes to Aquinas' explanation of his Second Way. In this, the answer demonstrates an understanding of the idea, even if it has not used Aquinas' own words.

(5) The third way, argument from contingency, argues that everything in the world is contingent, not necessary, as everything in the world relied on something else to create it. The world itself is contingent as the world relied on something to will it into existence. An example of this is us. We are contingent because we rely on our parents to make us. Without our parents we would not exist. Aquinas did not believe in an infinite universe as the universe had a beginning and was caused by an uncaused cause which was not only non-contingent but necessary. This is because if the thing responsible for creating the universe was only 'possible', then it may not have existed and therefore the universe would not have existed either. Therefore this thing must have been necessary in order to bring the universe into existence. He also existed outside of the universe. This necessary, non-contingent being was God.

(6) Leibniz then created the 'principle of sufficient reason' to prove God's existence and used the example of geometry books to show how you could trace each book back to the previous edition and eventually to the first, original author. He related this to the universe and said that the succession of states in the universe only gave a partial reason for the universe's existence, therefore there needed to be a sufficient reason to explain the universe's existence, which Leibniz said was God.

(7) William Lane Craig then developed the kalam argument, kalam meaning to argue or discuss. He separated the argument into two parts and argued that the universe cannot be infinite as the universe had a beginning. He believed that there must be an external agent outside the universe who freely chose to will the universe into existence and created the universe ex nihilo – out of nothing. Craig also argued that if the universe was created out of nothing then the beginning of the universe was also the beginning of time. This personal agent existing outside of the universe was God and Craig argued that because the past is there, it is evidence that the world cannot be infinite.

(5) The description of the Third Way uses an example of parents and children to illustrate the concept of contingency – this demonstrates clear understanding and is an apt use of an example for this purpose. There is also a presentation of the ideas of possibility and necessity, fundamental to Aquinas' explanation of the Third Way.

(6) A concise but highly accurate explanation of Leibniz's principle of sufficient reason. Linking the chain of logic to God is often missed in student responses, but not here.

(7) The final paragraph ends with an explanation of Craig's Kalam argument – again, presented concisely, but accurately.

Summative comment

Seren produces a well-written answer that presents the key facts and ideas of the cosmological argument with evidence of clear understanding, almost throughout. A clearer and more detailed explanation of Aquinas would have given this the additional information it required for the 'thorough understanding' of Level 7. It is awarded Level 6, 27 marks for AO1.

Q&A

1a Examine the cosmological argument for the existence of God.

(30 marks)

Tom's answer:

① The cosmological argument is an argument for the existence of God and it is an *a posteriori* argument. St Thomas Aquinas was a Greek philosopher who supported the design argument and he came up with three ways which were motion, cause and contingency.

② The first way was motion. He believed that nothing can move by itself, it has to be moved by something else, he uses an example of 'the arrow is directed by the archer' this means that the arrow cannot move by itself it needs the archer to guide it. He believed that the universe had a first mover to be God.

③ The second way was from cause, He believed that nothing can cause itself, it needs a first cause, he used the example of wood being hot because it cannot cause itself to be hot, it must have potential and the potential is fire. The fire becomes the first cause because it makes the wood hot. Aquinas believed that the first cause of the universe was God because it couldn't just cause itself.

④ The third way was from contingency. He believed that we are contingent because we are not needed for the world to exist but Aquinas believed that God was not contingent but necessary as the world could not exist without him.

⑤ Gottfried Leibniz was a famous philosopher who believed in the cosmological argument and he came up with sufficient reason. He used an example of the geometry books that you have to look at ones from the past to get the right information because over the years as the book gets published it gets changed so you would have to look back to the author. David Hume believed that it is far more probable for the universe to be designed but he doesn't believe that it was God who designed it.

Examiner commentary:

① Tom's introduction to the essay starts well but the second sentence demonstrates poor understanding of the subject by firstly wrongly accrediting Aquinas as a Greek philosopher and secondly naming the argument as the 'design' argument. This sort of mistake indicates to the examiner that the candidate has a patchy understanding of the topic.

② Tom recognises that he should be discussing Aquinas' Three Ways but he does not seem to know precisely what these are. The example of the archer/arrow is from the Fifth, not the First Way, although Tom attempts to make it fit into his understanding of the concept of motion. He also states that God has to be the first mover.

③ Tom's explanation of the second way further illustrates his basic/patchy understanding of the topic as he mixes up Aquinas' example from the First Way as an exemplar for explaining the Second Way. However, he correctly identifies Aquinas' assertion that the universe cannot be the cause of itself and attributes its cause to God.

④ Whilst very concisely written, Tom has understood and described the concept of contingency with accuracy.

⑤ Tom attempts to explain Leibniz's example but becomes confused in his explanation. The idea of the principle is there but is only partial. The reference to Hume is neither pertinent nor accurate.

Summative comment

Tom clearly has an appreciation of the cosmological argument, although his understanding of it is basic. His answer is better (just) than outline and low level accuracy and fits more comfortably into the basic/patchy understanding level criteria – but only just! He gained a Level 4, 15 marks for AO1.

1b 'The strengths of the cosmological argument clearly outweigh its weaknesses.' Assess this view. *(15 marks)*

Seren's answer:

① The cosmological argument has many strengths that make the argument more persuasive and believable. The argument is an a posterior argument using evidence around us to show evidence of the universe having a beginning. Even if science is an easier option to take, scientific experiments have proven the world to have a caused beginning and this makes the cosmological argument more plausible. Also, Ockham's razor supports the argument and states the belief that God is the simplest explanation for the beginning of the universe. Also, the argument is part of a cumulative case and with another argument, for example the teleological argument, becomes stronger.

② However, the cosmological argument has its weaknesses and there are four major known oppositions of the cosmological argument. David Hume argues that just because everything in the universe is caused doesn't mean that the universe itself is caused or that the personal agent who caused it is the God of classical theism. John Stuart Mill poses the question of 'If the world is caused, then why is the cause of the world uncaused?' This poses many doubts of the cosmological argument as it is hard to believe that the cause of the universe caused itself and that was that. Immanuel Kant argues that we do not have sufficient human knowledge to conclude that there was a beginning to the universe or that the universe was caused by an uncaused cause and to do so is wrong. Bertrand Russell presented his brute fact and agreed with Hume and Kant. He argued that 'I should say the world is just there and that is all'.

③ To conclude, there are equal numbers of strengths and weaknesses for and against the cosmological argument but many people in today's society will find a scientific explanation easier to understand such as the world was created by the Big Bang and therefore God is not needed. In my opinion, I believe the weaknesses outweigh the strengths as scientific explanations clearly state how the world was made and can incorporate experiments to prove the scientific theory but religion explains why the world was created, which in my opinion, people find hard to contemplate.

Examiner commentary:

① A number of arguments that are considered strengths are presented in this first paragraph. Explanation of each is partially supported by reasoning. The paragraph as a whole is coherent and presents the ideas with accuracy, without repeating information unnecessarily from part 'a' of the question.

② The second paragraph does the same as the first, although this time looking at the weaknesses of the argument. Again, further explanation would have benefitted Seren as she clearly understands the issue.

③ The concluding paragraph, again, gives a concise account of the preference (in this case the weaknesses) and the reasons for this.

Summative comment

Seren's part b demonstrates a clear appreciation for the issues and she clearly understands the debate. However, there is insufficient comment to warrant a Level 6 or higher. The answer was therefore awarded Level 5, 11 marks for AO2.

Q&A 1b 'The strengths of the cosmological argument clearly outweigh its weaknesses.' Assess this view. *(15 marks)*

Tom's answer:

① Some philosophers would agree with this statement because it has many strong points such as it is 2,000 years old and it's also a logical explanation for the existence of God and it's an *a posteriori* argument therefore it is based on evidence and with evidence it must be a strong argument Aquinas, Paley and F.R. Tennant would all agree with this statement.

② There are not as many weaknesses to the cosmological argument. Immanuel Kant would disagree with this statement because he believed we have no knowledge of the creation story so it must not have happened.

③ In conclusion I would agree with this statement because I believe there are many more strength than weaknesses that have evidence to back them up.

Examiner commentary:

① Tom starts well and sums up accurately two of the supporting arguments for this issue. However, again, he confuses cosmological argument and design and his scholars are more commonly associated with the design argument. He also says that they would support it but doesn't explain why.

② Kant's criticism is poorly explained and demonstrates a limited attempt at an argument.

③ The conclusion is basic and does nothing more than state a perspective without supporting it with any evidence.

Summative comment

Tom's response is limited and, again, shows that he only partly understood the issues. He was given Level 3, 5 marks for AO2.

Teleological Argument

2a Explain the teleological argument.

(30 marks)

Seren's answer:

① The teleological argument, originally started by Plato and Aristotle, is used to question design in the universe, based on observation.

② Aquinas argued design qua regularity and believed 'natural bodies' could not act in a regular fashion to accomplish their end without an intelligent force behind them. He developed the famous analogy of the arrow and the archer; the arrow being an item of no intelligence it needs the force of the intelligent archer, to move it towards the target (its end). This was the fifth of his five ways 'From The Governance Of Things', and when he used his analogy to refer back to the universe he said that God was the intelligent being behind the 'natural bodies' and the universe.

③ Following Aquinas, Paley wrote 'Natural Theology' where he argued both sides of the argument. His first point was made by his famous analogy of the watch; if you were to stumble across a stone on a heath you would disregard it as normal, but if you were to find a watch you would question where it came from and how it was made. Paley looked at the complexity and specific purpose of the watch and said it must have been designed that way by an intelligent watch maker. He then looked at the universe and concluded that it too must have an intelligent designer due to its complexity; 'This being we call God'.

④ The second part of Paley's argument was design qua purpose and to demonstrate this he used the human eye and its complex function, Newton's law of motion and even the simplest things like why birds have wings. He used these examples to state that surely, design is more probable than chance.

⑤ In later years, as a more recent development F.R. Tennant developed the 'anthropic principle', showing that this world is specific to our needs, that even if one molecule was different, things would be chaotic but they aren't. He developed three natural types of evidence; Firstly, that the world can be analysed in a rational manner. Secondly, that the inorganic world contains the basic necessities to sustain life. Finally, the theory of natural selection, that we can progress and develop.

⑥ Arthur Brown backed up this theory by stating that if the ozone layer was any thinner, the planet would be too hot, any thicker and it would be too cold.

⑦ F.R. Tennant, then also developed the 'aesthetic argument' that God wanted us to enjoy our lives by the simple fact that humans possess the ability to enjoy music, art and literature.

Examiner commentary:

① A simple introduction, Seren highlights the origins of the argument but does no more than reference Plato and Aristotle.

② This section deals very well with Aquinas's Fifth Way and very confidently and clearly explains how Aquinas saw God as the designer of the universe. The analogy of the archer and arrow is fully linked to Aquinas' argument.

③ A concise explanation of Paley and referring to both of his 'qua' arguments (regularity and purpose). Linking Paley's watchmaker to the universe's designer is an important part of this argument and one that many candidates fail to do. It is pleasing to see it done correctly here.

④ Explaining the 'qua purpose' argument in detail demonstrates Seren's clear understanding of Paley's contribution to the design argument. Reference to Newton is also apt.

⑤ Seren then progresses to discuss Tennant's contribution to the anthropic principle. This is accurately done and demonstrates that key facts have been presented with accuracy and relevance.

⑥ The reference to Brown's support of the argument is accurate but a little rushed. Further explanation, in terms of showing how this could not have occurred unless deliberately designed for human beings to exist, would have benefitted Seren's overall mark for the essay.

⑦ Again, Seren skims over Tennant's Aesthetic principle. Concepts of benevolent designer are missed here.

Summative comment

Seren clearly understands the subject and has written an essay demonstrating this. Some parts are explained well but this is not always balanced. Better explanation of Tennant's Aesthetic principle and Brown's ozone layer example would have allowed Seren to access additional marks and raise the overall standard of the answer to a Level 7. As it is Seren is awarded a Level 6, 25 marks for this AO1 response.

Q & A

2a Explain the teleological argument. *(30 marks)*

Tom's answer:

① The teleological argument is also known as the design argument, the word *telos* comes from the Greek word meaning end or purpose. It is an *a posteriori* argument because it is based on experience.

② St Thomas Aquinas also accepted the teleological argument who supported design qua regularity as he believed that the order and regularity in the universe must be evidence of a designer. In his fifth way, 'From the governance of things' Aquinas shows how God is like an archer aiming an arrow at a target when he designs the universe. William Paley was also a famous philosopher who supported the design argument. He came up with a watch analogy which was If you were walking through heath and you seen a rock you would think it was silly to ask yourself where it came from but if you came across a watch you would question yourself why it was there. Paley believed that the watch is like the universe, very complex thing, and that it must have been designed. The universe must have been created like the watch has a watchmaker. This shows how the teleological argument has developed because there are becoming more and more strengths to why it's true.

③ There are more recent developments to the teleological argument like the anthropic and the aesthetic principle. The anthropic principle states that the universe was created/designed for intelligent life and if there were a tiny minute change in the creation of the universe the development of human life may not have been formed. This shows how the argument has developed because newer additions are kept being added on.

④ The aesthetic principle was developed by F.R. Tennant who also developed the anthropic principle. He stated that because humans have the ability to enjoy music, art, literature, etc., but we don't need it for survival. This, according to Tennant, shows evidence of a omnibenevolent designer who wants us to enjoy the world that we live in.

⑤ Many people agree with the teleological argument but there are some weaknesses.

Examiner commentary:

① Tom makes a positive start to the essay by outlining the basic points relating to the type and form of argument that can be found in the teleological argument for the existence of God.

② Tom makes reference to Aquinas and his ideas related to the argument. He does not explain these in any depth. He makes an accurate identification of the arrow/archer analogy but, again, this is not developed. The comments on Paley are heavily based on the narrative of the watchmaker analogy but here Tom makes the all too common mistake of not relating the watchmaker to God. He also strays into AO2 territory by offering an evaluative comment at the end of the paragraph.

③ The argument is developed by a reference to the anthropic principle and a mainly accurate comment is made relating to this concept.

④ The explanation of the aesthetic principle demonstrates clear understanding of Tennant's point about the presence of beauty in the universe.

⑤ The final comment does nothing to add to the AO1 objective.

Summative comment

Tom clearly understands the main points of the teleological argument and presents them in a systematic way, thus addressing the question. His argument is not consistent in terms of its explanations and depth but he does demonstrate an understanding of the main ideas and is mainly accurate in his account. Tom therefore gained a Level 5, 22 marks for AO1.

2b Scientific evidence strongly supports the teleological argument.' Assess this view.

(15 marks)

Seren's answer:

① The teleological argument is based on observation to find order and regularity in the world. The argument is also supported by some and disregarded by others in science.

② David Hume disregards the argument as it is flawed, he believed. He firstly argued against Aquinas saying that even if there was an 'intelligent being', it doesn't mean that it is 'the God of classical theism'. He suggested that this planet may have been developed by 'apprentice Gods'. Hume then argued Paley's watch analogy, stating a piece of machinery cannot be compared to something so vast as the universe, it would be more appropriate to compare it to something which was alive and grew – like an inert animal or vegetable.

③ Arthur Brown was a scientist who did support the teleological argument, saying surely the ozone layer, which is the perfect thickness for human life, cannot be merely chance but specific design. However, Charles Darwin's theory of natural selection, from his book 'The Origin of Species by Means of Natural Selection' stated that we can influence progress of species. That we developed through the mechanism of natural selection, not as the result of a divine designer. This led many to question God's relevance.

④ There are many scientists who support this argument, however, like Brown, Paul Davies and John Polkinghorne. Moreover, Anthony Flews analogy of 'leaky buckets' applies, that stacking flawed arguments will not give a sound argument.

⑤ To conclude I don't believe the argument is strongly disproven by science and until it is the teleological argument is a logical explanation for the existence of God.

Examiner commentary:

① A straightforward response is given as an introduction to the issue. The parameters of the argument are stated, Seren is therefore hinting at where the debate may arise.

② Whilst Hume may not normally be considered as a 'scientist' in the traditional sense, Hume's arguments are firmly based on the scientific principles of empiricism – the arguments as presented here, are entirely valid, and demonstrate Seren's understanding of the issue.

③ Contrasting views are given with Brown's ozone layer example being cited as strong scientific evidence to support the argument, whilst Darwin's theory of evolution via natural selection is used to demonstrate the flaws in the argument. Seren compares the two scientists with good effect, to show some of the tensions presented by the debate.

④ Seren presents a list of scholars but does not develop their views. She then gives the leaky bucket response as an argument against. This, however, is not, strictly speaking a scientific argument, even if it makes use of a scientific principle – all arguments should be based on sound evidence.

⑤ Seren gives a brief conclusion to support her argument, and includes a simple reason to evidence her view.

Summative comment

Seren deals competently with the issue and presents some good arguments. However, some of her analysis is limited and her ability to provide a balanced argument is lacking overall. More critical analysis would have improved the mark given to the response. Seren gained a Level 5, 11 marks for this AO2 answer.

Q&A

2b 'Scientific evidence strongly supports the teleological argument.' Assess this view. *(15 marks)*

Tom's answer:

① Most philosophers would disagree with this because a lot of scientists believe in the Big Bang as well as the theory of evolution. Richard Dawkins is a philosopher who would disagree with this statement as he followed Charles Darwin who came up with natural selection. Dawkins thinks it's non-scientific to believe in a designing God.

② David Hume argued against the teleological argument as he believed humans have no experience of the universe being designed so we cannot believe the teleological argument. Some weaknesses are the leaky bucket theory no matter how many buckets you have if they all have a hole in it won't carry water.

③ There are also strong points to the argument like it's a logical explanation; it's part of the cumulative case and it's a posteriori. In conclusion there are many strengths and also many weaknesses but they both are supported by views and have reasons/evidence to back it up.

Examiner commentary:

① A limited attempt to demonstrate how scientists have disagreed with the design argument is presented here. Names and ideas are, however, accurate although these ideas are not developed.

② Hume's argument and the leaky buckets argument are presented, again in a limited way. These ideas really need to be developed for Tom to gain a higher mark for AO2.

③ The final paragraph attempts to deal with the counter-arguments but unfortunately the points listed do not really address the question relating to scientific evidence. There is no clear conclusion presented in this part of the essay. For AO2 it is essential that a conclusion is always offered.

Summative comment

Tom has made a limited attempt at responding to the argument but, with no conclusion and minimal evidence to support his views Tom was awarded Level 3, 6 marks.

Evil and Suffering

3a Explain why the existence of evil poses a challenge to a belief in the existence of God. *(30 marks)*

Seren's answer:

① 'The problem of evil' is a problem put forward by non-believers to the believers of 'the classical God of theism' questioning why evil exists if the qualities they believe their God to have, (omnipotence – all-powerful, omnibenevolence – all-loving and omniscience – all-knowing) has.

② When discussing evil, we must define what we mean and here I am going to define evil as anything that causes suffering. We must also distinguish between natural and moral evil: 'Natural evil' is an evil outside of our free-will and control, an example being 'Hurricane Katrina' or the 'Lisbon earthquake'. 'Moral evil' is an evil that an individual or group chooses by exercising their free-will, for example the 'Holocaust' or the 'kidnapping of Madeline McCann'.

③ The inconsistent triad looks at each aspect. The triangle contains three statements of proposals: omnibenevolence, omnipotence and evil, only two of which can ever be true, according to Epicurus, developed by Hume.

④ If we take away evil we are left with the fact that God is all loving and all knowing. Due to the world that surrounds us it is evident that evil does exist, although some argue that evil is just an illusion and perspective and that what we see as evil, God does not. Non-believers argue that if God was all loving and all knowing, his creation would not suffer, even for 'temporary evil'.

⑤ Therefore either: God is all loving but not omnipotent and evil exists. That means he wants to take away the evil and suffering that we face but he lacks the power to do it. This is a problem for believers as it contradicts what they believe God is. Or, God is all powerful, not all loving and evil exists. This would mean that whilst God has the power to remove evil he chooses not to because he doesn't care enough, or, even worse, he may enjoy watching us suffer. Once again this poses the same problem of contradiction.

⑥ As Epicurus concluded, 'Either God wants us to abolish evil and cannot, or he can but does not want to. If he wants to but cannot he is impotent. If he can, but does not want to he is wicked.'

⑦ Non-believers also raise the argument of the amount of suffering needed; why didn't two million die in the holocaust as opposed to six million? The very fact that so many people died is appalling and this immense suffering seems to go against what believers think about God. They also argue why should animals suffer abuse? They cannot learn and develop; therefore their suffering has no meaning. If, as some religions (e.g., Christianity) teach, animals have no souls – how can suffering be useful or 'soul-making' likewise as animals are not descended from Adam and Eve, why should they suffer as humans do? It makes no sense. There is also the problem of innocent suffering, such as the children starving in the developing world. They are not improving their souls, they are slowly and painfully dying and this cannot be justified. Even if evil is temporary, it is not compatible with a loving God who wouldn't want innocents in his creation to suffer.

Examiner commentary:

① A good introduction which sums up why there is a problem of evil – defining the God of classical theism's characteristics demonstrates clear understanding on Seren's part.

② Seren then develops her answer by defining evil and the types of evil, with examples. Setting up the parameters of why there is a debate in the first place shows good understanding of the subject material and allows the main part of the argument to be developed upon a platform of agreed upon definitions.

③ Reference to the inconsistent triad is important to any essay of this type; however, more could have been done here to develop how the inconsistent triad came about and the nature of such a philosophical device.

④ The explanation of the illusion/problem of perspective of evil is apt and explained clearly. Seren continues her explanation by showing how this is an insufficient justification in trying to solve the problem of evil.

⑤ This demonstrates a very competent unpacking of the removal of the omnipotent/omnibenevolent characteristics and, again, shows why each of these 'solutions' is ultimately inadequate. This, again, shows evidence of good understanding. The key facts and ideas related to the inconsistent triad are presented with accuracy.

⑥ Using Epicurus' dilemma to underline the point made by the inconsistent triad is an intelligent application of a philosopher's viewpoint to support the reasoning of the essay answer.

⑦ Seren here deals with the particular problems raised by animal, immense and innocent suffering. All examples are apt and serve to illustrate the point being made.

⑧ As Hume stated, 'The gravity of suffering is too much'.

⑧ Again, using a philosopher's viewpoint to underline the points made in the previous paragraph demonstrates not only clear understanding but also the ability to organise the material in a clear and coherent way.

Summative comment

Seren has produced a fairly full answer to the question in the time available. Her information is relevant and, whilst she does not always present information thoroughly (which would have given her a Level 7 mark), her presentation of material is sufficient to fully meet the criteria for Level 6. This AO1 response was therefore awarded Level 6, 26 marks.

3a Explain why the existence of evil poses a challenge to a belief in the existence of God. *(30 marks)*

Tom's answer:

① The existence of evil poses a challenge to belief in God's existence for many different reasons.

② Augustine's theodicy questions the existence of moral and natural suffering. Evil causes suffering and many people question why our loving God would let this happen, if he has the power to stop it. Augustine believed that we were all developed from Adam. He argued that everyone deserves to suffer because we are being punished for Adam's original sin, eating the fruit in the Garden of Eden. He believed that we were all made in the image of God; however, some people choose to disobey him and sin.

③ Irenaeus believed that God made a world free from flaws. He created us all in his image and gave us our own free will. By giving us this it gave us a chance to disobey him. This is why we experience evil and suffering. This is known as the free will defence.

④ David Hume believed that there were three errors in the problem of evil. The first one was the logical error; the second error was the moral error; the third one was scientific error.

⑤ David Hume also argued about the God of classical theism being all knowing, all powerful and all loving. He put his idea forward by using the inconsistent triangle. He believed that God could not be all three as they cannot exist alongside each other.

⑥ If God was all powerful and all loving then would it not make sense for him to stop evil? He believed that God was either omnipotent or omniscient or omnibenevolent and evil does not exist. He concluded that evil is not a substance but it is a deprivation of good.

Examiner commentary:

① A very brief introduction, limited in scope.

② Referring to a theodicy (a justification of God, you may remember) in a question that asks you to explain why evil is a challenge to God's existence, seems to be misplaced. Tom seems to be using this as a platform to explain why evil exists, rather than it being a challenge to God's existence.

③ Tom repeats his previous device, only this time referring to Irenaeus.

④ Comments on Hume are inaccurate. Tom is confusing Hume (who did comment on the problem of evil – only not in this way) with the traditional criticisms of Augustine's theodicy as stated by Schleiermacher *et al*. These criticisms are not explained nor exemplified. If he had done so, Tom would have gained some credit.

⑤ Hume is referred to again and a problem of evil is stated. This clearly states the problem and, in doing so, relates directly to the question set.

⑥ A limited unpacking of the problem of evil makes up the final paragraph in this section. This demonstrates not just limited knowledge but also limited understanding of the problem of evil.

Summative comment

Tom has some concept of what the question is asking him but his responses are limited in nature. This would therefore qualify as an 'outline' answer, with limited knowledge and understanding. There is very little in the way of relevant evidence or examples and the references to the theodicies at the beginning lack direct relevance to the question that has been asked. Tom was therefore awarded Level 3, 11 marks for this question.

3b 'Religious solutions to the problem of evil fail to convince anyone.' Assess this view.　*(15 marks)*

Seren's answer:

① The 'problem of evil' is an argument that believers in the 'God of classical theism' face. The religious solutions to the argument are put forward by Augustine and Irenaeus.

② Augustine's 'justification of God in the face of evil' is that as we are all seminally present in Adam when he committed the first sin, we are all to be punished (moral evil) and in taking the fruit the natural balance was destroyed giving us natural evil. God is not to blame as it was our choice to disobey him and evil is not a substance, but a privation of good.

③ This theodicy is criticised on three counts: logical error (e.g., how can a perfect world go wrong?); scientific error (how is it possible that all human beings are biologically descended from Adam and the theory of evolution and natural selection contradict the idea of a 'perfect creation'?) and moral error (the fact that hell seems part of the design suggesting God knew it would go wrong – did he therefore set us up to fail? How is that compatible with his goodness?)

④ Irenaeus' theodicy of 'The vale of soul making', and that due to our free will that God wouldn't compromise, meaning he knew it could go wrong is another religious 'answer'. Irenaeus argued that our suffering was 'temporary' and necessary for us to develop from God's image to his 'likeness' and it is part of God's plan that, eventually, we would all go to Heaven, and this was the justification for that evil we suffered.

⑤ This theodicy is also criticised on many accounts especially that everyone goes to Heaven. A murderer surely isn't worthy and this notion leaves no incentive for people that do good. Also, why do some people suffer far more than others? Why is there so much suffering?

⑥ To conclude I agree with the view that these religious 'solutions' fail to convince, as even though they contain nice ideas, both arguments contain logical flaws that make the idea of evil co-existing with of the 'God of classical theism' unlikely.

Examiner commentary:

① The answer starts with a simple but effective introduction. Introductions do not need to be long winded. Generally speaking they do not, of themselves, gain the candidates any marks, it is the way in which they 'set the stage' for the rest of the answer that makes them important, and, they are a necessary part of a well-structured essay.

② Augustine's theodicy is summed up in brief – demonstrating that Seren is aware of the main points of the argument.

③ This section shows, again in relative brevity, the criticism of Augustine's theodicy and why it is not considered to be a convincing response to the problem of evil.

④ Again, the same device is used to set up the Irenaean theodicy, summarising the main points and demonstrating awareness of how the theodicy works.

⑤ This effectively lists the criticisms, almost suggesting that the answer has a 'rushed' quality, possibly due to time pressures within the exam. It is essential to be aware of what time you have available to you when you go into an exam, and how long you should spend on each part question!

⑥ The conclusion offers a response to the question in a clear manner.

Summative comment

Seren's answer is concise and to the point. The information provided is all accurate but, because of the brevity of the material, the analysis and reasoning are limited. The argument is partially supported by reasoning and evidence and, as such, gains a Level 5, 10 marks for this AO2 response.

3b 'Religious solutions to the problem of evil fail to convince anyone.' Assess this view. *(15 marks)*

Tom's answer:

① Religious solutions to the problem of evil do not always convince. Many people will question why God, if there is even a God at all, would let suffering become so extreme and not put a stop to it. For example, immense suffering such as what the Nazis did to the Jews in the Holocaust is one of the biggest types of evil that has occurred. Why would an all loving God let millions of people die?

② Innocent suffering such as the children and families in Africa, who struggle for survival in their everyday life, Would an all-powerful God not want to use his power to give them better quality of life? Also animals suffer because they have less authority and are smaller than humans, is this fair?

③ Religious solutions such as Irenaeus and Augustine's theodicy are convincing arguments to prove God's existence in the problem of evil. It is our choice as humans to disobey our God who made a world free from flaws. And this is why he designed heaven and hell, for the good and the bad to go to. Also, evil is not a substance and therefore it cannot be claimed that God created it.

④ In my opinion, I think that religious solutions are unconvincing. I feel that there are far too many errors in the argument for the problem of evil and If God created the world and everything in it, then I feel that it is wrong to say that God the designer did not also design the evil that we have to face. The main critique is for the God of classical theism as it seems impossible to say that he or any other God can be all knowing, loving and powerful, if evil still exists in the universe.

Examiner commentary:

① The introduction starts well but then just uses information which is AO1 in nature. An opportunity to make this more evaluative is missed and it is important that, as an introduction to an evaluation, such an opportunity should be grasped.

② Again, similarly to (1), Tom is restating information that he has already used in AO1. So far the question set has not been answered.

③ Augustine's and Irenaeus' theodicies are skimmed over and a superficial analysis of what they state is given. This is limited and would need to be expanded on significantly to contribute adequately to the evaluation.

④ The concluding paragraph (it's always essential to have one in an AO2 response) provides a personal point of view, based on evidence, but is limited in scope. The inconsistent triad is restated but, overall, reasoning is simplistic and basic.

Summative comment

This answer demonstrates that the issues were only partly appreciated and the analysis was limited. Evidence provided to support the reasoning was minimal and therefore this response was awarded Level 3, 5 marks.

Religious Experience: Mysticism

4a Explain why some people question whether mystical experiences are authentic. *(30 marks)*

Seren's answer:

① There are many reasons why philosophers and scientists alike might question the authenticity – that is, the empirical reality and God-given nature – of mystical experiences wherein the recipient experiences a transient, passive, noetic, ineffable union with God.

Examiner commentary:

① Seren demonstrates a high level of understanding straightaway in the response. A concise paragraph that offers an insight into the heart of the subject. Reference to James' characteristics also demonstrates that her form and style of writing are, thus far, highly suitable.

② Firstly, the idea of such a union with a divine power goes against the currently accepted laws of science. The human brain, and all the chemicals, zones and pathways therein, has been accounted for by biologists and neuroscientists, and it is not believed that the brain has any capacity whatsoever for telepathic, long-distance communication with any living being – let alone a being whose existence is already extensively historically challenged by other scientific laws such as evolution and the Big Bang theory. Thus, all 'mystical experiences' reported are more often than not believed by scientists to be the result of non-religious, biologically grounded chemical processes in the brain, often induced by drug use or mental illness. Such explanations decrease the authenticity of mystical experiences as truly God-given in the eyes of many.

③ Another reason for questioning the authenticity of mystical experiences might be the theological evidence which suggests they do not occur. John Hick's idea of God's 'epistemic distance' from humankind, as an explanation for his non-intervention against evil and suffering, poses such a problem – if God exists at an intellectual distance from humans, experiences wherein humans believe he visits their mind must be imagination or wish fulfilment. Conversely, if mystical experiences *are* assumed to be authentic, God's policy of not intervening against evil is called into question – surely, posit philosophers such as Dawkins, if he can step into the mind of a recipient, he could also negate the excess of sin in the world? Furthermore, if William James' definition of mysticism as a transient experience – that is, the idea that a mystical experience, while fleeting, will 'stay with' its recipient and cause them to look at the world in a more religious light – is to be believed, God's desire to preserve our free will (including the choice to believe in him or not) is also called into question.

④ Mysticism can also be seen to violate the modern Christian view of God as a being who exists simultaneously within everything and outside time and space. If God is such a formless entity, argue critics like Dawkins, how can experiences wherein he takes form of an 'angel bearing a spear of light' (St Teresa of Avila's account of her experiences) or possesses a 'voice' ever be considered authentic?

⑤ In addition to reasons why mystical experience might not be authentic, there are also numerous popularly cited reasons why their 'recipient' might have cause to invent them. One such reason would be the instilment of a sense of purpose in life and a feeling of being 'special' and 'chosen' by God. Another might be the gaining of religious and social influence, as in the case of modern-day would-be 'saints' who declare their mystical experiences at least partly in hope of being recognised and praised by the Church.

⑥ Finally, according to some critics, such as Hume, the very nature of mystical experiences as 'ineffable' detracts from their plausibility: if their recipient could describe the experiences with accuracy and scientific conviction, scientists might have to consider their authenticity more seriously, but, with only half-baked descriptions, mystical phenomena cannot be afforded this luxury by the scientific community.

② This paragraph deals intelligently with the main reasons why scientists might be one group who would challenge the authenticity of the experiences due to them being experiences that cannot be qualified by scientific enquiry. Key concepts are referred to accurately to support the response.

③ Having dealt with the more obvious area of challenge – i.e. empirical science, Seren then progresses onto the challenge offered by the theological arena. Again, highly intelligent use of language, examples, evidence and scholars are intertwined to produce an accurate and relevant treatment of the topic.

④ A further philosophical point is established and highlighted by separating it from the previous collection of theological objections. Seren is demonstrating very high levels of relevance and accuracy in her work by following this coherent pattern in her response.

⑤ Seren now offers arguments based on socio-psycho-anthropological debates in order to further support her argument. Excellent skills being continually developed, this answer is thoroughly logical and demonstrates the excellent level of understanding that Seren has on this particular topic.

⑥ The final paragraph deals the 'devastating blow' to the question asked. Seren's confidence in dealing with this subject produces a superb, highly relevant and well-chosen example to round off her thoughts on the subject.

Summative comment

Seren has produced an ideal response to this question. It fully meets the demanding criteria of Level 7 for AO1 and was awarded 30 marks. Superb!

Q&A

4a Explain why some people question whether mystical experiences are authentic.

(30 marks)

Tom's answer:

① Mysticism is an experience of the divine. Bauderschmidt described it as an 'altered state of consciousness' that results in 'unity with the divine'. Mystical experiences cannot be physically measured, which leads many to question whether they are authentic.

② Firstly, philosopher William James, who outlines four characteristics of mystical experiences, shows how some question whether they are authentic. James first characteristic is ineffability; this is that the recipient cannot explain what has happened to them. Mystic Rabbi Israel Tov stated he 'couldn't authenticate' his experience. Immediately people question whether mystical experiences are authentic as how can something which cannot be described be real. Equally some suggest that if God is omnipotent, all-powerful, then why can't he show himself to everyone and not just a select few. Followers of Joseph Fletcher's ethical system, Situation Ethics, may say that the most agapeistic thing to do would be to show himself to everyone. This leads people to question the authenticity.

③ Secondly, some people question whether mystical experiences are authentic as they can be deceptive. Psychologists Carl Jung and Sigmund Freud note how these religious images can be merely things conjured up through our lives. We see what we want to see, it is 'wish fulfilment'. They believe our mind conjures up images to combat fear and inner psychological stress. Teresa of Avila believed she saw Jesus and that a golden spear pierced her heart repeatedly and inflicted spiritual pain upon her which resulted in 'love for God'. Psychologists have advocated this as sexual frustration. The spear that caused her to 'moan' was conjured up as a figment of her imagination. This leaves the question of whether they are authentic. Equally the 'miracle of the sun' in which thousands of people in Fatima, Portugal, declared they saw God when looking at the sun has been explained by scientists that looking at the sun for prolonged amounts of time can result in hallucinogenic conceits. This can question authenticity. Finally scholar Walter Stace believes some people can have extrovertive mystical experiences in which the divine is transgressed physically. An example of this is the 1994 evangelical Christian neo-charismatic group Toronto Blessings. Characteristics include laughing hysterically and weeping uncontrollably. They state it is the physical manifestation of the Holy Spirit. Yet many believe these people are secretly drunk and are emphasising these experiences for show. This also questions the authenticity.

④ In conclusion it appears that other explanations can explain mystical experiences, which is why some people question whether they are authentic.

Examiner commentary:

① A very good, clear and focussed introduction to the subject with a scholarly quote to support the introduction. This is good practice and sets the stage for the rest of the response.

② Reference to William James and Rabbi Israel Tov are usefully inserted to support the point of view that the very nature of mysticism makes it difficult to authenticate. However, the ethical references are a little dubious and Tom is stretching the point to include this. I would suspect that he is also studying the ethics module and was trying to find ways to fit what he's revised to a subject that he was not as confident on. Whilst this practice is occasionally desirable (it can be a synoptic skill) it should be used in an obviously relevant manner in order to convince the examiner that it is a pertinent response to the question asked.

③ A number of relevant examples are now given in the next section of the response. These are highly relevant, although Tom needs to explain precisely how they challenge authenticity rather than just writing the sentence *'this questions the authenticity'*, which shows only partial understanding. A missed opportunity to impress the examiner with his subject knowledge.

④ The 'conclusion' is unnecessary for AO1; it is only in AO2 where conclusions are required.

Summative comment

Tom presents information that is mainly accurate. He clearly has an understanding of the topic but here it is only basic and occasionally patchy. He would need to extend his explanations in order to improve his overall mark. Tom was awarded Level 4, 18 marks for AO1.

4b 'A mystical experience should not be devalued by the challenge of authenticity.' Assess this view. *(15 marks)*

Seren's answer:

① Some Christians and mystics argue against the idea that 'authenticity' should devalue the worth of an experience, certainly. For example, F. C. Happold, one of the prime defenders of mysticism, claimed that 'mysticism exists in a different sphere of experience to science altogether', thus implying that scientific evidence against the existence of authentic mystical experiences should not detract from the sense of religious authenticity the recipient might attribute to their experience.

② Some, however, have argued against this view of the value of mysticism, such as A. F. King, and have instead posited that, if one considered any experience valid based simply on the fact that the recipient underwent it in their own mind, in a non-scientific 'sphere of thought' then the views of mentally ill people and hallucinatory drug users would have to start to be taken seriously alongside defenders of mysticism – after all, such people also have experiences and visions which seem real to them but are scientifically dubious, and are locked away in hospitals or prisons, not listened to and praised by the Church for having encountered God first-hand.

③ This argument can be refuted, however, by defenders of mysticism fairly easily via the idea that mental patients and those who have hallucinations are often the recipients of such negative experiences – one of the reasons mystical visitations are considered valuable is because they are not irrational, but serve to heighten the recipient's well-being and impart useful spiritual knowledge onto them (James' 'noetic quality'). Indeed, William James further defends mysticism against the aforementioned argument by stating that the transience of an experience – its ability to stay with the recipient and change their life despite its fleeting nature – is the quality which proves it is of worth and distinguishes it from the hallucinations by mental patients, who normally forget.

Examiner commentary:

① The use of scholarly names adds support to Seren's opening argument. Supporting the claim in the question, Seren provides appropriate critical analysis and comment.

② The next paragraph sees a direct response to her first argument and, again, uses scholarly evidence to promote the point being made.

③ The final paragraph counters the counter argument and provides a more sympathetic approach to the issue. The final sentences imply a conclusion but this is not directly focussed on the original question. It is often good practice to refer to the question in the final conclusion so as to demonstrate to the examiner that the issue has been fully understood and responded to.

Summative comment

Seren makes an intelligent response to the question but does not develop her answer sufficiently. The implied conclusion is not directly relevant to the question and this weakens the evaluation as a whole. As such, Seren meets the criteria for Level 5 as it 'addresses the main issues' and her argument is 'partially supported by reasoning and/or evidence' and she was given 11 marks. To get a higher mark Seren needed to add to her arguments with additional material and provide a clear and focussed conclusion.

Q&A

4b 'A mystical experience should not be devalued by the challenge of authenticity.' Assess this view. *(15 marks)*

Tom's answer:

① The view that 'a mystical experience should not be devalued by the challenge of authenticity' is a compelling one.

② Firstly, some of the world's largest religions have come about by people who have had a mystical experience. Buddhism, which has approximately 347 million followers, came about by Buddha's experience when deeply absorbed in meditation. Equally, Islam came about when the final prophet Muhammad was visited by an angel, Jibrael, who told him to 'Recite!'. This now makes up the first portion of the Qu'ran and today Islam is the world's second largest religion. If these experiences were devalued by the challenge of authenticity, the world's largest religions would not have come about.

③ Equally, scholar Richard Swinburne in the 'Principle of Credulity' believes that we should believe what people say. He states it is illogical to not believe what people say, and as empirical recent evidence has found, almost 40% of people can be said to have had a religious mystical experience. To doubt all these people by challenging the authenticity would be wrong, Swinburne suggests that unless there is overwhelming evidence to the contrary, we should believe them.

④ However, some people would disagree with this. Many people take drugs in order to experience the divine. These drug-induced mystical experiences are not counted as 'real' religious experiences and can be explained by drugs and not the divine.

Examiner commentary:

① Tom starts by rephrasing the question and offering an opinion on it. He does nothing more than this and thereby does not demonstrate any level of comment beyond the very basic.

② The second paragraph states, with two examples, relevant material that supports the argument. Tom also offers an analysis of this information albeit in a relatively limited way.

③ The use of Swinburne to further Tom's argument is useful and good practice; however, some of the statistics quoted are not entirely accurate, neither does Tom state where the statistics come from.

④ The counter argument is presented in a limited fashion in the final paragraph. Tom's response begins to lose coherence at this point and he uses the word 'religious' rather than 'mystical' which is a different issue. No conclusion is offered.

Summative comment

Tom's response demonstrated that he had some grasp of the main issues but, due to limited analysis and comment and the fact that the argument has not been presented convincingly, with a balanced answer and a clear conclusion, he was awarded Level 4, 8 marks for AO2.

Natural Law

5a Explain why some religious believers reject the use of Natural Law whilst other religious believers accept its use.

(30 marks)

Seren's answer:

① The Christian denomination that has been most influenced by Natural Law is the Roman Catholic Church. Their theology follows the strict rules and guidelines set out by Aquinas. Catholics believe in Natural Law when it states that all moral decisions can be made using our God-given reason. Aquinas developed Aristotelian ideas that everything has a purpose describing this as our 'telos'. Aquinas, unlike Aristotle, believed this purpose was given by God. Our 'telos' is to reach fellowship with God through the decisions we make using our ability to reason. Any action that does not bring about causality or fulfil its final purpose is wrong.

② Aquinas determined that Natural Law has five primary precepts: worship God, self-preservation and preservation of the innocent, live in an ordered society, to learn, continuation of the species through reproduction and to defend the defenceless. He then explained the secondary precepts which demonstrate the primary precepts in action. For example, in order to live in an ordered society we need the secondary precept 'do not kill'. Many Catholics still accept the use of Natural Law because it gives them a clear set of rules by which to lead their lives. The Roman Catholic Church upholds the precept of 'an ordered society' by maintaining an absolutist approach to issues such as abortion and euthanasia that would break this precept. The primary precepts are also supported by the Bible, for example in Genesis it states that one of our main purposes is reproduction.

③ As a deontological theory Natural Law focuses on the action that is performed and Aquinas described both 'exterior' and 'interior' acts. The exterior act is the act itself and the interior act is its motive. For an act to be good both the exterior and interior acts must be good. Many Catholics still accept his ideas and believe that doing the right action for the right reasons will improve oneself and enable humans to get closer to God. Aquinas also encouraged the development of cardinal virtues such as inner strength, fortitude or temperance (everything in moderation). Scholars such as Peter Vardy agree that the idea of improving the self and soul is very appealing to religious believers who aim to get closer to God.

④ Aquinas believed that the main purpose of sex was reproduction – as outlined in the primary precepts. Any sexual activity that frustrates this final cause, such as homosexual sex, is therefore wrong. This is why many Catholics hold the view that homosexual sex is not permissible because it does not lead to the fulfilment of the 'telos' of sex – reproduction.

Examiner commentary:

① Although Seren has answered the question in an unorthodox manner by answering the second part of the question first, she does successfully answer the entire question overall. She has carefully selected accurate and relevant information. Specialist vocabulary is also used accurately.

② Seren has clearly linked the primary and secondary precepts here, not only to each other, but also to Catholic teachings and to biblical evidence.

③ Seren has clearly defined interior and exterior acts here and explained why these concepts are important to religious believers. In addition to this she has identified the cardinal virtues and their link to a human's personal development. She has supported the points she has made with a scholarly opinion.

④ Here Seren has clearly identified why Catholics would support Natural Law's view on homosexual acts. In the next paragraph she contrasts this with the Quaker view.

(5) However, some denominations, such as the Quakers, adopt a more liberal and relativistic approach and argue that it is the quality of the relationship that determines whether homosexual sex is meaningful or not. Many Quakers prefer to adopt Situation Ethics as a means of making moral decisions as it focuses on the most loving outcome and the situation people find themselves in. They would argue that homosexual sex can be both an expression of love and develop a bond between the couple. They would also argue that Natural Law's legalistic approach fails to consider the situation people find themselves in and is very prescriptive, giving them no real choices. Many Protestants would support Martin Luther's view and disagree with the fact that Natural Law sees humankind's ability to reason as being more important than the teachings of the Bible (which they believe are the words of God). They would argue that since the Fall mankind has developed a sinful nature and this has corrupted our ability to reason. They would stress the importance of Divine Authority over rationality.

(5) Seren now begins to address the issue here of why some religious believers reject Natural Law and adopt other approaches such as Situation Ethics. She uses the issue of homosexual sex to support the view she has given. She demonstrates a mature understanding of Lutheran theology by explaining why Luther and many Protestants would reject Natural Law – due to the fact that it appears to give priority to rationality over Divine Authority and humankind's sinful nature.

Summative comment

Seren has given a thorough answer and presented key facts accurately. She has also shown a thorough understanding of the issues given. She makes effective use of well-chosen examples. She scored 30/30 Level 7 for AO1.

Q&A

5a Explain why some religious believers reject the use of Natural Law whilst other religious believers accept its use.

(30 marks)

Tom's answer:

① Religious believers might accept the use of Natural Law as the primary precepts link with a number of Christian Teachings. The Catholic Church has used Natural Law as a means of making moral decisions for over seven hundred years and this shows that the theory is still accepted by some religious believers. For example, the primary precepts include worship God, which is referred to in the Ten Commandments. Another precept is 'to reproduce' which is one of God's first commands to humans. As a result of this primary precept the Catholic Church rejects the use of artificial contraception and homosexual sex as both would break this precept. This view on homosexual sex is also supported by the Bible in Leviticus

② However, it might also be rejected by Christians as they think as an absolutist theory it is too strict. Some Christians would allow abortion if it was the most 'loving thing to do'; for example, Baptists would allow it in the case of rape. However, if a woman had been raped Natural Law would not allow abortion as this would break the primary precept 'to reproduce'. Also some Christians believe that Jesus rejected legalistic approaches like Natural Law when he broke laws to help people, e.g. when he healed on the Sabbath. Gay Christians may also reject Natural Law on the basis that they claim it treats them unfairly by not allowing them to express their sexuality through sexual activity.

Examiner commentary:

① Tom has started well linking his answer to the question. The link he has made between the precepts and Christian teachings shows relevant knowledge. His reference to the Commandments could be more specific, e.g. – in Exodus 20 it says, 'you shall have no other Gods before me'. This is also the case with his reference to God's command to reproduce which is in the Bible – Genesis 1v28. The reference to Leviticus, whilst correct, could also be expanded – Leviticus 18v22 states that gay sex is 'an abomination'. There are many other reasons why some Christians accept Natural Law which could be developed here such as the fact that it recognises the place of the divine creator in establishing order in the Universe, it promotes the uses of the theological virtues listed by St Paul, etc.

② The 'absolutist' claim about Natural Law is true, but what does it mean? Why would it mean that some people consider the theory to be too strict? Why do some Christians adopt the attitude that they should do 'the most loving thing'? The distinction made about the issue of abortion because of rape demonstrates some understanding of the views of different denominations towards Natural Law. Tom could also have developed the last two points he made further; for example, he could have provided evidence of Jesus breaking Sabbath laws such as when he healed the man with the withered hand on the Sabbath (Mark 3v1–6). In addition to this he could have explained that many homosexual Christians would support the view in the Bible in Genesis 1v27 that they were made in God's image and had no choice about their sexuality.

Summative comment

Overall, Tom's answer was partially adequate. Whilst his knowledge was accurate, his answer lacked a deeper understanding of the main ideas. His answer was almost a 'list' and he needed to expand further on the points he made. He achieved 17/30 Level 4 for AO1.

5b 'Natural Law provides an excellent basis for making moral decisions.' Assess this view.

(15 marks)

Seren's answer:

(1) For many believers across the world Natural Law does provide an excellent basis for making moral decisions. Its absolutist approach determines that some actions are always right or always wrong. This provides people with clear-cut consistent rules. Natural Law echoes the Ten Commandments in the Bible such as 'do not kill'. Natural Law is still used by the Catholic Church, the largest Christian denomination in the world. It must therefore provide an excellent basis for making moral decisions as it is still used by many as part of their faith. The Pope criticised relative theories as 'moving towards a dictatorship of relativism' where the individual only looks out for themselves, whereas Natural Law is based on goodness for all humanity. It promotes precepts such as promoting 'an ordered society'. It also promotes the Golden Rule of Christianity 'Do unto others as you would have them do unto you' through cardinal virtues such as justice.

(2) However, many have criticised Natural Law's absolutist approach. For example, Kai Nelson stated that what is 'good' or acceptable varies within different cultures and believed that 'there is no such things as a universal human nature'. The idea that all of humanity is given the gift of reason also seems unrealistic as not everyone has the ability to reason. Reformist Protestants such as Martin Luther also criticised Natural Law and Catholic theology for the emphasis they place on human reason as he believed that the Bible was the highest form of authority.

(3) Many also believe it is outdated in its views on abortion and euthanasia and its strict rules prevent people from doing what they believe to be right. Natural Law had led to the Pope condemning the widespread use of contraception in poverty-stricken African countries when surely allowing this would be the most loving answer providing a better quality of life, to stop the spread of HIV, for example.

(4) Whilst many favour the rules-based approach given by Natural Law and the way it allows them to have a clear moral stance on many issues, I think it is fundamentally flawed as people's perception of what is a rational decision will vary according to their cultural background – what is considered rational and right in one culture may not be in another.

Examiner commentary:

(1) Seren has clearly focussed on the question and has made a valid point on the benefits of Natural Law's absolutist approach. The link between Natural Law and the Bible could have been more clearly stated, e.g. one of the primary precepts is live in 'an ordered society', which supports the rules within the Ten Commandments such as 'do not kill'. The second half of the paragraph displays clear understanding of one of the core principles of Natural Law and of one of the virtues.

(2) Some good examples of evaluation are given here, pointing out two of the major weaknesses of Natural Law. The fact that not everyone has the ability to reason could be developed further with an example. The reference to Martin Luther shows a mature understanding of the issue of the importance of scriptural authority over Natural Law.

(3) Whilst the points raised here are perfectly valid, they could be developed – what are Natural law's views on abortion and euthanasia and why are these views held? Why, according to Natural Law, would contraception not be allowed?

(4) An appropriate conclusion has been drawn – perhaps an example could have been used to illustrate the point made?

Summative comment

Overall, Seren's answer shows a thorough response to the issues raised. Different views have been analysed and evaluated. Arguments have generally been strongly supported and a conclusion drawn. She scored 14/15 Level 7 for AO2.

5b 'Natural Law provides an excellent basis for making moral decisions.' Assess this view. *(15 marks)*

Tom's answer:

① Some disagree with this statement as how can we be sure that the 'telos' or purpose of a particular object/action as defined by Natural Law is correct? For example, Natural Law says the main purpose of sex is reproduction, but what if its main purpose is pleasure? A Utilitarian might well argue that this is the case.

② Also Natural Law is based on the belief that God created a world and everything within it for a purpose, but many people would challenge this idea. An atheist would have no reason to follow this theory as they don't believe in God. They might argue that modern science has challenged the need for a creator God.

③ Aquinas' theory is based on the false assumption that all of mankind has the same universal nature, but is there such a thing as a universal human nature? For example, Eskimos think it is acceptable to allow elderly relatives to die in the cold to stop them becoming a burden on their family.

Examiner commentary:

① Whilst the point raised here is valid, it could have been explained more clearly. Why is the concept of the 'telos' so important within Natural Law? God designed everything with a purpose and therefore fulfilling its intended design is good. Tom could develop the valid point he has made about Utilitarianism by explaining why a Utilitarian might argue that sex for pleasure is acceptable.

② A valid point partially supported by reasoning. How has modern science challenged the idea of a creator God? For example, Darwin's idea of evolution some claim challenges the idea of there being a designer God.

③ The candidate needs to explain 'Why did Aquinas believe there was a "universal human nature" here?' – We were all created this way by God. Also why do scholars such as Kai Nelson reject this idea? He rejected it because from the study of the various cultures around the world there doesn't appear to be a universal human nature. Tom could explain how modern science has challenged the need for a creator God, e.g. are we part of the evolution process?

Summative comment

Overall, Tom's answer shows some grasp of the main issues here, but analysis or comment is limited. The arguments given are only partially supported and lack deeper evaluation or analysis. His answer also lacks any argument which supports the 'agree' viewpoint and a conclusion. He scored 8/15 Level 4 for AO2.

Situation Ethics

6a Outline the four working and six fundamental principles of Situation Ethics.

(30 marks)

Seren's answer:

(1) The principles of Situation Ethics provide guidelines for those who want to make moral decisions based on agape or selfless love.

(2) The first of the four working principles is pragmatism – there must be a clear chance of success. The action must be practical and have the possibility of agape as the consequence. Positivism is the idea that we must have faith and hope that 'God is love'. Like we accept God is real without proof so we must accept that love is also real. Relativism means that 'love relativises the absolute'. Personalism means the focus should be on the person not the law.

(3) The six fundamental principles also help us to a loving outcome. The first principle is that agape is the only intrinsic good – nothing is good in and of itself than agape. The second principle is that 'Love is the ruling norm' – this shows that we must do away with legalistic approaches as Jesus said, 'the Sabbath was made for man and not man for the Sabbath' – love is now the guiding principle. The third principle is 'Love and justice are the same' – this shows that if we bring about agape in each situation we also bring about justice. For example, Mother Theresa showed agape love to the poor and therefore fought for equality and justice. The fourth principle 'Love wills thy neighbours' good' suggests that we should not be swayed by our own personal interests or egos but put the person at the centre using agape, which is a selfless love, loving even our enemies. The fifth principle is the 'end justifies the means' – this means our actions may be overlooked if the outcome is agape. For example, Mrs Bergmeier committed the act of adultery; however, this was overlooked due to the fact that the act was an expression of agape love which allowed her to return to her children and family. The sixth principle is 'Love's decisions are made situationally not prescriptively' – this shows that Situation Ethics has the ability to be used in any situation. No two situations are treated the same.

Examiner commentary:

(1) Seren's answer gets straight to the point and she doesn't waste time on irrelevant background material. She also clearly defines agape love.

(2) By numbering each principle Seren is able to check she has included all four working principles. She uses specialist vocabulary accurately and has recognised that the trigger word in the question is 'outline'. Relativism could be defined more clearly as 'there are no moral absolutes only the guiding principle of love'.

(3) The paragraph starts by stating why the fundamental principles are also needed. Seren has demonstrated her understanding of the third and fourth principles particularly effectively by using examples – although this is not a requirement of an 'outline' type answer. The fifth principle should be 'the loving end justifies the means' and the sixth principle although listed is not clearly defined here.

Summative comment

Overall, Seren's answer is a thorough one in the time available. The material she has used is organised clearly and coherently. She has also used specialist vocabulary accurately. The answer scored 27/30 – Level 6 for AO1.

Q&A

6a Outline the four working and six fundamental principles of Situation Ethics.

(30 marks)

Tom's answer:

① There are six fundamental and four working principles within Situation Ethics. These principles help to decide how to produce the most loving thing.

② One of the six fundamental principles is that 'you should love you neighbour even if you like them or not' – this means you should love everyone. The second principle is 'only one thing is intrinsically good which is love' – this means that nothing is good except love. The third principle is the Christian decision making in the norm is loving. The fourth is that the ends will always justify the means – this means if the outcome is loving then the action you took was good. The fifth principle is that love and
③ justice are the same.

One of the four fundamental principles is personalism this means when you put the person before the rule. For example, Jesus allowed his disciples to pick corn on the Sabbath day because they were hungry even though the Sabbath rules forbid it. The second principle is pragmatism – the outcome must be practical, e.g. the adulterous woman, when Jesus saved her from being stoned to death because he felt it was the loving thing to do. Relativism means that it is more about the consequences than the action itself. Finally the fourth principle, positivism, means that you may not be sure what the most loving thing to do is.

Examiner commentary:

① A weak start here as the first sentence is just repeating information given in the question. Also the second sentence is vague. There needs to be a clear link between Situation Ethics and doing the most loving thing. No reference is made to agape or selfless love here.

② The first two of the six principles given here are only partially defined – the first actually means setting aside any personal emotions and even loving your enemy. The second means only love is good in and of itself. The third principle is misquoted and not defined at all – it should be 'The ruling norm of any Christian decision is love, nothing else'. This refers to the fact that Christian decisions should be based on the Golden Rule – 'Love one another as I have loved you'. The fourth principle should be 'The loving end justifies the means'. The fifth principle is not defined and means justice is love at work in the community. The sixth is not even listed – it is 'Love's decisions are made situationally, not prescriptively'. This means humans are not tied to following rules, but must 'do the most loving thing' in every situation.

③ Good knowledge and understanding shown of personalism and pragmatism here (using examples although this is not a requirement of an 'outline' type answer). The definition of relativism is wrong and positivism is only listed here. There is no real knowledge and understanding shown of either principle. Relativism means you need to always respond in love to each unique situation. One cannot use words like 'never' as circumstances can always throw up exceptions. Positivism means accepting that love is the right thing to do through faith rather than by reason or proof.

Summative comment

Overall, Tom's answer is only partially adequate. It demonstrates mainly accurate knowledge but only basic/patchy understanding. He has also made some accurate use of specialist vocabulary. He scored 15/30 Level 4 for AO1.

Q&A

6b 'Situation Ethics is entirely compatible with religious belief.' Assess this view.

(15 marks)

Seren's answer:

① This statement is true as Situation Ethics puts people first before rules and Jesus' opposition to legalistic morality is evident in the New Testament. For example, Jesus healed the paralysed man on the Sabbath (John Chapter 5) which could be seen as an example of personalism, one of the four working principles of Situation Ethics. In this example Jesus puts healing the man before breaking the Sabbath law (working on the Sabbath). Jesus also showed love and compassion towards the socially outcast and this is compatible with Situation Ethics which is based on agape – selfless love. Jesus told people to 'Love your neighbour as yourself' (Luke Chapter 10) and this is compatible with one of the six fundamental principles which says 'Love wills thy neighbours' good'. Love has been major feature of the teachings of several religious leaders, e.g. St Paul taught love as the highest principle above the Law – 1 Corinthians 13.

② On the other hand this statement is regarded by some as false because Situation Ethics has no set laws. Pope Benedict condemned this type of ethic, speaking in April 2005 he said, 'We are moving towards a dictatorship of relativism which does not recognise anything as for certain and which has as its highest goal one's own ego and one's own desires …'. He said we should remain steadfast to our faith and not give in to society's constantly changing ideas on morality. The Bible also states that there are other qualities which are just as important as love, e.g. St Paul stated, '… the fruit of the Spirit is love, joy, peace, patience, kindness, goodness, faithfulness, gentleness, self-control; against such there is no law' Galatians 5v22–23. Situation Ethics due to its relative nature would also allow you to break the Ten Commandments given to humans by God. For example, using Situation Ethics, I could help someone to die if it was the most loving thing to do, but the Commandments clearly state 'Do not murder'. Situation Ethics therefore puts humankind's free-will above God's divine laws which many would claim is sinful.

③ In conclusion, I think that Situation Ethics is not compatible with Christianity as it has the potential to promote selfishness by allowing us to make selfish moral choices which we can justify by saying they were done for loving reasons. For example, killing an elderly relative claiming she was in pain and this was a loving act when really I did it to gain an inheritance. Such acts are not only contrary to the Ten Commandments, but also go against the Christian message of selfless love 'love one another as I have loved you'.

Examiner commentary:

① Seren has from her opening sentence clearly focussed on the question. The arguments given in this section are strongly supported by reasoning or evidence with clear links being made with the Bible and Christian leaders.

② Seren has organised her answer into two clear sections. The second section considers different views on the issue and demonstrates good analytical and evaluative skills. Arguments are once again strongly supported by reasoning or evidence with clear links being made with the Bible, Christian leaders and the issue of divine authority.

③ An appropriate conclusion has been drawn here. Seren has raised a new and valid point in her conclusion and justified her opinion using both reason and evidence.

Summative comment

Overall, Seren's answer showed a thorough response to the issues raised. Different views have been analysed and evaluated. Arguments have generally been strongly supported and a conclusion drawn. Seren achieved 15/15 Level 7 for AO2.

6b 'Situation Ethics is entirely compatible with religious belief.' Assess this view.

(15 marks)

Tom's answer:

① Situation Ethics is compatible with Christianity as Jesus often preached about the importance of love "Love your neighbour as yourself" (Luke Chapter 10) and this is the central belief of Situation Ethics. Jesus showed selfless love towards others through his actions, e.g. healing the sick. It is also used by some Quakers as a basis for making moral decisions.

② However, Situation Ethics can justify acts that are seen as wrong by some Christians. For example, it can justify abortion in the case of rape if it is the most loving thing to do; whereas Roman Catholics who follow Natural Law would say is wrong. Situation Ethics also allows you to breaks religious rules if is the most loving thing to do, which many would regard as wrong, e.g. to steal food to feed a starving family.

Examiner commentary:

① An attempt has been made to construct an argument here, but many of the points raised are only partially supported by reasoning or evidence; however, Tom has failed to explain how love is central to Situation Ethics. A more detailed example of a healing (such as the healing of the paralysed man) could be linked to the principle of personalism in Situation Ethics. Also the final point lacks any clear detail, e.g. the Quaker view of homosexuality is based on the idea that it is the quality of the love expressed in the relationship that is important not whether or not it is a heterosexual relationship.

② Again the points made are only partially supported – Catholics would not allow abortion because it breaks the primary precept of reproduction. Tom needs to refer to other reasons why Christians might reject Situation Ethics, e.g. it puts too much emphasis on a person's right to make their own moral decisions rather than aiming to fulfil God's will.

Summative comment

Overall, Tom's answer shows some grasp of the main issues here, but his analysis or comment is limited. The arguments given are only partially supported and lack deeper evaluation or analysis. His answer also lacks a conclusion. He scored 8/15 Level 4 for AO2.

Utilitarianism

7a Explain Bentham's Act Utilitarianism. *(30 marks)*

Seren's answer:

① Bentham stated in his book 'An Introduction to the Principles of Morals and Legislation' that 'Nature had placed mankind under the governance of two sovereign masters, pleasure and pain'. Bentham believed that humans aim to seek pleasure and avoid pain. This is the idea on which he based his principle of 'utility' or 'usefulness' – to aim for the 'the greatest happiness for the greatness number'. He developed the relativistic and teleological theory known as Act Utilitarianism. It was called 'Act Utilitarianism' because it treats each situation as being unique and believed that consequences of an action are what make our actions right or wrong.

② However, he realised that this was hard for an individual to work out what the happiest consequences might be, so he devised the hedonic calculus to help people discover this. The calculus consisted of seven criteria which would be used to judge whether an action was right or wrong. The first of these seven criteria was intensity and refers to how intense the happiness will be. The second is duration and this means how long the happiness will last. The third criterion is certainty, how sure are you that what you are going to do will lead to happiness? The fourth is propinquity or remoteness, meaning how far your happiness will reach. The fifth criterion is fecundity, which means how likely your original action which initially leads to happiness is likely to lead to further happiness. The sixth is purity, which means how free from pain this action is likely to be? The seventh criterion is extent and refers to how many people will receive happiness.

③ To give an example, imagine there was a burning house and trapped inside were a scientist who has the cure for cancer and your elderly father? Who do you save? Bentham would say you should save the scientist because saving her will bring strong happiness (intensity) to the millions of people suffering from cancer (extent). It would also allow the cancer suffers to live longer – the duration of their combined happiness would last longer than the happiness of your elderly father. Saving the scientist would definitely lead (certainty) to pleasure, as millions of people would be happy to be saved from a previously terminal disease. The initial happiness from saving the scientist and therefore the cancer suffers will lead to further happiness for their friends and family (fecundity). The action would not be completely free from pain (purity) as your father will die, but the happiness will be far reaching and many people will experience the happiness if you save the scientist (extent).

Examiner commentary:

① Seren has started well by accurately quoting from Bentham's book. She then successfully defined the principle of 'utility' and used key terminology such as 'hedonist' and 'consequentialist' accurately. The terms 'relativistic' and 'teleological', although correctly related to Bentham's form of Utilitarianism could have been clearly defined here.

② Seren has clearly defined the purpose of the hedonic calculus. She could, however, have stated why it is called the 'hedonic' calculus and explained that the term 'hedone' is the Greek work for 'pleasure'. She has also been able to list the seven criteria it contains and to accurately define five out of the seven criteria. 'Intensity' is not correctly defined and means how strong is the happiness? In addition to this propinquity or remoteness actually means how close in time is the happiness?

③ In this paragraph Seren has demonstrated a clear understanding of how Act Utilitarianism can be applied to a particular situation using six out of the seven criteria. Seren has also actually shown an understanding of 'intensity' here even though her definition in the previous paragraph was not clear. The only criterion that has not been successfully applied here is 'remoteness'.

Summative comment

Overall, Seren has given a fairly full answer and presented key facts accurately. She has also shown a clear understanding of Act Utilitarianism overall. She scored 26/30 Level 5 for AO1.

7a Explain Bentham's Act Utilitarianism. *(30 marks)*

Tom's answer:

① Bentham's Act Utilitarianism is based around his idea that humans aim to achieve pleasure and avoid pain. The only important principle is that people must achieve 'the greatest happiness for the greatest number'. It is a relativistic theory and allows us to break laws if they fulfil the 'greatest happiness for the greatest number'.

② Bentham focussed on the quantity of happiness rather than the quality. Act Utilitarianism is a theory which treats individual situations as unique and each act is considered to be right or wrong based on the consequences it produces.

③ Bentham devised the hedonic calculus to provide a way of ensuring we achieve 'the greatest happiness for the greatest number'. It contains seven criteria such as Intensity – how strong is the happiness? Duration – how long does the happiness last? Certainty – how sure are you that the happiness will actually happen?

④ So, for example, if there was a girl who loved chocolate and she had a large chocolate bar and she could either share it with her four friends or eat it all herself, Bentham would say she should share it in order to create 'the greatest happiness for the greatest number' as more people would experience the happiness (extent) if she did this.

Examiner commentary:

① Tom has defined Bentham's main principle, but could have made it easier for himself by stating it was also known as the principle of 'utility'. He could then refer to this rather than having to repeat the whole principle throughout the essay. Also he could explain why this principle is called the principle of 'utility'. The term 'relativistic' is not clearly linked to the definition given in paragraph (2).

② Act Utilitarianism is clearly defined here, but Tom fails to use key terms such as 'consequentialist' or use and define the phrase 'teleological'.

③ Tom explains how the hedonic calculus is used, but can only define three out of the seven criteria. Why is the calculus called the 'hedonic' calculus? As the question specifically focusses only on Act Utilitarianism he has sufficient time to define all seven criteria here.

④ Tom's example is very simplistic and he fails to apply all the criteria he has given to his example. He only applies the 'extent' criterion to his example. The answer he gave could also be wrong – if the girl's pain in not having the chocolate all to herself outweighs any pleasure her friends might have then Bentham might have said she should eat the chocolate all herself.

Summative comment

Overall, Tom's answer was partially adequate. Whilst his knowledge was accurate his answer lacked a deeper understanding of the main ideas. His answer also failed to demonstrate correct use of terminology. Tom achieved 15/30 Level 4 for AO1.

Q&A

7b 'Utilitarianism has too many weaknesses to make it useful.' Assess this view.

(15 marks)

Seren's answer:

① Act Utilitarianism is essentially concerned with fulfilling the 'greatest happiness for the greatest number' and as a result allows a minority to suffer if it would fulfil this principle, which is a major weakness. This could lead to the justification of acts such as slavery or torture, e.g. two sadistic prison guards attack an innocent prisoner as this brings them happiness. They are able to justify their actions using criteria from the hedonic calculus. They claim that they gain a strong happiness (intensity) from beating the prisoner and their happiness will be received instantly from watching the prisoner suffer (remoteness). Their happiness will also last for several months as they can enjoy re-telling the story to each other about their cruel deed. Whilst the prisoners will experience pain, their physical pain will only be temporary (a short duration). The fact that there are two guards experiencing happiness and only one prisoner receiving pain means that the extent of the happiness (number of people receiving the happiness) also favours them. The theory also fails to consider the fact that we have duties/emotional ties to certain people like our friends and family. Realistically, if a ship was sinking and I only had time to save one other passenger – a doctor with a cure for AIDS or my mother, I am more likely to save my mother as she has reared and cared for me for many years as opposed to a stranger. Act Utilitarianism, however, would favour saving the doctor as this fulfils the principle of utility. Another weakness is that 'happiness' is subjective – what brings each person happiness is different; for one person, watching football brings happiness, but for others it might bring pain and boredom.

② However, Utilitarianism has a number of strengths. For example, using Mill's idea of higher pleasures (intellectual pleasures of the mind) being superior to lower pleasures (pleasures of the body) it would be very hard to justify the sadistic guards example given above, as the pleasure they have gained cannot really be classed as an intellectual pleasure. Also this takes away the 'subjective' nature of happiness, as he clearly defines that intellectual pleasures are superior to any other form of pleasure. In addition to this, even Act Utilitarianism, despite having weaknesses, has been used by many organisations as a means of making decisions. For example, a hospital with a limited budget cannot please/treat everyone as it might have liked, so it has to adopt the idea of achieving 'the greatest happiness for the greatest number'. Many people would see the fact that Utilitarianism as a teleological theory aims for the goal of happiness as being realistic as this is what many people claim is their aim in life.

③ In conclusion, whilst Act Utilitarianism does have a number of weaknesses, the fact that it forms the basis of modern political democracy shows that it must have some considerable strengths. Using Act Utilitarianism everyone has the right to vote initially, but it is the majority's views that determine the outcome of the election. You cannot possibly please everyone so you might as well please the majority. Although happiness is subjective, Utilitarianism does at least allow us to make decisions for ourselves without being forced to obey rules. Mill's version even encourages us to strive for intellectual pleasures, which would be useful in terms of helping us to becoming more fulfilled human beings.

Examiner commentary:

① Seren has clearly focussed on the question set and her arguments are strongly supported by reasoning/evidence. Specialist terms such as parts of the hedonic calculus have been used accurately here.

② Seren now goes on to give different views on the issue; again her arguments are strongly supported by reasoning or evidence. Her answer is well organised, clear and coherent.

③ An appropriate conclusion has been drawn and the view given is again supported by strong evidence/reasoning.

Summative comment

Overall, Seren's answer shows a thorough response to the issues raised. Different views have been analysed and evaluated. Arguments have generally been strongly supported and a conclusion drawn. Seren achieved 15/15 Level 7 for AO2.

7b 'Utilitarianism has too many weaknesses to make it useful.' Assess this view. *(15 marks)*

Tom's answer:

① Utilitarianism as an ethical theory has many flaws. For example, when you fulfil 'the greatest happiness for the greatest number' principle, a minority are allowed to suffer, e.g. the public smoking ban. Also this principle allows the justification of any act which goes against religious teachings such as the commandments. Many people would argue that Act Utilitarianism's lack of rules would lead to moral chaos. In addition to this, many people have different ideas of what happiness is, so how can you make a judgement on this basis? Utilitarianism as a consequential theory asks us to predict consequences, which is impossible.

② On the other hand, Utilitarianism is fairly useful as a means of making moral decisions, as most people want to aim for happiness. Hospitals and medical practices have shown Utilitarianism can be useful by making decisions using Utilitarian principles as they often cannot afford to treat everyone. Using Utilitarianism could be useful in that it helps to promote a 'community spirit' through the pursuit of the common goal of happiness.

Examiner commentary:

① An attempt has been made to construct an argument here, but the points raised are only briefly made. For example, the argument about a minority being allowed to suffer is correct, but the argument is only partially supported by evidence and no further reasoning to support this or any of the other arguments given here. His answer here is almost 'list' like and as a result his analysis is limited.

② Whilst there is recognition of more than one view here the points raised continue to be only partially supported by reasoning or evidence. For example, how do hospitals make decisions using Utilitarian principles? How does Utilitarianism promote a community spirit through happiness?

Summative comment

Overall, Tom's answer shows some grasp of the main issues here, but his analysis or comment is limited. The arguments given are only partially supported and lack deeper evaluation or analysis. His lack of analysis means that he is also unable to produce an appropriate conclusion to his answer. He achieved 8/15 Level 4 for AO2.

Applied Ethics

8a Explain the ethical teachings of one major world religion on adultery.

(30 marks)

Seren's answer:

① Adultery means to have voluntary sexual intercourse between a married person and another person who is not his or her spouse. Adultery is condemned by Christians for several reasons. One form of religious authority for Christians is the traditional teachings of the Church, which state that adultery goes against the sacramental nature of marriage. A sacrament is 'an outward and visible sign of an inward and spiritual grace'. For example, in an Anglican wedding service the priest joins the couple together with their stole to show by the outward sign that God has spiritually joined these two people together. This teaching is supported by the Bible as in Mark 10v7–8 it states, 'For this reason a man will leave his father and mother and be united to his wife, and the two will become one flesh.' So they are no longer two, but one. Adultery breaks this spiritual bond and undermines the sanctity (or holiness) of marriage referred to in Mark 10v7. Also when you get married, you make promises to your partner and to God that you will remain faithful to them. The vows include 'to love and to cherish' and to remain faithful 'till death us do part'. By committing adultery you are breaking both of these promises by having sex with someone other than your spouse.

② In addition, another form of religious authority for Christians is religious leaders and notable Christian leaders like Jesus have condemned adultery. For example, Jesus said in Matthew 5v27–29, 'I tell you that anyone who looks at a woman lustfully has already committed adultery with her in his heart'. By this he meant even having adulterous thoughts about another person is a sin. Also in Matthew 19 Jesus states that adultery is the only grounds for divorce – which shows how serious a sin this is. St Paul wrote in Ephesians 5v22–25 that a husband's love for his wife should reflect Christ's love for the Church. 'He who loves his wife loves himself. After all, no one ever hated his own body, but he feeds and cares for it, just as Christ does the Church – for we are members of his body'. Therefore if anyone commits adultery they are not only betraying their spouse but going against Jesus' teachings. Adultery is also seen as a sign of promiscuity and lust. In 1 Corinthians 6v9 St Paul stated, 'Do not be deceived: neither the sexually immoral, nor idolaters, nor adulterers … will inherit the kingdom of God'. This passage emphasises how serious a sin adultery is.

③ Another source of authority for Christians is in the Bible; one of the Ten Commandments clearly states, 'Thou shalt not commit adultery' (Exodus 20v14). Also in Deuteronomy 22v22 it states, 'If a man is found sleeping with another man's wife, both the man who slept with her and the woman must die.' So both these passages condemn adultery and even go so far as to say the punishment for the adulterers should be death.

④ Roman Catholics also condemn adultery as it breaks several of the precepts of Natural Law. For example, it breaks the precept 'ordered society' as it could lead to the break-up of a family. It also generally breaks the precept 'to reproduce' because those committing adultery are usually not having sex with the intention of creating a child and even if they were, any child would not be brought up within marriage, again breaking the 'ordered society' precept.

Examiner commentary:

① In this paragraph Seren has clearly defined adultery which clearly demonstrates to the examiner that she knows about the issue she is referring to. She then goes on to explain why one form of religious authority – traditional teaching – is against adultery. She makes effective use of evidence and uses specialist vocabulary accurately.

② Seren refers to another form of religious authority here – religious leaders. She provides accurate and relevant information on what religious leaders have said and she then explains what these sayings teach people about adultery.

③ She then moves on to her third form of religious authority and accurately quotes and explains passages from a religious text – the Bible.

④ Seren then moves on to her final form of religious authority – Natural Law – and correctly identifies how adultery breaks several of its precepts. She could also if she wished have referred to Situation Ethics here provided she clearly linked this theory to a major world religion.

⑤ Christians would state that we all have a conscience — the voice of God within, which provides us with an intuitive awareness of right and wrong. They must also follow their conscience which would tell them that adultery is sinful as it threatens the family as a cornerstone of society as it often leads to divorce. Adultery may also it cause stress for the family (including children) it affects, distrust and bitterness. Adultery is harmful because it damages, even destroys, the special relationship between the spouses.

⑤ In her final paragraph Seren provides general principles about why adultery is wrong including the harmful effects it can have on a spouse and the family.

Summative comment

Seren has given a thorough answer and presented key facts accurately. She has also shown a thorough understanding of the issues given. Her material is organised clearly and coherently. She makes effective use of well-chosen examples. Specialist vocabulary is also used accurately. She scored 30/30 Level 7 for AO1.

8a Explain the ethical teachings of one major world religion on adultery.

(30 marks)

Tom's answer:

① Christianity is against adultery, as Christians believe that marriage is God's gift and involves one man and one woman (Genesis). They believe it should be respected therefore and not broken by adultery. Christians also believe that adultery can lead to divorce, which is a sin and is not recognised by Catholics. They believe that marriage is a sacrament that should not be broken: 'therefore what God has joined together, let man not separate'. Christians also frown upon adultery because it promotes promiscuity and it can lead to a multitude of problems such as STDs and problems in future relationships.

② Also during the marriage service the couple make vows to God, which include remaining faithful. These vows are sacred and made both to God and your partner.

③ Adultery is also wrong because when a married couple join together they become one. As it states in Mark 10v7–8, 'For this reason a man will leave his father and mother and be united to his wife, and the two will become one flesh'. If you commit adultery then you are breaking this bond.

④ Jesus stated that you should 'love one another as I have loved you' (John 13v34). However, if you commit adultery, you are not acting according to Jesus' commandment.

Examiner commentary:

① Tom starts by referring to the Bible, but the example he gave is a brief one and could be further developed as could the quotation given later. He then goes on to refer to the Christian concept of marriage as a sacrament and could perhaps have explained what a sacrament is. He could also explain why Catholics reject divorce as this is relevant – they see marriage as a life-long commitment between a married couple. The points he makes about STDs and future relationships are also valid, but again they could be developed further to show clear understanding. For example, adultery might cause a person to have problems with relationships in future because their husband/wife has cheated on them and now they find it difficult to trust others. Also he might have started his essay by defining what adultery is as this immediately shows he knows what he is writing about.

② The reference made to the vows here is valid but could be developed further by specifying the vows and Tom could have also referred to other actions that take place within the marriage service which show that marriage is a bond not to be broken by adultery. For example, the giving of rings symbolising the couple's eternal love for each other.

③ Another valid point made here. This could have been supported further by Tom referring to one of the Ten Commandments – 'Thou shall not commit adultery'.

④ Tom's final point, whilst again valid, is not sufficiently explained. Adultery is a selfish act rather than a selfless act as it is based on putting your needs/desires before those of others. He could also have said that lust is a sin – it leads us away from the ideal human nature that God intended.

Summative comment

Overall, Tom's answer was partially adequate. Whilst his knowledge was accurate, his answer lacked sufficient detail to show a deeper understanding of the main ideas. He achieved 16/30 Level 4 for AO1.

8b 'Traditional attitudes towards adultery are unfair.' Assess this view.

(15 marks)

Seren's answer:

(1) Many people would agree with this statement for a number of reasons. Firstly some would say that you cannot judge all instances of adultery in the same way and that you have to consider each unique situation. For example, if someone has committed adultery because they are seeking love from another person as they are being physically abused by their spouse then this is not the same as another person who commits adultery simply to satisfy their own sexual desires. Joseph Fletcher, the founder of Situation Ethics, took this relativistic approach to ethics and even gave a pertinent example of when adultery may be the most loving thing to do. During World War II Mrs Bergmeier was captured by the Russians and placed in a POW camp. In order to return to her family Mrs Bergmeier realised that she would only be released if she was pregnant. As a result of this, she committed adultery with a camp guard in order to become pregnant and return home to her husband and children. In this case Fletcher said her adulterous act could be excused by the fact that the outcome was a selflessly loving one.

(2) Secondly, a Utilitarian also would say that if a married couple both consent to each other committing acts of adultery, they should be allowed to do so. This is provided that such acts were in private and harmed no one because this would fulfil the principle of 'the greatest happiness for the greatest number'. An atheist would argue that traditional attitudes towards adultery are unfair as they assume that such acts offend God, but if you don't believe in God why should you not be free to do as you choose?

(3) Thirdly, in Deuteronomy 22v22 it states, 'If a man is found sleeping with another man's wife, both the man who slept with her and the woman must die' but some people would say that such attitudes are unfair as no one has the right to take another's life. The idea that adultery should result in the death penalty still exists in parts of the world because of teachings like this.

(4) However, many religious believers would argue that traditional attitudes towards adultery are not unfair as they are designed to protect a spouse and any other members of the family from harm, disappointment and to ensure people can be trusted. They would argue that you made promises to God and to your spouse to remain faithful 'till death us do part' and that was your free choice. If you cannot keep the promise then you should never have made it in the first place. They would also argue that just because society appears to be more accepting of adultery today it does not mean that this is right. Having clear rules on issues such as adultery, like the Ten Commandments, actually promotes fairness as everyone is aware that it is unacceptable. A Catholic, for example, would argue that adultery is justifiably condemned because it breaks several of the primary precepts including 'to reproduce' as this is not the primary intention of the majority of people who commit adultery.

Examiner commentary:

(1) Seren has clearly focussed on the question and has made a valid point about adopting a more relativistic approach to this issue. The example given demonstrates a clear understanding of one of the core principle of Situation Ethics – agape love.

(2) Seren has now gone on to explain the Utilitarian position on adultery using the main principle of Act Utilitarianism to support her view. In addition to this she has logically argued that an atheist should not be forced to follow a religious code based upon a God they don't believe in.

(3) Here Seren continues to support her current line of argument by showing how some Biblical texts promote harsh punishment for those who commit adultery which seem to have been judged unfair even by Jesus.

(4) Seren now goes on to explain why some religious believers hold a different view to the one expressed in the question. She supports her arguments with reasoning and evidence.

⑤ In conclusion, whilst I recognise the views of those who claim that traditional views on adultery are unfair I do not agree with them. It is illogical to make the claim that you should by definition keep a promise, but then allow people to break some promises in certain circumstances. I agree with Pope Benedict, who said in 2005 'We are building a dictatorship of relativism that does not recognise anything as definitive and whose ultimate standard consists solely of one's own ego and desires'. The only person who would consider traditional attitudes to adultery unfair is the person who wishes to commit adultery but is not willing to accept responsibility for their actions – for breaking their marriage vows.

⑤ Finally an appropriate conclusion has been drawn – the conclusion demonstrates a mature approach to the question and again Seren's closing arguments are strongly supported by reasoning or evidence.

Summative comment

Overall, Seren's answer showed a thorough response to the issues raised. Different views have been analysed and evaluated. Arguments have generally been strongly supported and a conclusion drawn. She achieved 15/15 Level 7 for AO2.

Q&A

8b 'Traditional attitudes towards adultery are unfair.' Assess this view.

(15 marks)

Tom's answer:

① Some Christians would disagree with this statement as they say your body belongs to your spouse only and therefore adultery should be regarded as wrong as you are betraying them. Christians would also say that it is inappropriate to commit adultery as this can lead to unwanted pregnancies and that the traditional strict view against adultery tries to prevent this. Traditional views promote happiness within an ordered society and therefore are fair.

② However, some people will say that traditional attitudes are unfair as in the Old Testament adultery was punishable by death but this is not recognised by law within the UK so cannot be fair. Some may also feel that modern society has moved on and adultery is more accepted within society. Society is more relativistic and will look at the circumstances of the adultery.

③ Ultimately I think traditional views towards adultery are fair as you shouldn't break your marriage vows.

Examiner commentary:

① Whilst Tom's first point is valid, he could begin by providing evidence of his opening statement; for example, quoting 1 Corinthians 7v4, 'The wife's body does not belong to her alone but also to her husband. In the same way, the husband's body does not belong to him alone but also to his wife.' Again the second point is valid, but could be further developed – adultery can lead to the breakdown of the family unit in many cases and this can in turn have an impact on society. The final point here about the traditional view of adultery promoting happiness could be expanded by saying that traditional view helps to promote an ordered society where a spouse can trust their partner and this promotes happiness.

② Tom has initially given some evidence to support what he has said. The point about society being relativistic could be developed if the person who committed adultery had done so out of love, this is more acceptable than if they had done it out of lust. The link could have been established here with relativistic theories such as Situation Ethics or Utilitarianism.

③ Tom's conclusion is weak and does nothing more than state a perspective without supporting it with any evidence, e.g. what vows does a person break when they commit adultery?

Summative comment

Overall, Tom's answer shows some grasp of the main issues here, but his analysis or comment is limited. The arguments given are only partially supported and lack deeper evaluation or analysis. His answer also lacks a conclusion. He scored 8/15 Level 4 for AO2.

Quickfire answers

Philosophy

1 The Cosmological Argument

① The fact that the universe exists.

② St Thomas Aquinas.

③ The unmoved mover.

④ The object or person that brings about the change from potentiality into actuality.

⑤ The law of cause and effect.

⑥ 'If there be no first cause among efficient causes, there will be no ultimate, nor any intermediate cause.'

⑦ A contingent being is one that does not have to exist and depends on something else for its existence. A necessary being must exist and depends only on itself for its existence.

⑧ *Ex nihilo, nihil fit.*

⑨ It has a cause.

⑩ An actual infinite has no beginning and no end, a potential infinite may have a beginning and can therefore be added on to.

⑪ The evangelical churches of North America.

⑫ That an actual infinite universe is impossible.

⑬ It need not be the God of classical theism.

⑭ Sir Isaac Newton.

⑮ That infinity is impossible yet God is infinite.

⑯ Why is there something rather than nothing?

⑰ Cumulative arguments that are not sound arguments individually are more like leaky buckets – no matter how many you stack together, water will still get out, i.e. an unsound individual argument remains unsound when added to other unsound arguments.

2 The Teleological Argument

① The demi-urge.

② The marvellous handiwork that can be seen in earth, seas, and the sky.

③ The natural workings had no intelligence themselves to move towards their ends or purpose.

④ He stated that the stone occurred naturally but the watch had not.

⑤ Watchmaker is the intelligence behind the design of the watch whereas the universe-maker is the intelligence behind the design of the universe.

⑥ The way in which the eye works; the fact that moths and butterflies lay their eggs on the correct food plant for their larvae, etc.

⑦ Brendon Carter.

⑧ 1 The very fact that the world in which we live provides precisely those things necessary for life to be sustained.

　2 The fact that the world in which we live can not only be observed but holds itself up for rational analysis from which we can deduce its workings.

　3 The fact that the process of evolution, through natural selection, has led to the development of intelligent human life – to the degree that that intelligent life can observe and analyse the universe that it exists in.

⑨ Humans were meant to enjoy the world they lived in, not just exist in it.

⑩ Seven.

⑪ Human analogies are weak as the point of comparison between human designs and the universe's design is not credible enough to prove the point.

⑫ It denies the possibility of an omnipotent AND omnibenevolent God.

⑬ That life developed according to a process of adaptation to its environment, not as part of some divine plan.

3 Evil and Suffering

① The God that possesses the characteristics of omnipotence, omniscience and omnibenevolence. Also the God worshipped by the three main Western religions of Christianity, Islam and Judaism.

② The incompatibility of an omnipotent and omnibenevolent God allowing evil to exist.

③ Where the three statements: God is omnipotent; God is omnibenevolent and Evil exists cannot co-exist without a logical contradiction.

④ Moral evil and natural evil.

⑤ Any suitable response according to stated definitions – e.g. murder and earthquakes.

⑥ 1 Pain is a necessary event for any living thing to learn how best to survive within the natural order.

　2 The suffering caused as part of natural selection benefits the species as a whole in terms of evolution.

⑦ Any suffering undergone by an individual or group who have done nothing to deserve it.

⑧ God chose to create this world as the one that had the optimum conditions for humanity to grow towards Him.

⑨ The concept that the world contains no real suffering, or pleasure, as every decision made in it has a limited effect.

⑩ Genesis 1v26: 'Let us make man in our image after our likeness'.

⑪ The lack or absence of something that should be present in normal circumstances.

⑫ It allowed God to send Jesus into the world to atone for humankind's sin and to provide a way back to perfect harmony with God.

⑬ How can a perfect world go wrong?

⑭ It contradicts the idea that humankind was originally created perfect.

⑮ Genesis 1 v26.

⑯ To allow humankind to grow into God's likeness by understanding that all actions have consequences – both positive and negative.

⑰ It takes no account of animal suffering; the immensity of suffering or the unfair distribution of suffering; neither does it encourage individuals to choose to do good in the here and now if all people will eventually end up in heaven.

4 Mysticism

① Transcendent; ineffable; noetic; ecstatic; unitive.

② The sorely wounded Christ.

③ A watered garden.

④ Seven – they represent the deepening levels of prayerful union with the Divine.

⑤ Mystical marriage.

⑥ The Dominicans.

⑦ Four.

⑧ Siddhartha Gautama, the historical Buddha.

⑨ Poetry.

⑩ As mystical gateways to the Divine.

⑪ A sacred dance, practised by Sufis.

⑫ Apophatic – cannot be described; Kataphatic – can be described.

⑬ W T Stace.

⑭ Like a drop of water which is poured into a large portion of wine.

⑮ Ineffability; noetic quality; transciency and passivity.

⑯ Such experiences are neither analytic *a priori* nor synthetic *a posteriori* experiences; neither can they be verified or falsified.

⑰ Description-related; subject-related and object-related challenges.

⑱ Any from science, anthropology, sociology or psychology. E.g. Connection in pre-industrial societies between the incidence of religious ecstasy and the need of individuals and groups to legitimatise claims made upon the larger society; all mystical experiences were nothing more than the result of the repression of sexual urges; use of alcohol and drugs such as LSD, which can stimulate the brain into hallucinating and experiencing so-called alternative realities, etc.

⑲ Any two from those listed in the 'irrelevance' section in the evaluative issues.

⑳ Any two from those listed in 'do not devalue' section in the evaluative issues.

Ethics

5 Natural Law

① Aquinas said that rationality (the ability to reason) was a key element of human existence.

② The four types of inter-related law identified by Aquinas were eternal, divine, natural and human.

③ The Five Primary Precepts are To Worship God, To Live in an Ordered Society, To Reproduce, To Learn, and To Defend the innocent/self-preservation (W.O.R.L.D.)

④ They identify humankind's main purposes in life. They help people get closer to God and their ultimate goal of eternal life with God in heaven.

⑤ These are rules derived from the primary precepts which uphold the primary precepts, but can be overruled in some extreme circumstances.

⑥ They help humans to fulfil the primary precepts.

⑦ They help people to fulfil their true human nature.

⑧ Prudence, justice, fortitude and temperance.

⑨ Faith, hope and charity.

⑩ The interior act is the motive and the exterior act is the act itself.

⑪ People should develop 'real' goods as they help them to become closer to the ideal human nature that God has planned.

6 Situation Ethics

① Joseph Fletcher.

② Agape: it means 'selfless love'.

③ It literally means 'against law'. A situationist attitude is based on the idea that people are under no obligation to obey the laws of ethics or morality as presented by religious authorities. The situation will provide the solution, which can be found through intuition/use of a person's conscience.

④ Fletcher rejected this as he said with no guiding principles there could well be moral chaos.

⑤ An attitude that exalts laws above all other considerations.

⑥ Fletcher rejected this approach as he said it gave people no choice but to follow the rules.

⑦ Personalism, positivism, pragmatism and relativism.

⑧ Agape provides justification not proof for an ethical decision. People must accept that acting in the most loving way is the right thing to do.

⑨ Belonging naturally to or essential to.

⑩ One must achieve a loving end, and one can perform any action in order to achieve this.

7 Utilitarianism

① Jeremy Bentham.

② A form of Utilitarianism associated with Bentham that treats each moral situation as unique and applies the hedonic calculus to each 'act' to see if it fulfils the 'principle of utility'. Any action is right if it produces 'the greatest happiness for the greatest number'.

③ The main principle of Utilitarianism – 'The greatest happiness for the greatest number'.

④ Pleasure.

⑤ Bentham's means of measuring happiness. It contains seven criteria.

⑥ The seven criteria are: the intensity, duration, certainty, extent, remoteness, richness and purity of the happiness.

⑦ The quality of the pleasure.

⑧ Higher pleasures of the intellect or mind and are superior pleasures. Lower pleasures are pleasures of the body and are inferior pleasures.

⑨ Which general rules promote the greatest happiness for the greatest number?

⑩ In extreme circumstances, when breaking the rule would actually fulfil the 'principle of utility'.

8 Applied Ethics

① The traditional Christian view of sexual orientation is that heterosexual orientation is the 'norm'.

② No, although they believe those with homosexual orientation are 'disordered', they do not discriminate against people because of their sexual orientation.

③ No, there are differing views within the denomination. Some accept homosexual orientation and some do not.

④ To create children, to bring a married couple together physically, to strengthen their bond and for pleasure.

⑤ A temple of the Holy Spirit.

⑥ The way sex is used in a loving relationship.

⑦ They have condemned it because they see heterosexual sex within marriage as the norm.

⑧ That a man having sex with another man is an 'abomination'.

⑨ Biblical writers failed to recognise that homosexual partnerships can be between loving, monogamous and faithful Christians.

⑩ That the person committing adultery and the person they committed it with must die.

⑪ Jesus also condemned anyone having adulterous thoughts.

⑫ Adultery breaks the following precepts: 'an ordered society' and 'to learn/educate children'.

⑬ Any two answers from:
- To provide a relationship that reflects God's relationship with humanity.
- To creates a spiritual bond between a man and a woman.
- To create a life-long commitment.
- It also creates a new stable social unit in which children may be nurtured.

⑭ Any two answers from:
- To express faithful intimacy.
- Providing an outlet for sexual desire.
- Their spiritual duties.
- To create a physical bond between a couple.
- To fulfil God's command to reproduce.

⑮ Any one of the following:
- The vows (promising to be faithful).
- The giving of rings (eternal love).
- The proclamation (the creation of a spiritual bond declared by the priest).

⑯ Marriage is part of God's intended design and purpose.

⑰ One example from:
- To worship God: humans are worshipping God by fulfilling his commands in the Bible to marry.
- To reproduce: one of the main purposes of marriage.
- To live in an ordered society: having children within marriage creates a family unit which provides order for society.
- To learn: as a family unit provides children with an environment in which they can: learn to become good citizens, develop their sense of morality and where they learn about the importance of relationship.

⑱ One example from:
- Such relationships cannot lead to reproduction.
- They also cannot provide a traditional 'nuclear' family unit, which many argue is the basis of society.

⑲ One example from:
- Reproduction is only one of the purposes of marriage and that other purposes such as creating a loving bond between two people can be fulfilled within a civil partnership or gay marriage.
- A gay or lesbian partnerships/marriage may actually provide a more loving/stable environment for children than some heterosexual marriages.

⑳ Any two from :
- The Quakers
- Methodist Church
- The United Reform Church

Index